Musings of a Southern Lawyer:

A Collection of Commentary and Observations from the New South

Volume II

J. WESLEY CASTEEN, ESQ., CPA

NOTICE TO THE READER

I never submitted the whole system of my opinions
to the creed of any party of men whatever,
in religion, in philosophy, in politics, or
in anything else, where I was capable
of thinking for myself.

Such an addiction is the last degradation
of a free and moral agent.

- THOMAS JEFFERSON
to Francis Hopkinson
March 13, 1789.

TABLE OF CONTENTS

Volume II - A

"In polite company, one does not discuss politics, religion, sex, or money."

The foregoing admonition is one, which many persons would likely take to heart. Avoiding such topics of conversation makes family dinners more palatable and social gatherings more harmonious. However, shying away from those topics under all circumstances means that we gain little insight into other human beings and only a cursory understanding of the factors, which often define the persons that we are.

Often, we tend to believe and expect that what we deem "right" in our own lives should be readily accepted and applied in the lives of all other persons.

The topics listed above are deemed taboo because the impacts, which these issues have on every individual's life, are inescapable; however, the manner and degree, to which the underlying information and principles are applied by disparate peoples and individuals, vary greatly. Any discussions, which venture onto these topics, will almost certainly result in a wide divergence of opinions and may include vociferous disagreements among any number of parties.

However, few persons attempt to explain of even understand why it is that they believe the things, which they hold true. Often, we simply regurgitate that which we are told without critical analysis or thought. Trying to synthesize our core beliefs and to understand the mosaic, which makes each one of us the individual that we are, is not an easy task.

There is a nearly universal fear that, in challenging core beliefs, we may discover that the foundations for those beliefs are not solid. It is a disconcerting experience looking into a mirror and not fully understanding the person looking back. While absolute certainty and truth may be unattainable, a greater understanding and appreciation can be had through self-examination, as well as through discussions and even disagreements with other persons.

Introspection and debate are worthy tasks. In challenging our beliefs and opinions, we come to understand those things better. Even if those beliefs prove true under intense examination and close scrutiny, we develop a deeper appreciation for perspectives, which may differ from our own, and better understandings about other persons, who may hold differing beliefs and opinions.

Much has transpired since I compiled Volume I of *Musings*, which was subtitled, "A Collection of Commentary and Observations from the New South." In the interim, the American public weathered an election season, which included a heated Presidential contest. We continue to suffer through the malaise of the Great Recession. The Affordable Care Act ("ACA" a/k/a "Obamacare") is being implemented, and there have been a series of disclosures and revelations, which has fundamentally changed the way that many persons view government

For these reasons, Volume II is heavy on politics and legal issues. In fact, this volume consists of two (2) parts:

- Volume II-A - *Addled, Agitated, Aggrieved, Amazed, and Amused*, covers – Politics & Government; and Laws & Crimes; and

- Volume II-B - *Befuddled, Beguiled, Bemuddled, Bemused, & Bewildered*, covers – Social Commentary; Business & Taxation; and Religion & Philosophy.

The delineations of topics are not exact. Some themes are repeated, and many topics bleed over into multiple sections. It is impossible to discuss many of these issues in a vacuum, and acknowledging the interrelatedness of the topics, makes it easier for the reader to appreciate, and perhaps better understand, the complexities of such issues.

While I have given consideration to continuity and flow, the reader should not feel obliged to read the essays and articles in succession or from cover-to-cover. The major sections and even the essays themselves are intended to be self-contained. The reader should feel free to pick and choose those sections or readings that may be of most interest and to proceed in any chosen order.

I do hope that in reading *Musings* you benefit from joining me in a continuing journey, which for me has been filled with wonder and discovery.

\- J. Wesley Casteen, Esq., CPA
January - 2014

PREFACE – VOLUME I

I have no notable talents in the arts beyond appreciation. Any avocation that I have arises from my fascination in the power derived from the spoken and written word. I do not mean the power of poetic verse, which may cause one to emote over some aspect of life or our surroundings. Instead, I make reference to the prose of philosophy and reason. It is the ability of words to convey the contents of men's hearts, souls, minds, and characters that I find most fascinating.

By reading and listening carefully to the sincerely expressed words of others, we come to understand those things that are important to the writer or speaker. We are allowed a glimpse into the processes of their minds.

My talents and skills, such as they are, come from education and learning. I was first trained as a Certified Public Accountant ("CPA"). Today, I practice as an attorney-at-law in southeastern North Carolina and my vocation continues to involve issues related to business, finance, and taxation.

I have been fortunate to have had the opportunity to learn from noted academics and scholars. I have learned also from fellow students and colleagues from points all over the country and globe. Most importantly, I have been afforded the privilege of living in this great state of North Carolina and learning from its people, who are my family, friends, and neighbors. Each of these experiences is a part of the tapestry that makes me who I am today.

Over the last several years, I have shared some of my thoughts on issues that I believed were of general interest to others in the community. My thoughts and words were shared in articles, letters, and commentary. The audience was at times limited and at other times quite broad.

Some of the writings were intended to be more scholarly and included significant research and analysis. Other pieces, like the blogs entries contained herein, may have arisen off the cuff in response to a particular question or event. Still other pieces have been culled from series of online discussions or communications with friends and colleagues.

It is my hope that these articles and essays convey sincere thought and reason; although, emotion and personal opinion can never be completely removed from the equation. I do not write to impose any commandment or to offer any special enlightenment. It is only through discussion and debate that we can glean truth and understanding. That is my goal: A better understanding of people, life, and myself.

As you read some or all that follows, I am certain that there are parts with which you will not agree. It is not my objective to convert anyone to a particular way of thinking. I would prefer that each person reaches his own conclusions based upon his own careful reflection, thought, and contemplation.

Consider the essays an invitation to start a dialogue. I have provided the opening lines. From those opening lines, you have a better understanding of how I would approach the subject or address the issue. However, definitive "yes" or "no" answers are rarely included in the writings. If the questions were that easily answered, no discussion or debate would be required.

I am certain that I have a great deal more to learn, and I look forward to the discussions and experiences that will confirm my observations or provide a better insight and perspective on developing truths.

"Debate ...is not the celebration of common thought. It is the purification and forging of ideas through the smelting fires of discourse."

- J. Wesley Casteen, Esq., CPA
February - 2012

Volume II-A

Addled, Agitated, Aggrieved, Amazed, and Amused

The Erosion of the Bill of Rights

Introduction -

The provisions of the Bill of Rights (not to mention the Revolutionary War) were instituted to combat tyrannical powers of government. I would argue that tyranny under British rule differed, if at all, only in degree when compared to the ever expanding and intrusive powers of our federal government:

- The First Amendment is meant to assure the free flow of information, ideas, and political discourse, unless of course the current government is inconvenienced or embarrassed by the dissemination of such "speech." In which case, the government will likely deem any derogatory information "Top Secret" thereby making it a criminal offense to disseminate information, which is otherwise true and accurate.

  This, of course, is done under the guise of promoting "safety" and "national security." However, free speech protections are abandoned all too often in favor of supposed government efficiencies and job security for government power brokers.

- The Third Amendment was intended to address the British Quartering Acts, which required colonists to house soldiers of the crown in their private homes. Today, we have the government effectively in our homes (not mention our hip pockets) spying upon our telephone communications, internet traffic, financial transactions, e-mail, "snail mail," *etc.* The government has found the domestic surveillance programs of the NSA and FBI to be a much more efficient way to chill dissent, quell domestic unrest, and to keep tabs on the populace.

If agents of the government were stationed in our homes at least we would have notice of their existence and would have the option and opportunity to remove ourselves from their presence and out of earshot. With the current "Top Secret" surveillance programs, we are not even supposed to know that we are being spied upon much less know and appreciate the extent to which our most personal secrets and private information are being laid bare.

- The Fourth Amendment was added specifically to address British issued Writs of Assistance, which authorized agents of the crown to search for contraband generally and without a requirement of probable cause. I am sure that the now familiar refrain from current government officials was uttered back then as well, "If you're not doing anything 'wrong' then you don't have anything to worry about, and you should have no problem with us snooping into your personal business."

The government trawls channels of communication supposedly in search of (foreign) "wrongdoers." However, the net is being cast excessively wide, and the bycatch entangled in the nets includes domestic innocents. Even if the innocent are able to escape the harrowing confines of the net, the chilling psychological effect, which impairs the rights of free speech and free association, is a price much too high to pay.

- If administrative efficiencies and enforcement of government defined "right" are the prime directives of government, then we should certainly abolish the inefficient, cumbersome, and apparently misguided protections of the Fifth, Sixth, Seventh, and Eight Amendments in all criminal and civil law matters.

    The government cannot be bothered with individual rights and personal property interests when it is the protection of the sovereign and the expansion of its wealth and powers which are paramount.

- As to the Ninth and Tenth Amendments, they were the first casualties of the Leviathan, [1] and they lost

---

[1] In these essays, *Leviathan* is used in the same context as the book of the same name, which was written by Thomas Hobbes (1588–1679) and published in 1651. The name derives from the biblical Leviathan, which is a sea monster referenced in the Tanakh, or the Old Testament. The monster is described extensively in Job 41 and mentioned in Isaiah 27:1. Hobbes' book concerns his views regarding the structure of society and legitimate government (the "sovereign").

their intended meanings and import long ago. Their deaths were hardly mourned in the rush to centralize the cumulative powers of the people in the hands of the political classes, and the resurrections of these reservations of powers to those outside the federal government would certainly be opposed by those whose present powers would be greatly curtailed by their rebirths.

- So, that leaves only the Second Amendment, which prohibits infringement upon the preexisting right of the people to bear arms, as being the last front between the people and a government of unbridled tyranny.

    The Second Amendment is a political right, not a recreational privilege, and the amendment exists to remind those in government that their powers, such as they exist, are derived from the people and that their positions along with their incumbent powers are subject to being taken away at the behest of the people, by force if necessary. The Second Amendment provides an admonition, which politicians ignore at their own peril.

Sovereignty or Liberty -

Of course, the government, through those who wield its formidable powers, would argue vehemently that the expanding actions and scope of government (and the concurrent demise of

6

freedoms and liberties) are entirely for the collective benefit and continuing "safety" of citizens. The minions of government argue:

> *If only you were smart enough, you would understand and accept that government knows what is best for all 300 Million of its citizens.*

In their zealous pursuits of those, who dare to expose the improper aims and abuses of government, officials reveal their own belief that the people cannot be trusted with the truth. Government seemingly acts consistent with the belief that there is an inverse relationship between freedom and safety. In limiting the freedoms of the people, we can be deemed "safe" from all but government itself.

Mark my words: There is a deliberate and systematic effort to abolish any "legitimate expectation of privacy" in the names of "safety" and "national security." Once there is no expectation of privacy, many if not most of the protections contained in the Bill of Rights become superfluous. Without the pesky protections and prohibitions, which are contained in the Bill of Rights (and elsewhere), the government would thereafter be free to usurp sovereign power from the people.

As a sovereign, the government would then be able to allocate and dole out "privileges" (as contrasted with inalienable "rights") in return for sworn allegiance and the faithful performance of duties for the benefit of the sovereign (government). Similarly, the government could reject and remove such "privileges" at will, particularly from those, who do not support the actions, programs, and aims of government.

Eventually, the definitions of the various "threats to national security" would be expanded to include anyone or any act, which threatens the job security of those in power. Does this sound like the United States of America, for which our forefathers and ancestors fought and died to establish and maintain?

Submission to Just Laws -

Some would contend that we do a disservice to our country when we question the objectives, power and authority of government. However, an unjust government has no legitimate authority.

In a "Letter from a Birmingham Jail," Dr. Martin Luther King, Jr. wrote:

> *[T]here are two types of laws: just and unjust. I would be the first to advocate obeying just laws. One has not only a legal but a moral responsibility to obey just laws. Conversely, one has a moral responsibility to disobey unjust laws. I would agree with St. Augustine that "an unjust law is no law at all."*

We owe no allegiance to any particular administration, party or political leader. To the contrary, any allegiance that we have as Americans (including our political leaders) is to the Constitution of the United States. Our political leaders take oaths to support and defend that Constitution, including the parts which restrict and impair the powers of government. Acting in a manner contrary to the Constitution is a violation of every politician's oath of office, and such acts destroy the legitimacy of their positions and acts. The exercise of powers and the usurpation of authority in contravention of the Constitution need not be supported or tolerated by the people.

Thomas Jefferson wrote on November 29, 1775:

Believe me, dear Sir: there is not in the British empire a man who more cordially loves a union with Great Britain than I do. But, by the God that made me, I will cease to exist before I yield to a connection on such terms as the British Parliament propose; and in this, I think I speak the sentiments of America.

Less than a year later, Jefferson penned the Declaration of Independence, which provided in the Preamble:

When in the Course of human events, it becomes necessary for one people to dissolve the political bands which have connected them with another, and to assume among the powers of the earth, the separate and equal station to which the Laws of Nature and of Nature's God entitle them, a decent respect to the opinions of mankind requires that they should declare the causes which impel them to the separation.

Patrick Henry said it much more succinctly, "Give me liberty, or give me death!" George Washington, Thomas Jefferson, Patrick Henry, Benjamin Franklin, *et al.*[2] were "traitors" to the British crown, and had the Revolutionary War ended differently, they would have been executed as such.

History is written by the victors, and the deciding factor between whether one dies a traitor or is celebrated as a patriot turns on which side fires the final shot. Or, to quote Bertrand Russell, "War does not determine who is right – only who is left."

_____

[2] Meaning: "…and others."

Many persons argued then (as others do today) that success against such a formidable foe would be impossible. However, a battle for "independence" is not a war that must be won through absolute victory. Guerrilla tactics rather than demonstrations of brute force are generally the *modus operandi*.[3]

(Un)Civil Disobedience -

Just imagine the chaos and inefficiencies that might be inflicted upon the United States from a small but determined band of domestic "revolutionaries." For nearly twenty-four hours, a major metropolitan area was put on lock-down because of the two Boston Bombers. For several days, much of California was in chaos because of the actions of one disgruntled former police officer. The impact of these events far exceeded the limited means of the actors.

The "victory" comes in exposing the weaknesses and shortcomings of government and by forcing government to narrow its focus and rein in its scope. The Revolutionary War was not fought to conquer Great Britain. Instead, the battles were fought to rid the colonists of the intrusions, which the British imposed upon their lives and affairs.

By exponentially increasing the costs and inefficiencies of governance, victory ultimately goes to those capable of self-sufficiency and self-rule. No government can successfully govern a people, who do not voluntarily subject themselves to the authority of that government. However, "revolution" and "resistance" need not take on the form of armed conflict or

---

[3] Meaning: Mode of Operating – "M.O."

violence. The mechanisms of insurrection and change can be more subtle.

For example, our country's tax and revenue policies are based upon self-reporting and voluntary contributions. Should large segments of the population simply refuse to report income and neglect to pay taxes (*a la* Greece) the mechanisms of revenue collection would grind to a halt and tax enforcement agencies would be overwhelmed. Even if the enforcement mechanisms could keep pace, the result would be even more overcrowded jails housing otherwise law-abiding citizens.

In the absence of public shame and rebuke, criminal codes quickly lose their deterrent effect. Thereafter, the moral imperative is nonexistent. The only issue involves weighing the potential benefit of noncompliance versus the potential punishment should one get caught and be convicted.

The result could look much like the current by-product of this nation's decades long "War on Drugs." That perennial war effort has been ineffective in stopping the influx and distribution of drugs, but it has succeeded in establishing an underclass of persons, who are recreational users or drug addicts. Few would harbor sympathy for drug lords and kingpins, who prey on the weaknesses and addictions of other men; however, the net, which is cast by government, more often sweeps up recreational users and those suffering from dependency and addiction.

One eventually has to ask, "Is it a reasonable and effective use of government resources to pursue and punish persons, through incarceration or otherwise, for personal choices (even if such choices relate to vices and addictions)?"

Government has taken the position that it is appropriate to protect persons from themselves. However, rather than taking steps and implementing programs to lessen drug dependence or to address addiction, the government's tactic is to convict and incarcerate such persons thereby branding the "victim" as a criminal and assuring that his contributions to society and his self-sufficiency will be hampered even further. Government would argue that it has been engaged in pursuing the supposed "good" of lessening in the impact of illicit drugs on society; nevertheless, the incessant costs of enforcement must be weighed against the limited benefits to society at large.[4]

Prohibition (as instituted by the 18th Amendment to the Constitution and subsequently repeated by the 21st Amendment) is the textbook example of government action, supposedly for the collective benefit of the people, which was entirely ineffective because it did not have the support and assent of the general population. In attempting to control a vice (*i.e.* limit a liberty), which was favored by the people, the government faced ineffective police enforcement and courts that were overwhelmed by the number of "criminals" being processed and jailed. Organized Crime had the incentive and a mechanism

---

[4] On August 29, 2013, the U.S. Justice Department advised that it would essentially turn a blind eyed regarding enforcement of marijuana restrictions in states, which have legalized the recreational use of cannabis (specifically Washington and Colorado). This is true despite federal prohibitions extending back seventy-five (75) years and classification of marijuana by the Drug Enforcement Administration (DEA) as a Schedule I Drug, supposedly having no beneficial application or accepted medicinal use. A Pew Research Center poll found that sixty percent (60%) of Americans opposed enforcement by the Justice Department in such cases.

through which to grow in scope and power, and corruption ran rampant throughout law enforcement and government agencies.[5]

What is the utility in the government pursuing a course of action, which may be legitimately opposed by a significant segment of the population or espoused by a mere majority?

Consider this in regards to persons, who are willing to risk potential conflict with foreign foes rather than suffer the certain loss of liberty and freedom. Should those, who value liberty over illusions of safety, sit back quietly while their rights and liberties erode?

Also, consider this in regards to entitlement programs or government benefits, which have at their core the objective of redistributing wealth. Should "producers" silently acquiesce to the demands of government that they give up their wealth for the exclusive benefit of others within society?

Or, it is entirely appropriate that one use all reasonable means to protect his property and to assure his rights of life, liberty, and the pursuit of happiness in whatever ways that he chooses to define such rights?

Citizens do not have a duty to aid in the efficiencies and to assure the smooth operations of government. Therefore, persons are free not to subject themselves to such processes, and if they are willing to endure the wrath of government, they may choose to actively oppose the actions and to hinder the mechanisms of government. Every objector, protestor, and dissident increases the ineffectiveness and inefficiencies of government.

---

[5] It was in response to this exponential increase in the workload of the courts that the use of "Plea Bargains" became commonplace in order to clear cases.

13

When increasing energies, efforts, and monies are expended for regulation and enforcement, fewer resources are available for the more productive aims of government. These things fall under the rubric of, "Civil Disobedience," and the aim is to effect change through nonviolent (even if disruptive) means.

Of course, I am not advocating armed revolution; however, I am not so confident so as to discount the effects that current policies have in sowing seeds of discord and insurrection, and if nourished by continuing strife and conflict, those seeds may ultimately grow to fruition. The import of my words is intentional.

I do not believe that either a Nanny State or Big Brother government is capable of insuring the "peace" and "safety" that our government supposedly protects so zealously. Within a free society, the people must accept mutuality of obligations and commit themselves to self-restraint and self-regulation. In the alternative, no amount of government restraint and enforcement would be sufficient to impose laws, to which the people choose not to be subjected, no matter how "beneficial" they may be.

Government fears the resulting chaos and inefficiencies arising both from armed rebellion and nonviolent Civil Disobedience. Such acts exacerbate the ineffectiveness and inefficiencies of government and expose the fragile illusions of harmony and safety. The current government chooses to identify, as malcontents, criminals, traitors, and perhaps ultimately "terrorists," those who highlight its flaws and who dare to point out its breaches, excesses, and abuses.

A more prudent and effective government would recognize such "threats" as a failure of the mechanisms of government and would work diligently to assure the wellbeing of the citizenry rather than haphazardly pursuing the pacification of the populace. Government must do a better job of "selling" the collective benefits of government and its associated programs.

Consideration in some form must flow not just to those, who directly benefit from the government's largesse, but also to those, who are less dependent upon government and from whom the wealth of government is conscripted. Only when citizens personally buy into the social contract and feel that they are receiving the benefits of their bargains will they forego the urge to breach that contract and not seek ways to evade their respective duties and obligations.

The Lesser Evil: *Impeachment* -

President Obama and his congressional co-conspirators (from both sides of the aisle) are involved in repeated and deliberate abdications from their constitutional duties and obligations. Some have called for the removal of the President (and others) by Impeachment based upon his abuses of power and deliberate violations of the Constitution. However, any action for Impeachment would be in vain.

The Democratically controlled Senate, with which the power to convict rests following the issuance of Articles of Impeachment by the lower House, could never secure the two-thirds vote required for conviction and removal from office.

In reports on the debates during the Constitutional Convention, it is stated:

15

Dr. [Benjamin] Franklin was for retaining the clause [on impeachment], as favorable to the executive. ... What was the practice before this, in cases where the chief magistrate rendered himself obnoxious? Why, recourse was had to assassination, in which he was not only deprived of his life, but of the opportunity of vindicating his character. It would be the best way, therefore, to provide in the Constitution for the regular punishment of the executive, where his misconduct should deserve it, and for his honorable acquittal, where he should be unjustly accused.

The complicit nature of the government actors and the ingrained desire to protect the *status quo* power structure assure that meaningful changes to the underlying structure and behaviors of government are unlikely. We are seeing evidence of why the federal government was intended to be a government of limited enumerated powers. Awaiting the implementation of "corrective actions" by government itself would be like putting a finger in a low dike while awaiting the onslaught of a racing tsunami.

Other persons have questioned, "Why does the Supreme Court of the United States ("SCOTUS") not act to rein in the abuses and deficiencies in the other branches of government?"

Our Supreme Court is not a "Constitutional Court." SCOTUS does not (and arguably cannot) give advisory rulings on the constitutionality of any action or proposed law, much less impose its will on the other two co-equal branches of government when those branches choose to act in concert. Only in response to a *bona fide* dispute or controversy in the actual application of law, can SCOTUS rule.

Nevertheless, acknowledging and highlighting the illegal and unconstitutional acts of this administration (and the government in general) are imperative to effect change. Complacency and blind acceptance cannot be tolerated.

The battle for America cannot be won so long as the average man on the street continues to believe that abuses of government are "legal" or "constitutional":

- The selective enforcement of federal laws by the President (and by the Justice Department headed by the President's minion, Eric Holder);[6]

- The unwarranted expansion of executive and administrative powers;

- The unprecedented erosion of the right of privacy; and

- The blatant disregard for numerous provisions of the Bill of Rights.

Citizens are being spat upon by government, and many persons believe it when the minions of government offer assurances to them that it is only raining.

Conclusion -

Some strife and conflicts, armed or otherwise, are inevitable in life. The primary issues are whether we as individuals rise to meet life's challenges or whether government ultimately succeeds in depriving us of the tools necessary to fend for ourselves so that we are all collectively wards of the state.

---

[6] "[T]o contend that the obligation imposed on the president to see the laws faithfully executed implies a power to forbid their execution is a novel construction of the Constitution, and is entirely inadmissible." *Kendall v. U.S.* ex rel. *Stokes*, 37 U.S. 524, 525 (1838).

Government can either adopt the proper role of fostering the individual rights, liberties, and freedoms of its people or government can attempt to expand its own power and can allow its agencies to expand their fiefdoms in contravention of independence, self-determination, and self-sufficiency of the people.

A government, which is intent upon self-preservation rather that protection of individual rights, guarantees the demise of those rights, and the resulting losses of personal rights and individual liberties ultimately will assure the downfall of that government.

It is time that we as a people shore up the foundations of our society and stop the erosion of our individual rights. It is imperative that we take back the reins of government so that government is once again a shield in defense of personal liberties and individual rights rather than a weapon to be wielded by those fortunate enough to lay temporal claim to its powers.

The superior powers and authority of the people can be exercised by voting into office those, who recognize and respect the rights and freedoms of the people, and by exposing those who would use the powers of government to curtail and suppress such freedoms. Now is not a time to be timid or complacent. Now is the time to stand up, to speak unwaveringly, and to be heard across this great land.

Bill of Rights

Half Truths are Whole Lies:
A Government no longer for the People

Introduction -

On June 6, 2013, the British newspaper, *The Guardian*, reported that the United States National Security Agency ("NSA") and the Federal Bureau of Investigation ("FBI"), had secured an Order from the Foreign Intelligence Surveillance Court ("FISA") related to the business records of Verizon, one of the nation's largest communications carriers. The cited authorization for the Order is the euphemistically titled, "Patriot Act," which was adopted during the furor following 9-11.

The FISA court nearly always meets in secret. The only party represented before the court is the U.S. Government. No adverse or "opposing" positions are represented or heard at such hearings. The court rarely, if ever, issues written opinions explaining its rulings, and most of its rulings are classified as "Top Secret."

Some would argue that the FISA court simply "rubber stamps" government requests. The process can be compared to a Grand Jury proceeding, where only the prosecutor presents evidence in seeking a criminal indictment. At the recommendation (or insistence) of the prosecutor, grand juries almost always indict the alleged perpetrator. Given the one-sided presentation of evidence, very rarely does a grand jury find that the proposed indictment is "not a true bill."

From 1979-2006, a period of nearly three (3) decades, 22,990 applications for warrants were made to the FISA court, of which 22,985 were approved, and only five (5) were definitively rejected. Since Obama took office, only ONE (1) application has been rejected by the FISA court, and ten (10) others were apparently withdrawn by the government.[7]

The Verizon Order directs the telecommunications company to make transfers on an "ongoing, daily basis" of "telephony metadata" for essentially ALL of Verizon's wireless and traditional landline customers. "Metadata" are the collections of information that include: Originating number, number called, duration of call, locations of parties, *etc.* This vast amount of personal information is stored in government maintained databases, which can be mined in order to establish associations among callers. Verizon has nearly 100 Million domestic cell phone customers, whose records would be covered by this order. Certainly, it is safe to presume that there are similar standing orders for AT&T and other national telephone and communications carriers.

Initially, the White House would "neither confirm nor deny" the existence of any such order(s), but under pressure from an outraged citizenry and faced with the obvious truth, the White House unapologetically acknowledged the program. The administration attempted to defend the need for such secret domestic spying, and officials vigorously condemned the disclosure as being a purportedly certain but nebulous threat to "national security."

The disclosure of this "Top Secret" domestic surveillance program was followed later the same day [06/06/2013] by a

---

[7] SOURCE: www.epic.org.

20

similar report in the *Washington Post*, which was quickly confirmed by *The Guardian*. This later report identified a second secret domestic spy program, which is operated by the NSA and codenamed, "PRISM." This program is even more vast and sweeping than the warehousing of all domestic telephone records.

While most of us are casually familiar with the functions of the FBI, some persons may not know that the NSA is an intelligence gathering agency. Its history goes back decades, but it is tasked with gathering and analyzing data and intelligence in the name of national security. The NSA is an agency of the U.S. Military, and as such, its personnel answer to the President. It is part of the Executive Branch of the Federal Government. The NSA's stated targets are "foreign," but in the name of "efficiency" the NSA accumulates information domestically on essentially all Americans.

The Death of Privacy -

PRISM allows the government to connect directly to the information "pipes" utilized by the country's largest Information Technology ("IT"), social networking, and internet service companies: Microsoft, Apple, Google, Yahoo, FaceBook, Twitter, Skype, *etc.* PRISM has been described as utilizing a technology, which "splits" the information flow coming into and going from the servers operated by these IT companies. You can quite literally imagine a "prism" which splits the light traveling via fiberoptic cables (and thus bifurcating the flow of information).

This concept of siphoning from the flow of information versus utilizing the company servers to analyze and manipulate the information allows a notable distinction evidenced within the adamant (and nearly identical) denials from several "corporate partners" of the NSA. The companies issued statements and press releases, which provided the disingenuous assurance "that the government does not have DIRECT access to our SERVERS." [Emphasis added.]

The government does not need access to the servers if it is capable of duplicating the data flow going into and coming out of the various sites. The duplicated and redirected flow of information can then be housed on government computers awaiting mining by one of the many alphabet agencies involved in "intelligence" and "law enforcement," the latter sometimes being euphemistically called "justice."

More than a decade ago, a computer technician, with whom I consulted professionally, described the technology that would allow the NSA to use computer readers to "scan" internet traffic (*e.g.* E-mail, file transfers, photographs, web-based communications, *etc.*). The process is similar to the program by which the government is said to "listen" to international telephone communications. While it is impossible for human beings to "eavesdrop" on all such calls, computers can scan the communications for key words and digital elements. Upon identifying one or more of these pre-defined "red flags," the computer can then record or redirect the communications and send the information to be reviewed by a human technician.

I remember being somewhat incredulous when I initially heard of such supposed capabilities. These programs seemed to be the creations of overactive imaginations, conspiracy theorists, or spy novelists. In the intervening years, I have heard similar reports from sources that I deemed sufficiently knowledgeable and well informed so as to give credence to the existence of such technologies and capabilities. My only lingering questions related to the extents to which these powers and abilities were actually utilized and whether such expansive powers could be harnessed and controlled so as to be used only for "good."

Willkommen to Amerika -

Some persons, both within the government and among the citizenry, have endeavored to downplay the government's hoarding and mining of personal data. They argue that the treasure trove is only useful if you focus and filter it related to a limited number of targets. This argument proceeds that the volume of information is too immense to allow it to be used against citizens in general. The belief is that there is not a computer or storage facility big enough to make use of the voluminous information, which the NSA and FBI are allegedly siphoning from the internet. It should always be remembered, however, "Where there is a will there is a way."

The U.S. Government is constructing an NSA Data Center in the Utah desert. The cost estimates for the buildings and infrastructure alone approach $2 Billion, and that number does not include computer equipment and operating costs, which will also likely be measured in the billions. The government is using tax moneys that you pay in order to spy on you, and the Utah

23

Data Center is not unique. That center is one of network of similar operations with pods scattered throughout the United States. The Utah Data Center will have computing power and data storage well beyond the comprehension of the average citizen. The storage capacity is rumored to be as much as **Five (5) Zettabytes of data.** That capacity means little without a point of reference, but it is equal to the storage capacity of **312 Billion iPhones**. It is official; the United States government is the world's largest computer hacker.

By way of analogy, all of us have used the United States Postal Service in order to deliver written communications. We routinely deposit letters into the mail. Thereafter, an agency of the government has access, custody, and control of our mail. Yet, we do not anticipate or expect government agents to read our mail. It is interesting that the government has to have a court issued warrant to read the mail, which we deposit voluntarily into its custody. Nevertheless, the government supposedly needs no justification whatsoever to accumulate and store every bit and byte of e-mail and data transmissions that go across the Internet.

PRISM is the functional equivalent of the federal government photocopying every piece of mail that goes to the U.S. Postal Service ("USPS"), sticking it in a filing cabinet, and saving it just in case they need to use it to incriminate you later.[8] Does anyone believe that the public would stand still and allow the Post Office to be used in that way? Why should our

---

[8] Subsequent leaks by Edward Snowden led to the revelation that the USPS systematically scans and catalogues the "TO" and "FROM" information from the face of nearly every mail piece, which it handles.

computers and the Internet be any different? Can we not reasonably expect privacy in our personal communications whether written or digital?

The visual of papers and documents protruding from overstuffed filing cabinets is reminiscent of stories from Communist Eastern Europe. In those countries, the people feared the government and the government feared losing its slippery grip on power. Paranoia abounded on all sides, but one could not say that all fears were unfounded. This strained relationship between the state and its people was the subject of the German movie, *The Lives of Others*, which won the 2006 Oscar for "Best Foreign Language Film."

The film tells the story of The Stasi, East Germany's feared secret police. The Stasi kept copious records, which included minute details of the mundane lives of ordinary East German citizens. The Stasi employed 100,000 persons, and it had twice that number of informants, who were counted on to spy on their friends and neighbors.

I hear the retort, "But, this is America not a Communist state!" Recent history need only go back so far as the administration of George W. Bush and his Attorney General, John Ashcroft. Ashcroft proposed the Terrorism Information and Prevention System ("TIPS") whereby Americans would be recruited to spy on each other. Although the TIPS program was ultimately prohibited under the Homeland Security Act of 2002, PRISM makes this process much more covert and efficient, but no less intrusive and offensive. In the case of East Germany, and likely much of the Communist world, the government paranoia was a cancer that ate away from the inside. In the words of *Pogo* cartoonist, Walt Kelly, "We have met the enemy, and he is us."

Language and the Art of Deception -

The Obama Administration is completely unabashed and without contrition. Officials came out with guns blazing to defend and justify both recently disclosed domestic spy programs. The President and his minions quickly condemned the leaks, which opened the eyes of Americans to the existence and potential scope of these "Top Secret" surveillance programs. Rather than apologizing for obvious abuses and overreach, the administration dismissively described such government actions as an inalterable part of the *status quo*, and they directed the American citizens to accept this loss of privacy as the supposedly necessary cost to be paid for the illusion of safety from enemies of the state, both foreign and domestic.

Before becoming President, Dwight D. Eisenhower was a Five-Star General and Supreme Commander of Allied Forces in Europe during World Ward II. I would offer that President Eisenhower knew a thing or twelve about national security, military secrets, and what he termed the "Military-Industrial Complex." In his last televised address before stepping down from the Presidency, Eisenhower warned:

> *This conjunction of an immense military establishment and a large arms industry is new in the American experience. The total influence — economic, political, even spiritual — is felt in every city, every statehouse, every office of the federal government. We recognize the imperative need for this development. Yet we must*

26

not fail to comprehend its grave implications. Our toil, resources and livelihood are all involved; so is the very structure of our society. In the councils of government, we must guard against the acquisition of unwarranted influence, whether sought or unsought, by the military-industrial complex. The potential for the disastrous rise of misplaced power exists, and will persist.

We must never let the weight of this combination endanger our liberties or democratic processes. We should take nothing for granted. Only an alert and knowledgeable citizenry can compel the proper meshing of the huge industrial and military machinery of defense with our peaceful methods and goals so that security and liberty may prosper together.

[Emphasis added.]

The revelation of these domestic surveillance programs must be viewed in the light of other recent stories involving apparent government overreach and abuses (*i.e.* Benghazi "Talking Points," IRS v. "Tea Party," and Justice Department subpoenas of media records). In responding to the most recent disclosures, government officials again used "talking points" to explain and defend the domestic surveillance programs, and the arguments propounded by such officials were consistent and adamant, if not sincere and convincing:

- *These programs are "legal."* – As defined by whom … the Administration … the Justice Department … the "Top Secret" FISA Court? The Administration and Eric Holder's Justice Department have developed "opinions" as to the legality of certain actions undertaken and positions adopted by the

27

administration. These "opinions" have not been subjected to independent judicial scrutiny and are certainly less than universally accepted.[9]

- ***These programs are subject to "vigorous" judicial scrutiny.*** – It is hard to argue convincingly that a "Top Secret" court, which has denied less than a dozen government requests out of tens of thousands of applications in thirty-five (35) years, provides oversight, which may be described as either "zealous" or "vigorous."

- ***These programs are "necessary" for national security.*** – If that is the case, what are the limits, if any, on the government's infringement upon or curtailment of personal liberties and privacy in the interests of safety and national security?

- ***The scopes of these programs are "reasonable."*** – As determined by whom … those who insist on them being secret … those responsible for enforcement and implementation? The citizens can hardly pass judgment on programs that arc not even known to exist.

---

[9] See Nakashima, Ellen and Ann E. Marimow, "Judge: NSA's collecting of phone records is probably unconstitutional," *Washington Post* (December 16, 2013). U.S. District Judge Richard J. Leon found that the National Security Agency's daily collection of virtually all Americans' phone records is almost certainly unconstitutional. Leon ruled that Plaintiffs' "demonstrated a substantial likelihood of success" on the basis of Fourth Amendment privacy protections against unreasonable searches. The judge granted the request for an injunction, which blocks the collection of phone data, and he ordered the government to destroy any of Plaintiffs' records that have been gathered. However, the judge stayed action on his ruling pending a government appeal. For a strikingly contrasting ruling by another Federal Judge, see Horwitz, Sari, "NSA collection of phone data is lawful, federal judge rules," *Washington Post* (December 27, 2013).

- *The programs strike a "balance" between privacy and safety.* – The government certainly has its proverbial thumb on the scale in striking a balance of personal rights and individual liberties against apparently interminable "threats" against national security and in furtherance of illusions of safety.

In trying to understand what the government is actually saying about these programs, it is important to recognize how finely government officials and spokesmen mince words. Every statement must be parsed, and every word must be examined for meaning, context, and subtext. In what amounts to extreme creativity with and manipulation of the truth, the companies, which have been recruited into the PRISM program, consistently said that the government does not have "<u>direct</u> access to our <u>servers</u>." [Emphasis added.] More importantly, they did not deny that that government has access to the equally fruitful flows of information.

Imagine the potential reaction by users of the internet, when the nation's largest IT companies must admit that their so-called "Privacy Policies" are functionally nonexistent. Imagine the consternation of internet users when they realize that nearly every e-mail, telephone call, file transfer, text message, picture post, and social network site is accessible by and perhaps even stored on computers maintained by the government.

Intelligence officials disputed reports that PRISM was engaged in "data mining," and instead described the activities as "data collection." It was unclear whether the distinction between the two is substantive or simply a matter of semantics.

Forced to address the existence of these data hoarding programs, the Director of National Intelligence, James Clapper, declassified certain materials related to the administration of the programs. He was quick to condemn the leak of information and to state that portions of the media reports were "erroneous." However, Clapper failed to specify and correct any such errors, and he did not deny the scope and extent of the programs themselves.

In statements to the media, Director Clapper said:

> *[The Government] does this under protocols and internal controls that are approved in advance and must be reviewed by the FISA court periodically. This means that the tank can be accessed only for specific reasons -- not to generally roam through.*

In another report, Clapper, described PRISM as follows:

> *PRISM is not an undisclosed collection or data mining program. It is an internal government computer system used to facilitate the government's statutorily authorized collection of foreign intelligence information from electronic communication service providers under court supervision as authorized by Section 702 of the Foreign Intelligence Surveillance Act. ... The United States government does not unilaterally obtain information from the servers of U.S. electronic communication service providers.*

George Orwell, writing in 19**48**, chose the title of his prophetic novel, *1984,* by transposing the last two digits in the current year. He was only about thirty (30) years early in his predictions. George Orwell himself could not have crafted such *doublespeak* as Clapper demonstrates above.

I have twenty-one (21) years of education, doctorate and post-doctorate degrees, and two (2) professional licenses, but I do not have a clue what the latter statement from Clapper is supposed to mean. It is as if politicians and bureaucrats have contrived to distort and subvert the English langue so that it serves more as a weapon for obfuscation than an effective means of communicating facts and truth.

The audience for such lies and deception are those who would be confounded by the enormity of the present issues, those who would cower in fear of the Leviathan that is government, or those who are apathetic to a government, which of late appears more malevolent than benevolent. Clapper alternated between offering assurances to the public and demonstrating outrage regarding the leaks of politically sensitive information. However, such assurances are tepid at best, and the administration's outrage is entirely misplaced. It is the people, who should be outraged that their government treats them as serfs and pawns rather than the collective source of its derived powers.

Government feels that it has done and can do no wrong. The outrage that administration officials portray is not connected to any guilt or shame for the citizens' loss of privacy and freedom. Instead, their outrage comes from having been caught like a petulant child with his hand in the cookie jar. Their lies cannot stand the light of day, and the power afforded by those lies depends on secrecy and a compliant populace.

Caught red handed, their response is to blame the people for looking too closely. They tell us that, if only we would not look behind the curtain, then all would be well.

The current administration (and the federal government in general) is not competent enough to keep IRS agents from going "rogue" against Tea Party groups and those similarly aligned. Why would anyone believe that the same government can keep the nosey roaming fingers of hundreds, if not thousands, of civil servants and government contractors out of the cookie jar?

When considering the security of secrets, regardless of whether such secrets are personal or stem from classification by the government, it is important to note and remember a certain twenty-two (22) year old Army Private, who possessed a "Top Secret" Security Clearance. In the now infamous WikiLeaks disclosure, PFC Bradley Manning provided gigabytes of sensitive government materials to WikiLeaks, and that information eventually was published on the internet for all to see. If the government cannot control its own military personnel, why should it be trusted with implementing and enforcing extensive safeguards, which would be necessary to protect personal information on every U.S. citizen?

When Good Men become Enemies of the State -

On June 9, 2013, *The Guardian* newspaper identified the source of the leaks, on which its initial report on the secret Verizon order was based. The newspaper identified the man at his own insistence. The source stated in an interview that it was his hope that, in identifying himself, the focus would stay on the content of leaked documents and the underlying surveillance programs rather than on the hunt for the source of the leaks.

The twenty-nine (29) year old man, who was responsible for the leaks, is Edward Snowden, a computer technician, who worked with a defense contractor. He is one of thousands of technicians and employees working for hundreds of defense contractors, which make up the military-industrial complex and which benefit from the largesse of government outsourcing.

Snowden had experience working with the CIA and more recently with the NSA. He appears to be as All-American as anyone can be. His early childhood was spent in North Carolina. He and his family later moved to Maryland. More recently, he has lived with his fiancé in Hawaii, and the two of them had made plans to build a life together.

He risked his future, his freedom, and some would say his life to bring this information to light. Before turning over the information to *The Guardian*, he fled to Hong Kong, from where he hopes that extradition will be delayed and hindered.[10] Snowden spoke of the very real fear of rendition by the CIA or other covert operatives. He stated that he feared most for the effect and impact that his actions would have on his family and those whom he loved.

James Clapper, in his role as Director of National Intelligence, argued that whoever leaked that information broke a "sacred trust." Others, who have leaked classified

---

[10] Snowden sought and received offers of political asylum, but the U.S. government actively intervened to assure that Snowden could not travel to any country, which offered protection from extradition. Snowden traveled from Hong Kong to Russia, where after some diplomatic maneuvering, he was granted a temporary visa, which allows him remain in the country for up to a year.

information, have been charged under the arcane World War I era Espionage Act on the theory of their giving information to the enemy.

Snowden was not turning over secrets to the "enemy," unless you consider the American public to be an enemy of the state. He wanted U.S. citizens to know what the federal government was doing ostensibly on their collective behalf. He wanted those, who are most affected by the secret surveillance, to have the opportunity to decide whether the assurances of safety were certain enough to justify the costs already being paid in the losses of privacy, personal freedoms, and individual liberties.

Much to the consternation of those, who would argue vehemently that Snowden and PFC Manning violated some obligation or oath to keep the government's secrets, at any costs, persons who take oaths of allegiance generally aver to *support and defend the Constitution of the United States against all enemies, foreign and domestic.* Americans do not take oaths to serve an individual or even the government collectively. The President himself took an oath of office, in which he swore that he would to the best of his ability *preserve, protect and defend the Constitution of the United States*; although, there are certainly elements of the Constitution to which he is much more faithful than others.

Yes, PFC Manning took an oath to obey the orders of the President of the United States and his commanding officers. However, this oath taken by military personnel applies only so long as those orders are legal. What is "legal" these days tends to be in the eye of the beholder.

Even when there have been clear violations of law, the enforcement of laws by the executive branch is equivocal at times. The administration itself plays fast and loose with the concepts of legality, and it picks and chooses the laws by which to abide, or at least assures an interpretation of such laws, which is consistent with its goals and aims.

Based upon his public statements, Snowden sought to salvage the essence of what it is to be American before the government, which was installed to protect our natural and inalienable rights, usurps those rights permanently. If we relinquish the freedoms and liberties that define what it is to be Americans and relinquish our "inalienable" rights in vain pursuits of fluid concepts of national security and illusory safety, then the would-be terrorists, who have tasked themselves to destroy America, have won already.

Some persons may empathize with Manning and Snowden, but those same persons may also argue that their acts were improper. The actions of these whistleblowers were certainly "illegal" in the eyes of the current administration. Some persons may argue that their idealism was misguided. PFC Manning has repeatedly said that he undertook the actions that he did because he was appalled by the abuses and the calloused brutality that he witnessed from the war zone. Snowden, like Manning, felt that he did not have an avenue to adequately redress the wrongs that he perceived being committed. Whether one agrees with their actions or not, Manning and Snowden have allowed us to peep behind the curtains of the "war on terror" and domestic espionage, and the supposed Wizards of D.C. appear far from "wonderful."

To whom do you turn when there is no independent review within the chain of command? Who is the arbiter of right and wrong when government actions are done in secret with no meaningful oversight? What other forum is there besides the court of public opinion?

The words of Patrick Henry provide an inkling about what our Founding Fathers thought of the government, to which they gave life. Our Founding Fathers craved liberty and freedom from oppression. Patrick Henry was among those, who would likely describe government a necessary evil. Some of his inspiring words are more familiar than others, but many are apropos to the current situation:

> *The Constitution is not an instrument for the government to restrain the people; it is an instrument for the people to restrain the government - lest it come to dominate our lives and interests.*
>
> ***
>
> *The liberties of a people never were, nor ever will be, secure when the transactions of their rulers may be concealed from them.*
>
> ***
>
> *Is life so dear, or peace so sweet, as to be purchased at the price of chains and slavery? Forbid it, Almighty God! I know not what course others may take; but as for me, give me liberty or give me death!* [Emphasis added.]

Tyranny is rarely evidenced by a single over act. It is generally much more covert and subtle. Tyranny often builds from a series of small almost imperceptible acts until the backs of the people are broken. The actions of our government, which have been laid bare by Snowden (and Manning), are not minor or insignificant. Never in my lifetime have I witnessed more threatening and oppressive acts being undertaken so brazenly by our federal government.

I look upon the countenances of Snowden and Manning, and I hear their words. I do not perceive ego-maniacal personalities. I do not see traits of narcissism. I do not hear malice in their words. Instead, these are, by all indications, men of conscience, who were asked to do what all of us should consider unconscionable. Snowden and Manning looked at the actions of our government, and for themselves, they decided that they could no longer stand by in good conscience and facilitate oppressive actions of government. Some may call their actions courageous. Others may call such actions foolhardy, but these men responded to their convictions in favor of what they believed were the best interests of their fellow citizens.

I look once more to the words of Patrick Henry:

They tell us, sir, that we are weak; unable to cope with so formidable an adversary. But when shall we be stronger? Will it be the next week, or the next year? Will it be when we are totally disarmed, and when a British guard shall be stationed in every house? Shall we gather strength by irresolution and inaction? Shall we acquire the means of effectual resistance by lying supinely on our backs and hugging the delusive phantom of hope, until our enemies

37

shall have bound us hand and foot? Sir, we are not weak if we make a proper use of those means which the God of nature hath placed in our power.

Are Snowden and Manning properly compared to the likes of Judas Iscariot, Benedict Arnold, and "Tokyo Rose"? Or, should they be compared more closely to those, who were traitors to the British realm: George Washington, Thomas Jefferson, Benjamin Franklin, Patrick Henry, *etc.*? In an interesting twist, British Prime Minister, Winston Churchill, who was himself a noted historian, said, "History is written by the victors."

Our view of our Founding Fathers would likely be much different had the American Revolution been decided differently. The brush of history is fine and revealing. The portraits of Snowden and Manning are not yet finished, but I am confident that history will paint them in a much more favorable light than they are likely to be seen by the current government.

Each of these men sacrificed the life that he had previously known rather than to continue to live that life aiding and abetting in the destruction of liberty and in the oppression of their fellow man.

I for one would rather risk armed conflict with a foreign foe than to live in a new America, a country in which government is intent upon expanding its own powers and taking away the precious liberties and freedoms of its people. I feel more "unsafe" living in a country with a prying omnipotent government than I would in a country, which is free and poised to defend itself from a foreign adversary.

Politics Makes Strange Bedfellows –[11]

President Obama quickly responded to the growing public hue and cry by saying, "Nobody is listening to your telephone calls." It is fair to translate that statement to mean, *"No human being actively perceives the auditory portion of the telephone communications contemporaneously with the making of the call."* The President did not say that the government cannot and will not listen in on such conversations (or recordings thereof) or that the digital elements of such conversations may not be contemporaneously "scanned" by computer for key words, which may identify the communication or the speaker as a "threat to national security."

From a historical perspective, a "threat to national security" would have been synonymous with any "threat" to the *status quo* of government and to those, who control that government and wield its formidable powers. This would likely explain why strange bedfellows immediately rose to the defense of these domestic surveillance programs.

Sen. Diane Feinstein (D-CA) and Sen. Lindsay Graham (R-SC) were quick to make public statements, in which they uttered the same practiced talking points. I was aghast and appalled when I heard Sen. Graham say that, as a customer of Verizon, he was "OK" with the order commanding daily transmission of the Verizon metadata. Graham's words took on the same tenor and

---
[11] "Misery acquaints a man with strange bedfellows." - William Shakespeare - *The Tempest.*

tone as Attorney General Eric Holder in making recent self-serving statements defending overreach by his Justice Department.

The President should expect that many persons will take no comfort in his similarly self-serving assurances. Bureaucratic alphabet agencies may not be actively listening, but the government admits to having a list of every call that citizens make. It takes nearly no creativity or legwork for an agent of the government to show up brandishing a badge and to demand, from those with whom we may speak, the substance of our conversations. Such demands would be under covert threat of persecution, if not overt threat of prosecution, especially if it is supposedly in the interest of some nebulous concept of "national security."

The mantra, "Just trust us," rings hollow after the disclosure of: Multiple "top secret" domestic spy programs; "rogue" agents at the IRS; lack of respect for the First Amendment as demonstrated by the issuance of secret and excessively broad subpoenas; and a whole host of abject lies and half truths. No, Mr. President, the more informed and skeptical among us say, "We are no longer listening to YOU!" We tire of your lies and deceptions.

David Vladeck, formerly with the Federal Trade Commission ("FTC"), addressed the issue of data mining in typical bureaucratic fashion:

> *[The NSA] differs from a commercial enterprise in the sense that there are checks in the judicial system and in Congress. ... If you believe in the way our*

government is supposed to work, then you should have some faith that those checks are meaningful. If you are skeptical about government, then you probably don't think that kind of oversight means anything.

"Skeptical" is a monumental understatement, and to expect agents of government to serve with absolute altruism or complete selflessness is entirely contrary to historical experience and human nature. Government is not so far removed from commercial enterprises. Success, whether it be in government or business, requires many of the same personal traits and attributes, positive and negative. The overriding objectives of both are similar: Accumulate power and wealth.

Many politicians initially enter service full of idealism and as champions of noble goals. In their political infancy, those seeking public office often see themselves as Cincinnatus, being called upon to serve the people.[12] With few exceptions, barons of industry and politicians evolve to feed upon and to be motivated by the incessant accumulation of power and wealth, either directly or indirectly. Politicians supposedly do not reap direct financial reward from their services, but in growing their fiefdoms they do, in fact, accumulate power and control wealth.

That is not to say that government cannot do good things or that businessmen and politicians cannot have good intentions.

---

[12] According to legend, powerful enemies of Rome, the Aequians, were threatening an invasion of the capital city. The Roman Senate, finding the current consul unprepared to meet the crisis, voted unanimously to confer the extraordinary powers of dictatorship on their most distinguished former general, L. Quinctius Cincinnatus. At the time, Cincinnatus was living in retirement on his four-acre farm outside of Rome, and representatives from the Senate found him working in his field. When Cincinnatus learned of the emergency, which Rome faced, he left his plow standing in the field, bid farewell to his wife, and led the Romans to victory against the Aequians. Fifteen (15) days after assuming the dictatorship, Cincinnatus resigned and returned to his plow.

However, as men accumulate power and wealth, the actions and decisions, which must be undertaken to continue to feed the insatiable beast, tend to blur the lines between "right" and "wrong:"

> *Power tends to corrupt, and absolute power corrupts absolutely. Great men are almost always bad men.*[13]

Despite ideological differences, politicians from both the Democratic and Republican parties are more interested in protecting the current power structure than giving a tinker's damn about personal freedoms and individual liberties. The Executive Branch, through successive administrations, has demonstrated open disdain for any limitations on the President's executive powers. Despite oaths to protect and defend the Constitution, the rights enshrined by that document are hardly stumbling blocks to persons, who are intent upon the unlimited expansion of government powers and who favor restrictions on personal liberties.

Ultimately, a treasure trove of personal information will be too valuable and irresistible for the government and its various agencies not to mine. The more cynical among us will question whether the data could and would be adulterated and actively manipulated to effect the aims of government and to protect those in power. In the name of "national security," the accepted uses of this information will be expanded, and personal liberties will be curtailed and suppressed even further. Any semblance of privacy will be forever lost.

---

[13] John Emerich Edward Dalberg Acton - First Baron Acton (1834–1902).

"Security" will eventually mean "job security" for those in power. "Threats" to that security will include anything that interferes with government efficiencies or shines a negative light on those, who wield the intimidating powers of government. Even if the information is not used as a source of criminal "prosecutions," the threat of government "persecution" will be more than enough to have a tremendous chilling effect on personal freedom and individual liberties.

Ronald Reagan once said, "The nine most terrifying words in the English language are: 'I'm from the government and I'm here to help.'" Those in all levels of government parrot the admonition:

> *Just trust us. We have your best interests at heart. We will only use our immense powers for good. Besides, it is all legal.*

The latter statement comes with a knowing wink and a nod, which itself says:

> *It's legal, because we say it's legal. After all, we make and enforce the laws.*

In this context, "legal" means that the agents of government are unlikely to be subjected to prosecution by a complicit government. It does not mean that such actions are "right," or that those actions are consistent with fair interpretations of federal law.

Rep. Jim Sensenbrenner (R-WI), who authored the increasingly despised "Patriot Act," wrote to Attorney General Eric Holder in response to what the congressman charged was an "overbroad interpretation" of the Patriot Act. Sensenbrenner said he was "disturbed" by the report about the NSA's gathering phone records of Verizon customers and how such actions affect Americans' constitutional rights. The application of the Patriot Act gives new meaning to, "Give an inch ... take a mile." In this case, it was, "Give a mile ... and take away all semblance of privacy."

Transition to Tyranny -

Such unfettered powers are certainly inconsistent with the spirit of the Constitution; although, Obama, in his role as "Constitutional Scholar in Chief," has undertaken tortured and strained interpretations of that venerable document. These most recent government abuses trample all over the inherent and supposedly inalienable rights of all U.S. Citizens.

In a 2008 position paper, then-candidate Barack Obama wrote:

> *There is no reason we cannot fight terrorism while maintaining our civil liberties. ... As president, Barack Obama would revisit the Patriot Act to ensure that there is real and robust oversight of tools like National Security Letters, sneak-and-peek searches, and the use of the material witness provision.*

Even as disclosures of domestic spying filled media reports, a memo found on the White House website, and which bore the signature of President Obama, stated:

> *My Administration is committed to creating an unprecedented level of openness in Government. We will work together to ensure the public trust and establish a system of transparency, public participation, and collaboration. Openness will*

strengthen our democracy and promote efficiency and effectiveness in Government.[14]

President Obama has spent much of his presidency trying to distance and distinguish himself from his predecessor, George W. Bush. Obama rode into Washington on a tide propelled by the promise of hope and change. Unfortunately, it seems that the French novelist, Jean-Baptiste Alphonse Karr, was correct when he said, "The more things change the more that they stay the same."

The Supreme Court of the United States ("SCOTUS") first recognized an express "Right to Privacy" in *Griswald v. Connecticut*, 381 U.S. 479 (1965). That same constitutionally derived right is the basis for the controversial SCOTUS decision, *Roe v. Wade*, 410 U.S. 113 (1973). These are not concepts that should be foreign to the administration or to a Constitutional Law professor, as Obama is touted as being. Nevertheless, in an interesting juxtaposition, we have a federal government that wants to operate shrouded in secrecy with its actions hidden from the citizens, who are the source of its power. Yet, that same government, which is tasked with protecting the rights of its citizens, including the "Right of Privacy," has determined that the citizens are entitled to have nearly no secrets from that government.

Federal powers were originally enumerated and limited to avoid excessive concentration of government power and authority, which would lead to abuses. Where power is concentrated in the hands of a relative few, with no effective

---

[14] SOURCE: www.whitehouse.gov – Emphasis added.

45

oversight, it is not an issue of whether that power will be abused. It is only a question of when and to what extent. In the ultimate demonstration of hubris, Obama and his minions believe themselves to be immune to the temptations of absolute power. They believe that they will be unmoved by the irresistible Sirens' Song, and they believe themselves to be unsusceptible to the inevitable corruption, which would otherwise befall mortal men.

If you tell the same lies often enough with enough feigned conviction, the pliable sheeple are bound to believe and fall into line. Obama and his administration are taking yet another page out of the playbook of disgraced former President, Richard M. Nixon. In responding to an interviewer's question about Nixon's alleged crimes, the former President said, "When the President does it, that means that it's not illegal."

With apologies to Admiral David Farragut, the attitude of the administration seems to be, "Damn the Constitution, full speed ahead!" Administration officials remain committed to a script that defies reason and relies on the credulity of the general public.

A colleague used to say, "If you cannot dazzle them with brilliance, baffle them with [B.S.]" In the zealous adherence to government dogma and the use of deception, the administration follows in the footsteps of the most unsavory of historical figures, Adolph Hitler, who said:

> *By the skillful and sustained use of propaganda, one can make a people see even heaven as hell or an extremely wretched life as paradise.*

Truth: The First Casualty of an Undeclared War -

Rather than acknowledging abuse and overreach, the administration doubles down on a bet that it can survive this newest revolt by an oppressed citizenry and that it can maintain a desperate and weakening grasp on power. Even the co-equal branches of government are victims of subterfuge, lies, and deceit from those within the administration.

I will forego detailed examples unrelated to the instant issues, but I will note:

- Eric Holder being held in contempt of Congress related to the failed weapons sting, "Fast and Furious;"
- Holder also being less than forthright regarding his knowledge of and involvement in media subpoenas;
- Erroneous testimony by the IRS Commissioner regarding excessive scrutiny of "Tea Party" groups;
- An IRS official "pleading the Fifth" and refusing to testify to Congress; and
- Repeated delays and refusal by the administration to provide information on Benghazi "Talking Points."

As noted before, "rumors" about government spy programs and the extents to which government agencies can and do surveil and maintain records of nearly all citizens have circulated for years. When such information reaches the halls of Congress, members of Congress take the opportunity during Congressional hearings to inquire of administrative officials about the existence of such programs and government capabilities.

On March 20, 2012, General Keith Alexander, NSA Director, gave testimony to Congress. In response to repeated and detailed questioning by a member of the committee, the General unequivocally denied the existence of any program whereby the NSA could intercept and read internet traffic and other communications.

On March 12, 2013, Sen. Ron Wyden (D-OR), who sits on the Senate Intelligence Committee, asked the Director of National Intelligence, James Clapper, if the NSA collects data on millions of Americans. Clapper answered:

> *No, sir ... Not wittingly. There are cases where they could inadvertently perhaps collect, but not wittingly.*

I guess that "not wittingly" is government code for "**YES**."

In an interview with NBC's Andrea Mitchell, Clapper responded to questions about the veracity of his comments:

> *... I responded in what I thought was the most truthful, or least untruthful manner by saying no. ... And this has to do with of course somewhat of a semantic, perhaps some would say too-- too cute by half. But it is-- there are honest differences on the semantics of what-- when someone says "collection" to me, that has a specific meaning, which may have a different meaning to him.*[15]

Clapper seems to be channeling former President Bill Clinton, who during his 1998 grand jury testimony on the Monica Lewinsky affair, spoke the now infamous words, "It depends on what the meaning of the word 'is' is."

For his part, Sen. Wyden was asking questions, which were similar to questions that he posed to intelligence officials a year

---

[15] NBC News – June 10, 2013.

earlier but which were not fully answered. Sen. Wyden has said that he made Clapper's office aware that some form of the question was going to be asked during the hearing. Despite this "heads up," it was apparently impossible for Clapper to form an "entirely truthful" answer to the question.

How is it that such persons give testimony to Congress and make averments, which are full of overt lies and knowing half truths, but are not criminally charged with perjury? Let's see: President Obama, the renowned constitutional scholar, makes strained interpretations of laws in his favor, and his whipping boy, Eric Holder, dutifully agrees with his boss on such issues. Holder's Justice Department also has discretion in choosing who is charged with crimes. The administration has political cover provided by a clandestine court. That top secret court applies laws, which nearly no one understands, and the court makes decisions without the benefit of published rulings and opinions. All of this is comfortably hidden from public scrutiny and shielded from meaningful review and oversight. This sounds like a pretty sweet set up for everyone but the U.S. citizen.

If administration officials were required to abide by the familiar oath, "To Tell the Truth, the Whole Truth, and Nothing but the Truth," those persons, including Obama himself, would face accountability for lies and overt deception, not only to the American people, but also to Congress and likely to the judiciary, as co-equal branches of government.

Is the Loss of Privacy a Sunk Cost? -

The President and other government officials portray these assaults on individual liberties and personal freedoms as no big deal. They see only impediments and no benefits to the checks and oversights required by the Fourth Amendment (Searches and Seizures) and Fifth Amendments (Self-incrimination).

Search warrants are orders issued by courts allowing what would otherwise be impermissible infringements upon the rights of individuals. Such actions by the judicial branch are supposedly undertaken only after "independent" review of the facts. The burden is on the prosecution or executive branch to establish that probable cause exists to believe that a crime has been committed by the individual, who is the subject of the warrant. The government now argues that it cannot be bothered by things like "probable cause." The administration sees no problem with assembling the practical equivalent of "FBI Files" on all citizens without any requirement that the subjects are involved in a crime.

Generations of American citizens, including high level politicians, feared the power of the FBI and its power hungry Director, J. Edgar Hoover. Through the scourge of McCarthyism and through the decades of oppression leading up to the Civil Rights Act, citizens feared the "long arm of the law."

The fear of those citizens was unrelated to any sense of guilt arising from the commission of any act, which was inherently "wrong" or criminal. Instead, citizens feared finding themselves in the crosshairs of a government, which was intent upon maintaining an irrational and discriminatory *status quo*. The fear was that they would be devoured by a government, which is committed to its own expansion and self-preservation.

The FBI compiled expansive "files" and dossiers on individuals and groups. Many subjects had done nothing any more dangerous or subversive than attempt to exercise their constitutionally guaranteed rights of free speech and free association. These inalienable rights, which are enshrined in the Bill of Rights, do not exist to protect persons, who hold the reins of government. These rights do not exist to make government more efficient or "easy." Governing should be "hard" when the objectives of government include aims to deprive citizens of personal rights, individual liberties, and self-determination.

Some persons were fully aware or at least confident that they were subjects of heightened scrutiny: Dr. Martin Luther King, Jr. and others, who were fighting for acknowledgement of Civil Rights for racial minorities, and those in Hollywood and elsewhere, who were "blacklisted" for "anti-American Communist activities." No matter how "innocent" such person may have known themselves to be, these persons undoubtedly felt the "chilling" effects that such scrutiny put on their lives and their desired activities.

Other persons had no idea that by simply living their day-to-day lives they could be the subjects of government scrutiny. On November 8, 2013, ninety-eight-year-old Penn Kimball died. I am certain that most persons have never heard of him.[16]

---

[16] Portions of the following are adapted from: Schudel, Matt, "Penn Kimball, journalist and teacher, dies at 98," *Washington Post* (November 9, 2013).

Kimball, a journalist and longtime Columbia University journalism professor, sued the federal government in the 1980's after he learned that he was secretly declared a security risk decades earlier. ...
In the 1940's and 1950's, Kimball was a journalist with stints at Time, the New Republic, the New York Times, and CBS-TV.

In his 1983 book, *The File*, Kimball wrote:

I was stunned. I simply had no idea that for more than half of my life my name had been on file in Washington as a dangerous radical, a disloyal American, a national security risk, a subversive 'too clever' to be caught holding a membership card in the Communist Party.

This man, who was considered a "national security risk," would have been described by most persons outside of the paranoia fueled federal government as a model American:

Kimball was an Eagle Scout, a football player at Princeton University, a Rhodes Scholar, and a Marine Corps captain during World War II.

Kimball told the *Washington Post* in 1983:

There's nothing more precious to a man than his character and reputation, and what the United States government did is take that away from me.

In 1987, the federal government finally agreed to purge its files in return for Kimball dropping his lawsuit. Kimball spent years of his life in litigation trying to clear his good name and that of his deceased wife. Both of them had suffered from the presumptive guilt that the government placed upon them by naming them subversives four (4) decades earlier.

Kimball's story is not unique. A substantially similar story could be told by thousands, and likely 10's of thousands, of Americans. Those numbers include members of America's Greatest Generation and their children, Baby Boomers, who came of age during the tumultuous generation that spanned the 50's, 60's and 70's. Anyone, who expressed an original thought or who dared to question the efficacy and objectives of government, was likely to find himself subject to the prying and accusatory eyes of that government.

Today, every American citizen is presumptively guilty of subversion and "un-American activities." The NSA collects information and personal data using methods and in such a volume so as to make those copious "FBI Files" look like a cryptic note scribbled on the inside cover of a matchbook. The same discomfort and fear, which was felt by the former subjects of clandestine FBI operations, should be felt today by every American.

There is a huge difference between records being accessible via a court issued warrant (or even subpoena) versus a "Top Secret" program that stores essentially every digital bit (and byte) of information on all U.S. citizens without any prior showing of criminal behavior or wrongdoing. Even when the government meets its burden and establishes a reasonable need for the requested information, a judge generally orders warrants, which are narrowly tailored and limited to surveillance or seizure related to a single individual, or specified telephone number, address, *etc.* Judges generally do not issue broad open ended orders or warrants so as to allow constant surveillance of more than 300 Million U.S. citizens.

Upon learning of the Verizon order, former Vice President, Al Gore took to Twitter where he described such actions as, "Obscene." I would tend to agree with him. Power and hubris inevitably lead to corruption and tyranny. Just as Al Gore is not one from whom I would normally take my lead on political issues, I also find myself surprisingly aligned with the American Civil Liberties Union ("ACLU"). ACLU Deputy Legal Director Jameel Jaffer:

> *The stories published over the last two days make clear that the NSA – part of the military – now has direct access to every corner of Americans' digital lives. Unchecked government surveillance presents a grave threat to democratic freedoms. These revelations are a reminder that Congress has given the executive branch far too much power to invade individual privacy, that existing civil liberties safeguards are grossly inadequate, and that powers exercised entirely in secret, without public accountability of any kind, WILL CERTAINLY BE ABUSED. [Emphasis added.]*

In the Editorial, "President Obama's Dragnet," which was published June 7, 2013, the *N.Y. Times* finally joined the chorus bashing Obama and the policies of his administration:

> *Essentially, the administration is saying that without any individual suspicion of wrongdoing, the government is allowed to know whom Americans are calling every time they make a phone call, for how long they talk and from where. ... The administration has now lost all credibility on this issue. Mr. Obama is proving the truism that the executive branch will use any power it is given and very likely abuse it.*

In the 1986 horror film, *The Fly*, one character, despite his ongoing transformation into an insect, pleads to others that they not be afraid, to which Geena Davis' character replies, "No, be afraid; be very afraid." We would do well to heed that same warning as our federal government continues its transformation into something that is barely recognizable from its modest and benign historical foundation.

Safety at What Cost? –

A good friend, whose insight I appreciate, asked, "If the domestic surveillance programs might prevent terrorist attacks in the future, should U.S. citizens not accept the federal government tracking our telephone metadata and internet communications?"

If one has faith in opinion polls, his question and the sentiment evidenced thereby are echoed by the majority of Americans. The answer, which is clearly implied by the question, is similar to the often used rhetorical device, "If 'it' saves just one (1) life, then it will be worthwhile." The uncomfortable truth is that we will all die; therefore, no act "saves" a life. It merely delays the inevitable and avoids what may be argued is an "untimely" death.

Nevertheless, the reality is that society collectively is not willing to make the economic sacrifices or accept the personal inconveniences that would be required in order to prevent all untimely deaths. The real question is, "What costs are we as a society willing to pay for the protection of life and safety?"

As uncomfortable and unpalatable as it may be, we make cost-benefit decisions about life and death every day: Driving cars, flying on airplanes, *etc.* We long ago decided that the collective convenience and "freedom" afforded by these things outweigh the individualized proportionate risk. We ride in cars and fly in planes despite the fact that that the use of these means of conveyance assures that more persons will die untimely deaths, as compared to a world limited to pedestrian travel.

In recent years, cell phone use and text messaging while driving have been identified along with driving while impaired ("DWI" or "DUI") as scourges on the driving public and society-at-large. Media outlets carry ubiquitous warnings and incessant condemnation of "distracted driving," which not so obviously includes all acts or things giving rise to inattentive driving not just cell phones.

Given the continuing push to have government further restrict and punish these activities, one would expect that there are bodies littering the highways of America, but such is not the case.

In 2011, motor vehicle deaths were the lowest since 1949. This statistic is significant because it relates not just to proportional deaths (*e.g.* per miles driven) but also deaths in absolute numbers. There was roughly one (1) death per 100 Million miles driven. Even with a slight increase in 2012, the rate was still the lowest since 1950.[17]

It is unreasonable to establish an objective of "no untimely deaths" because accidents are inevitable with some degree of severity and with some frequency. Necessarily, there is a balancing test between "reasonable" (*i.e.* cost effective) safety

---

[17] Source: National Highway Traffic Safety Administration – www.nhtsa.org.

measures and the benefit derived from the ongoing activity, which gives rise to the risk.

Admittedly, for any individual, who suffers an untimely death, these statistics are meaningless. Nevertheless, the current accident avoidance systems and existing regulations seem to be effective. With such successes, the incremental costs, which are required for marginal additional safety, go up exponentially. Before incurring additional costs or imposing additional restrictions, it is appropriate to ask, "What is the real benefit, which is likely achievable, from such additional costs or restrictions (including losses of liberty and reduced freedom of movement)?"

In 2012, approximately Five Thousand (5,000) motorcyclists died on the nation's highways, and a similar number of accidental deaths are anticipated in 2013.[18] A dramatic reduction in untimely deaths could be had if motorcycles were outlawed on the nation's highways. The numbers would be even higher if highway use restrictions were extended mopeds and bicycles. With guaranteed decreases in accidental deaths, why does government not outlaw these inherently dangerous and unnecessary activities?

These activities have not been outlawed because there is a continuing, even if threatened, belief that persons should be allowed to exercise freedom and liberty even if, in exercising certain rights or privileges, the actor or some other persons may be occasionally injured or killed. Such risks and resulting losses are part of the costs of those rights and privileges (and of life in

---

[18] Source: Governors Highway Safety Association – www.ghsa.org.

general). Similarly, reductions in freedoms and liberties are costs, which must be considered in the pursuit of safety. Society can debate the reasonableness of such costs and debate the means by which we can lessen the risks, but it is unreasonable to expect or demand absolute safety at all costs.

It is a harsh reality of life that many conveniences, privileges, and rights come at the cost of human lives. Similarly, our rights, liberties, and freedoms were purchased at a high price, and we must be willing to pay a continuing price through defense and vigilance in order to assure the viability of those birthrights.

A reality of equal certainty is that some of us will die violent deaths at the hands of others, whether those others are domestic sociopaths or foreign terrorists. Rather than evaluating and valuing life by "quantity," more emphasis should be placed on the "quality" and intrinsic value of the lives that we live as individuals and as a people.

We must ask ourselves:

- What price are we willing to pay for illusions of safety?
- Are the liberties and freedoms that define what it is to be "American" inalienable or transient?
- Are we, as the heirs of the freedoms forged by our Founding Fathers, willing to fight and risk bloodshed in the furtherance and defense of those freedoms?
- Or, are we resolved to become subservient to a government, which has diminishing respect for those

freedoms and no respect for the necessary limitations on its powers?

My friend's suggestion that we just accept loss of freedom as part of the existing *status quo* can be answered with a quote, which is attributed to Benjamin Franklin:

> *Those, who would give up essential Liberty to purchase a little temporary Safety, deserve neither Liberty nor Safety.*

Should one have the utmost confidence that government is and always will be benevolent and that it will be restrained in the use of the immense power fueled by unlimited access to the personal information of citizens, then support for these programs is defensible. However, it is beneficial to remember that the Founding Fathers, who gave birth to this Country, were far less trusting of government and politicians, inclusive of their offspring and themselves.

We should respect and adopt the example of stern parenting given by the founders. Those Founding Fathers consciously and deliberately placed fetters on the federal government, and successive administrations have fought vigorously to loosen those chains. Presently, the Leviathan of government stands poised to take flight with its crushing powers unchecked by the Constitution or by the ultimate will of the people.

Centuries ago, the Protestant Reformer, Martin Luther said, "Peace if possible, truth at all costs." Truth is among the rarest of commodities, and thus, it has an incalculable value. The benefits and value of truthfulness are seemingly unappreciated by politicians and those in government today. Through legend, we tout the honesty of our favored Presidents, such as George Washington and "Honest Abe" Lincoln. Who today would be comfortable attaching the moniker, "Honest," to the names of any well known politicians, much less recent Presidents?

I have no reason to believe that today's political class is more selfless and enlightened than the Founding Fathers, whose words and actions have survived the tests of time. Unrestrained government today is no less contemptible than it was at the birth of our nation. A sovereign omnipotent government is inconsistent with the aims of liberty and freedom. While safety may be illusory, tyranny is a certain byproduct of the inevitable corruption, which is spawned by unchecked power.

The rights guaranteed in the Constitution came at a high cost. The freedoms and liberties enshrined in and guaranteed by the Constitution were purchased with the lives of more than ONE MILLION men and women. Those persons were true patriots, and they sacrificed their lives over more than two hundred (200) years to protect the freedoms, which many of us are now prepared to surrender. The federal government, in pursuit of illusions of safety, desecrates those lives lost and tarnishes the sacrifices, which continue to be made.

The Buck Stops Here -

By necessity, the President of the United States is afforded great power as Commander-in-Chief. It is among his responsibilities to assure that the country is protected from foreign threats and to command the vast resources of personnel and materiel, which comprise the world's only true military superpower.

Some curtailment of personal freedoms and individual rights in a time of war or in the face of an imminent and significant threat to national security is to be expected. In exercising the powers of Commander-in-Chief, Presidents have undertaken extreme acts, which have been rebuked with the benefit of hindsight:

- At the outbreak of the United States Civil War, President Lincoln unilaterally suspended *Habeas Corpus* (the right to a hearing upon arrest). That action by Lincoln was in contravention of Article I of the Constitution, which grants Congress the exclusive power to suspend *habeas corpus* in times of rebellion or invasion.

- During World War II, Franklin D. Roosevelt authorized "War Relocation Camps," in which approximately 110,000 persons of Japanese heritage were effectively imprisoned for the duration of the war without any justification other than accidents of birth.

- First reported on the front page of The *New York Times* in 1971, the "Pentagon Papers" exposed much of the government's policies and actions related to Vietnam. In 1996, the *Times* said that the Pentagon Papers "demonstrated, among other things, that the Lyndon Baines Johnson Administration had systematically lied, not only to the public but also to Congress."

- George W. Bush and his administration engaged the country in the war in Iraq, which lasted more than ten (10) years at a cost of more than FOUR THOUSAND (4,000)

American lives. Bush ordered the invasion of Iraq based upon allegations that Saddam Hussein possessed stockpiles of "Weapons of Mass Destruction," which upon closer inspection did not exist. In the wake of 9-11, it was also the Bush Administration which originally implemented "warrantless wire taps" and whose Attorney General, John Ashcroft, proposed the TIPS surveillance program.

- As President, Barack Obama quickly adopted many of the loathsome programs and policies of the Bush Administration. As Senator and later as candidate for President, Obama was very critical of Bush's actions. Such policies included the imprisonment alleged "enemy combatants" at the Guantanamo Naval Base in Cuba, many without the benefit of trial or formal charges. The Obama Administration also greatly expanded the breadth and scope of the previously "authorized" domestic surveillance programs. In prosecution of the "War on Terror," Obama has been responsible for the deaths of not less than FOUR (4) AMERICANS via his killer drone program.

Extremism in the face of imminent threat may be expected, but in the absence of an immediate and well defined threat, the justification of emergency police powers is also absent. There always have been and always will be "threats" to national security. The existence of such threats and the potential for attacks are insufficient bases for the erosion of liberties and freedoms and for the implementation and continuation of a perpetual police state.

All of the noted presidential actions were purportedly done in the interest of "safety" and "national security." Even if seemingly justified at the outset, many, if not all such actions, now are viewed as blights on the character of the United States. Such acts of oppression and abuses of power are reprehensible even in times of war, and they are contrary to the proper roles of government and detrimental to the freedoms that we are guaranteed as Americans. However, the actions noted above pale in scope and potential impact when compared to the current NSA domestic surveillance programs.

Do you trust your government to always use its immense powers for good? History has proven that trust to be naïve and unfounded. President Obama's former Chief of Staff, Rahm Emanuel, said:

> *You never let a serious crisis go to waste. And what I mean by that it's an opportunity to do things you think you could not do before.*

The federal government and the current administration stagger from crisis to crisis. The instant "crisis," which supposedly justifies these "emergency powers," is an incessant war on an ill-defined foe called "terror." This war has no end game, and it has no certain objectives other than perceptions of "safety."

The so-called "War on Terror" has become a scapegoat for unlimited government expansion and power grabs. It is inevitable that this false state of war (much like the ongoing and equally unsuccessful "War on Drugs") will be escalated to address evolving threats and heightened in response to eventual attacks by those who would destroy our freedoms and way of life.

In the midst of the present debates and discussions, I have been asked, "How would you do 'it' differently?" The short answer, "I wouldn't do 'IT'!" I would not support or tolerate domestic spying on American citizens without a prior showing of a crime or wrongdoing by the individual, who is the target of the search and surveillance. It is unfathomable that the entire U.S. population can be classified collectively as the "target" of any such investigation. The Fourth Amendment and judicial interpretations and applications thereof provide time-tested protections from and restrictions on searches and seizures by the government.

The rights and protections afforded to Americans by the Bill of Rights are sacrosanct. If the government wants to treat all foreigners as enemies of the state, then so be it. Such is within the power, authority, and purview of the federal government no matter how ill advised such a policy may be or how ineffective its implementation. Nevertheless, Americans have inalienable rights, which are guaranteed by the Constitution. Contrary to administration's propensities, the Bill of Rights is not optional or advisory. It provides continuing and absolute restrictions on the powers of government in favor of personal rights and individual liberties of its citizens. Not even the President should get to pick and choose the laws by which he abides.

Espionage and international intelligence gathering are not my areas of expertise. Nevertheless, contained within the "Just trust us" argument is the assertion and belief that those in government are smarter and more selfless than everyone else. I hate to disappoint the electorate, but politicians and those in public service on the whole are no smarter than others with similar aptitudes and experiences.

Politicians and government bureaucrats are not necessarily the crème de la crème. Collectively, they have the same talents, traits, and propensities as the population in general, both good and bad. While many may have the best of intentions, there are persons within the political class, who are just as narcissistic, egotistical, and selfish as any human being ever dared to be.

I do not object to any FOREIGN intelligence gathering, surveillance, or interventions, as may be in the interests of "national security." However, we succeeded in being in a state of "Cold War" with the Soviets and the rest of the Communist World for roughly half a century without destroying the rights of Americans. We did not "defeat" Communism by being more like the communists. The fall of Communism came because much of the rest of the world was envious of the freedoms that we have (or had) as Americans, and they wanted to be more like us.

From its inception, America has stood as a leader in promoting personal freedoms and democracy. For more than a century, the country maintained its position as the undisputed leader in industrial development and economic might. While the country was somewhat slower to advance causes of equality and civil rights, great strides have been made, and America is today a model for cultural development and social advancement.

America continues to be emulated in many respects; however, the example that our country, particularly our federal government, shows to the world today is less than stellar.

While we remain the standard bearer for democracy, there is little about our government for the world to envy. The federal government has become unresponsive, inefficient, bloated, and increasingly disrespectful of the rights of its citizens. If the U.S. government cannot fight "terrorism" without significantly curtailing and infringing upon the rights of Americans, then it is doing something wrong. If government gives in to the strictures and controls of a police state, we are no longer America.

Conclusion -

Before most of us heard of the FISA court or the PRISM program, many persons would have dismissed the allegations concerning these Orwellian surveillance programs as being the fruits of paranoia; however, it is not paranoia if it is true. The admitted existence of these programs confirms some of the worst fears of those, who are already skeptical and untrusting of Big Brother and a Nanny State government.

What is next? DNA inventorying, tattooing your Social Security number as a bar code on your arm, and/or embedded Radio Frequency ID chips ("RFID")? There should be little question that these yet-to-implemented steps are even more "convenient" and "effective" than the existing surveillance programs. There should be no question that implementation of such measures would improve "safety" and "national security" because no one would be able to make a move without government knowledge (and ultimately prior approval).

Do these things sound preposterous and far-fetched? Until recently, how many of us would have expected the NSA to be hoarding and mining the phone records, e-mail, and internet communications of innocent citizens without any prior evidence of a crime being committed?

The purported targets today are "foreigners." Tomorrow the targets may be "criminals." Eventually, the surveillance is likely to be used against whomever may be deemed an "enemy of the state." Government officials say, "If you don't do anything 'WRONG' [as defined by the government], then you do not have anything to worry about." The government is icing an already slippery slope.

In a now famous poem, Pastor Martin Niemöller was critical of the German intellectuals, who failed to respond and to object as the Nazi Party rose to power:

First they came for the communists,
and I didn't speak out because I wasn't a communist.
Then they came for the socialists,
and I didn't speak out because I wasn't a socialist.
Then they came for the trade unionists,
and I didn't speak out because I wasn't a trade unionist.
Then they came for me,
and there was no one left to speak for me.

Do not be naïve. You too are the subject of this surveillance, and you are already a victim of these abuses by government. We are carrying Big Brother around with us in our pockets (and paying for the privilege). Do we resolve ourselves to being subservient to government and falling compliantly into line at the command of that government? Or, do we take back the reins government and force it to relinquish the control and power improperly confiscated from the people? Speak now or forever commit yourself to indentured servitude.

Those of us, who feel that privacy and other personal freedoms are worth defending, have good company. Justice Louis D. Brandeis of the U.S. Supreme Court said:

> *They: The makers of the Constitution: conferred, as against the government, the right to be let alone -- the most comprehensive of rights and the right most valued by civilized men.*

Brandeis continued his admonition and warning:

> *Experience should teach us to be most on our guard to protect liberty when the Government's purposes are beneficent. Men born to freedom are naturally alert to repel invasion of their liberty by evil-minded rulers. The greatest dangers to liberty lurk in insidious encroachment by men of zeal, well-meaning but without understanding.*[19]

Stand up in unison and be heard to say, "Mr. President, let us alone!"[20]

TRUTH

---

[19] Dissenting in *Olmstead v. United States*, 277 US 479 (1928). Brandeis also co-authored with his law partner, Samuel D. Warren, an early law review article, which advocated for such a right: "The Right to Privacy," 4 *Harvard Law Review* 193 (December 15, 1890).

[20] This essay does not even consider or address whether a foreign state, such as China, already may have access to the same or similar information "pipes" from which the U.S. siphons internet data, or whether a malevolent state could hack into the information vault, which is maintained by the U.S. Government.

ADDITIONAL READING AND INFORMATION[21]

1. NBCNews.com, "NSA snooping has foiled multiple terror plots: Feinstein" – 06/06/2013 http://usnews.nbcnews.com/_news/2013/06/06/18796204-nsa-snooping-has-foiled-multiple-terror-plots-feinstein?lite

2. For those who haven't read Orwell's novel, *1984*:" http://www.sparknotes.com/lit/1984/

3. NBCNews.com, "How does the NSA's phone-record program work?" – 06/06/2013 - http://firstread.nbcnews.com/_news/2013/06/06/18803259-how-does-the-nsas-phone-record-program-work?lite

4. http://www.guardian.co.uk/world/interactive/2013/jun/06/verizon-telephone-data-court-order

5. NBCNews.com, "Sources: US intelligence agencies tap servers of top Internet companies" – 06/06/2013 - http://openchannel.nbcnews.com/_news/2013/06/06/18809021-sources-us-intelligence-agencies-tap-servers-of-top-internet-companies?lite

6. HuffingtonPost.com, "NSA Prism Data Mining Is All Up In Ur Microsoft, Yahoo, Google, Facebook, PalTalk, AOL, Skype, YouTube, Apple [UPDATE]" – 06/06/2013 - http://www.huffingtonpost.com/2013/06/06/nsa-prism-data-mining_n_3399310.html

7. HuffingtonPost.com, "NSA PRISM Program: Is Big Data Turning Government Into 'Big Brother?'" – 06/07/2013

---

[21] These publications and media sources were examined and reviewed in preparing the foregoing essay. The list is intended to provide general guidance as to where the reader can obtain additional material and information on the subject matter, but it is not intended to be a formal bibliography or complete list of source materials.

http://www.huffingtonpost.com/2013/06/07/nsa-prism-program_n_3401695.html

8. Forbes.com, "How The NSA Uses All Those Verizon Phone Records" – 06/06/2013 - http://www.forbes.com/sites/gregsatell/2013/06/07/how-the-nsa-uses-all-those-verizon-phone-records/

9. WashingtonPost.com, "NSA slides explain the PRISM data-collection program" – 06/06/2013 - http://www.washingtonpost.com/wp-srv/special/politics/prism-collection-documents/

10. http://www.youtube.com/watch?v=oYNXVgYhPOc

11. NBCNews.com, "Obama: 'Nobody is listening to your telephone calls'" – 06/07/2013 - http://usnews.nbcnews.com/_news/2013/06/07/18824941-obama-nobody-is-listening-to-your-telephone-calls?lite

12. NY Times Editorial, "President Obama's Dragnet," – 06/07.2013 - http://www.nytimes.com/2013/06/07/opinion/president-obamas-dragnet.html?pagewanted=1&ref=opinion&_r=0

13. http://www.youtube.com/watch?v=zRhjgynfhag

14. http://www.youtube.com/watch?v=44W0svJxCq8

15. NBCNews.com, "Intelligence chief declassifies PRISM details, slams 'reckless disclosures'" – 06/08/2013 - http://usnews.nbcnews.com/_news/2013/06/08/18850035-intelligence-chief-declassifies-prism-details-slams-reckless-disclosures?lite

16. http://sensenbrenner.house.gov/uploadedfiles/sensenbrenner_letter_to_attorney_general_eric_holder.pdf

Non est potestas Super Terram quæ Comparetur ei Iob. 41. 24.

LEVIATHAN

Or

THE MATTER, FORME

and Power of A COMMON-

WEALTH ECCLESIASTICALL

and CIVIL.

By THOMAS HOBBES

of MALMESBVRY.

London

Printed for Andrew Crooke

1651

If a nation expects to be ignorant and free,
in a state of civilization,
it expects what never was and never will be. ...
[W]henever the people are well-informed,
they can be trusted with their own government;
that, whenever things get so far wrong as to
attract their notice,
they may be relied on to set them right.

- THOMAS JEFFERSON

GOVERNMENT: The Beast Within

Introduction -

It is a fatal flaw to believe that one can tame the beast that is government. The power of the beast can be harnessed, but only if it is properly restrained. If it is fed incessantly, the beast will grow until it is powerful enough to break its chains. Rather than being inclined to restrain the beast or limit its powers, politicians and bureaucrats derive their own powers from their charge. Like the vampire's victims, they become enamored with the creature, and they are captivated by its powers.

The caretakers become foundered and drunk on overindulgence, and they are thereafter derelict in their duties. Unfettered, the beast first consumes those closest to it. It devours the politicians and other bureaucratic minions formerly responsible for its care and feeding. However, the beast is not sated by the consumption of those near, and it works to expand its territory and reach. It remains forever ravenous and insatiable.

Lessons Unlearned -

President Richard M. Nixon did not order the Watergate break-in. He was not forced to surrender the Presidency because of a "third rate burglary." Instead, Nixon faced impeachment, and he eventually resigned as a result of his role in the ensuing cover-up. Nixon's primary malfeasance was in fostering antagonism and animosity toward those, who he defined as enemies of his administration. To Nixon, his objectives were noble, and to persons who worked on Nixon's behalf, the furtherance of his prescribed ends justified the use of any means, even if those means were illegal. The administration, which Nixon fought so hard to maintain, ultimately collapsed not from the feared assault by outside forces but from the internal cancer seeded by his own policies. While not directly responsible for the initial acts, he was fully responsible for the environment that gave rise to them.

Histories Repeated -

Fast forward nearly forty (40) years. The current administration is in a nearly constant mode of damage control. Battles are being fought on not less than three (3) fronts. In each case, those within the administration argue vehemently that "high level officials" were neither knowledgeable of nor directly involved in the misdeeds. In these cases, those high level officials include President Obama, former Secretary of State, Hillary Clinton, and the Attorney General, Eric Holder. Should they get a pass? Should they shoulder no responsibility for the actions of others within the administration?

IRS v. "Tea Party" -

A [05/14/13] report of the Inspector General ("IG") confirmed that employees of the Internal Revenue Service ("IRS") targeted certain "Tea Party" and politically conservative groups for heightened scrutiny. Those groups were applying to the IRS for non-profit status under IRC § 501(c)(4). The increased scrutiny included burdensome requirements to provide additional documentation in support of the applications. Among the items requested were coveted but otherwise private lists of contributors. According to the IG's scathing report, the

74

additional requirements were not imposed upon groups described as "progressive" or liberal, and the affected groups argue that these actions had a chilling effect on political speech leading up to the most recent Presidential election.

Despite evidence of these activities as early as June 29, 2011, IRS Commissioner, Douglas Shulman, gave testimony before Congress on March 22, 2012, in which he flatly denied the existence of any such activities. It is possible that Shulman himself had no involvement in or knowledge of the activities. However, even if Shulman's 2012 testimony was the result of an innocent misstatement or honest error, no one within the IRS or the administration stepped forward, prior to the anticipated release of the IG's report, to acknowledge the error and to correct the record. Almost certainly, President Obama did not direct such actions; nevertheless, Obama is entirely responsible for a climate and environment within his administration in which this type of activity was deemed acceptable by persons acting in furtherance of his shared aims and objectives.

On May 20, 2013, the Obama administration acknowledged that White House legal counsel and the Chief of Staff knew, at least as early as April, about the IG's report on the illegal scrutiny given by the IRS to conservative political groups. Presumably, they were also aware that this report would contradict repeated assurances to Congress that complaints of such IRS activities were utterly unfounded. However, the administration remains adamant that the President was kept completely in the dark on the issue and that he knew nothing about the IRS activities until he saw television news reports.

Are we to believe that, notwithstanding damnable behavior by officials at the IRS, NO ONE in the administration thought it might be a good idea to give the President a "heads up"?

Such behaviors represent either an admission of abject incompetence on the part of administration officials or a culture of willful ignorance being pervasive within the White House. Such a culture would tend to indicate that the President would not WANT to know about such things presumably so that he could claim plausible deniability regarding actions within his own administration. Either way, that is no way to run a railroad. Willful ignorance is not excusable, and half truths are whole lies.

Benghazi and Beyond -

Then there is Benghazi, the lie that just will not go away. On September 11, 2012, an orchestrated terrorist attack resulted in the deaths of four (4) Americans, including Ambassador Christopher Stevens. Initial reports out of Libya were consistent in identifying the attack as the work of terrorists; however, the administration chose to blame the attack on a crude internet video, which supposedly triggered a "spontaneous demonstration" that got out of control. Afterwards, administrative agencies (*i.e.* CIA and State Department) carefully crafted talking points which were used by Ambassador Susan Rice, as she made the rounds on Sunday morning news programs five (5) days later.

Rice stepped in at the last minute substituting for her boss, Hillary Clinton, who fortuitously fell ill from a timely bout of exhaustion. (Clinton would later suffer a second episode, and she received medical treatment, which stalled her scheduled testimony before Congress on the same topics.) The talking points that Rice used have not only been discredited as being false, but material portions were intentionally fabricated. Removed from those talking points were any mentions of terrorists or a planned attack. The substituted explanation regarding the internet video was based upon the flimsiest of foundations.[22]

Neither Obama nor Hillary Clinton was in any way responsible for the attack itself. However, arguments have been made that the facility was inadequately defended and that the response to the attack was improperly restrained. Had the truth regarding the nature of the attack come to light immediately, the administration likely would have suffered a major public relations headache just two (2) months before the general election. As it was, the retiring Secretary of State and would-be Presidential candidate, Hillary Clinton, worked feverishly to distance herself from the circumstances in Benghazi and from the erroneous reports that followed the attack.

Persons within the administration chose to deflect responsibility from the administration, and its agencies, choosing instead to lay blame entirely upon the internet video.

---

[22] The *NYT* published a report more than fifteen (15) months after the attack, in which the writer concluded that the attack was "fueled in large part by anger at an American-made video denigrating Islam." While the *Times* article provides *ex post facto* corroboration for that portion of the government's official explanation, the writer concurs that portions of the government's initial explanations and descriptions were knowingly deceptive. As would be expected, critics of the administration expressed skepticism regarding the *Times* report. *See* Kirkpatrick, David D., "A Deadly Mix in Benghazi," *New York Times* (December 28, 2013).

The administration would be quick to note that "those at the highest levels" did not themselves perpetrate a demonstrable lie. However, persons at some level determined that allowing the administration to save face and protecting the image of the President was important enough cover up the truth. Those persons deemed it appropriate to lie on behalf of the President's administration. Obama and Clinton are entirely responsible for creating a climate and environment that fostered, if not condoned, this type of behavior.

A Tale of Two Executives -

As these two public relations crises were brewing, Obama took to his bully pulpit in the company of the British Prime Minister, David Cameron. [05/13/13] Unlike Obama, Cameron does not head an independent executive branch within the British government. The Prime Minister is himself a member of the British House of Commons. In fact, his position as Prime Minister has no constitutional basis whatsoever. He serves at the pleasure of the Queen and at the behest of Parliament. The Prime Minister derives his position and power from his ability to effectively steer legislation through Parliament. In performing his duties, the Prime Minister is answerable directly to his colleagues.

Perhaps, Obama would benefit from a couple of weekly sessions similar to the "Questions to the Prime Minister." Obama certainly does not envy the Prime Minister's obligation to answer directly for his actions. Obama considers Congressional inquiries and oversight an unwanted and unwarranted intrusion upon his expanding Executive Powers.

Regardless, Obama took to the podium to address the simmering crises. He acknowledged the scandal at the IRS, if for no other reason than it was about to be confirmed by the Treasury's own Inspector General. Still, Obama denied that he was personally aware of the "rogue" activities of "low level" employees. Perhaps, he should have consulted more closely with the acting Commissioner of the IRS. The newly installed Commissioner was aware of the prejudicial scrutiny over a year prior, but neither he nor any other member of the IRS staff stepped forward to correct the conspicuous and obviously false testimony that former Commissioner Shulman gave to Congress.

Obama was less inclined to acknowledge any substance to the continuing Congressional investigations related to the fiasco in Benghazi. He derisively described those proceedings as a "sideshow." Previously, the hearings and inquiries by Republicans have been alternatively described by the administration and similarly aligned Democrats as "inquisitions" and/or "witch hunts." In light of the IRS debacle, Republicans and those less trusting of government may be forgiven for not extending the benefit of the doubt, such as it may be, in favor of the President.

Had Benghazi been the only blip on the radar, it may have eventually drifted off the scope and out of the collective consciousness of the nation. However, the assurances and admonitions of the President ring hollow when there are active efforts by his underlings to limit access to information and to deliberately distort what should have been obvious truths. Benghazi is part of a one-two punch, which staggers the administration when combined with the admitted missteps at the IRS.

The Attorney General later deemed the IRS actions so abhorrent as to justify opening a criminal investigation, and the President asked for and received the resignation of the acting Commissioner of the IRS. The more cynical of us would question whether such actions represent just punishments for actual wrongdoing or whether those persons paying the price with their jobs (and potentially their freedoms) are scapegoats for the intractable misdeeds of others within the administration. What was a fog of uncertainty is replaced by what appears to be a smokescreen. Where there is smoke, fire (or at least some appreciable heat) is presumed to be close at hand.

Turning Up the Heat -

The heat was turned up even more when it was revealed on the same day [05/13/13] that the Justice Department had previously issued a secret subpoena covering calls for more than twenty (20) telephone lines utilized by the Associated Press ("AP"), as well as the personal phones of an editor and certain reporters. The information, which was obtained by the Justice Department, covered two (2) months in 2012 and included calls made by as many as one hundred (100) persons with the AP.

The AP is not just any media source. It is one of the oldest and most respected collaborative new organizations in the country. The objective of Justice Department investigation was to identify the source of a government leak that led to an AP story about a CIA operation, which intervened and stopped a potential terrorist bomb aboard an airliner.

The AP temporarily withheld publication of the story at the request of the administration, which cited national security interests. The story was eventually published with the knowledge of administration officials, but the administration demanded identification of the source of the leaked information. It was later revealed by the administration itself that the "bomber" was in fact a CIA operative, who had infiltrated a terrorist cell.

The Obama administration has been responsible for six (6) criminal prosecutions for leaks of information (more than all prior administrations combined). Those prosecutions have been brought under an arcane World War I era law related to espionage. The AP story was neither malicious nor libelous. It was published in good faith and factually sound, but the story directly contradicted prior public statements from the administration that there was no information supporting the likelihood of terrorist activity around first anniversary of the death of Osama bin Laden.

The administration contends that publication of the news story ended CIA access within the terrorist organization and constituted a threat to national security. However, the assertion by Attorney General Eric Holder that the AP report "put the American people at risk" is undermined by the White House's public comment about the operation. Then counterterrorism adviser John Brennan held a conference call in which he assured media representatives that the bomb plot was never a threat to the American public or aviation safety. So, was it a material threat, or much ado about nothing?

The administration had been caught in a lie as well identified as player in an international high stakes game of cat-and-mouse. Rather than reporting true facts, the administration would have had the AP become complicit in public deception. Apparently, truth is a casualty in the war on terrorism. However, its loss should not be viewed as acceptable collateral damage. Could the zealousness of the most recent search and the aggressive prosecutions that preceded it have anything to do with the repeated embarrassment felt by the administration as a result of internal leaks?

Trampling Upon the Bill of Rights -

The IRS scrutiny of conservative groups is viewed as particularly heinous, at least from a political perspective, because procedures have been developed and implemented over the years to assure that the Service has no political bias. Everyone recognizes the potential abuses concomitant with the power to tax. Chief Justice John Marshall famously sated, "The power to tax involves the power to destroy." The abuse of that power is particularly troubling when it is harnessed for the purpose of oppressing political opponents.

One of the Articles of Impeachment against Richard Nixon alleged that Nixon used the IRS in just such a way. Additionally, the Hatch Act prohibits federal employees from using their positions to further partisan political causes. Similarly, extensive procedures and guidelines exist to assure that Justice Department investigations do not impinge unnecessarily upon freedom of speech, as is argued in the case of the AP subpoena.

Intrusive government actions have a chilling effect on the sacrosanct First Amendment freedoms, which are afforded to individuals and to the press. The Justice Department's own guidelines provide that any subpoena be narrowly tailored and that the scope of investigations be limited. The guidelines also provide that subpoenas be used only when the information is not otherwise available and that prior notice of the subpoena be given, unless such notice would jeopardize the integrity of the information to be obtained. Finally, the procedures provide that the Attorney General himself must approve the subpoena. In practice, the Justice Department usually negotiates directly with the affected media outlet for the release of or access to information. The secrecy behind the AP subpoena and the subpoena's expansive scope were unprecedented.

Attorney General, Eric Holder, revealed [05/14/2013] that he had previously recused himself from the AP leak case. Upon further questioning, Holder acknowledged that there is no written documentation of his decision to recuse himself, and he was unable to identify a specific date on which that decision was made. Nevertheless, he justified his decision in that he had knowledge of the CIA operation as it was ongoing, and he previously testified before Congress regarding the leaks. Holder's self-imposed recusal conveniently excuses his lack of prior knowledge of the subpoena and insulates him from involvement in the investigation against the AP.

Holder's assurances that the Justice Department would investigate aggressively potential criminal behavior at the IRS carried the same familiar hollow ring that echoed from his self-serving assurances that all of the actions of his Justice Department were legal and entirely necessary for the protection of the American public. Nevertheless, there is no mistaking the parenthetical undertone, "Just know that Big Brother is watching you too!" The oft repeated meme, "Just trust me," loses its impact and effect when those words have to be uttered with ever increasing emphasis and frequency. Trust is a commodity, which is woefully lacking among the President, his administration, and the American people.

Persons Who Live in Glass Houses -

It is unlikely that the fingerprints of Obama, Clinton, or Holder will be found anywhere near the scenes of disinformation and cover-up. These persons give practiced lip service to "transparency" and "full disclosure" so long as such noble aims are consistent with their own policies, goals, and objectives. Those in "high levels" of government take comfort in the insulation provided by plausible deniability. At what point is ignorance of material facts deliberate and willful? At what point does poor management and lack of supervision become negligence or dereliction of duty?

Obama, and his minions, have definitely not shown themselves to be above the fray of late. That is not to say they are any worse than "the other side," but they are certainly showing themselves to be no better. Such is the curse of government. The siren's song of power leads otherwise good men onto to jagged reefs of deceit and corruption.

Administration officials, in the most favorable light, were derelict in their duties either in failing to direct subordinates in proper behaviors or in failing to investigate and respond properly to the actions of those subordinates once the misdeeds came to light. Those subordinates demonstrated egregiously poor judgment, willfully ignored the truth, and/or actively participated in the dissemination of propaganda and lies for the protection of the administration.

Where the defense to allegations of deceit and lying is that there was a grain of truth to what was said or that defense hinges upon the technical veracity of the words actually spoken, it should go without saying that a lie of omission is no less damnable. The administration is guilty of fostering a climate and environment in which it is acceptable to lie and to tell half truths.

Obama seemingly feels that he is bigger than the Presidency. He believes that anyone, who dares disagree with his philosophies and policies, is too ignorant or calloused to appreciate the rightness of his actions. Having demonstrated that he considers other points of view unworthy of debate and that those holding such points of view are beneath him, it should be expected that those, who do his bidding, will similarly hold those opposing views and persons, who would oppose the President, with disdain.

Once the world is viewed as us-versus-them, each decision takes on an unreasonable sense of urgency and every interaction is seen as a life-or-death struggle. In such an environment, the actors adopt the mindset of kill-or-be-killed. Political adversaries (and ultimately others) are devoured to provide sustenance in order to continue the fight. Having fostered that environment, does Obama have no responsibility for the actions that reasonably follow?

Obama feels inconvenienced by things like: Separation of powers, checks and balances, and that inefficient and pesky document called, the Constitution. He fails to recognize that the restrictions, which those concepts place on the institution of government, were intentional and necessary for the long-term health of that government and for the protection of the rights of its people. Rather than taming government, Obama consistently demonstrates actions and characteristics exemplified by none other than Richard Nixon and a host of other tawdry politicians, who preceded him. Although he may deem his ends noble, his means and those of his agents carry the familiar hallmarks of hubris, tyranny, and corruption.

Conclusion –

Corruption is part of the nature of the beast. Any person or institution that possesses (or asserts) great power, and which is not subject to effective oversight, is apt to be beset with corruption. To expect someone, who wields such power, to act in a contrary manner is tantamount to demanding a man to act in contravention of his human nature. At our base, we are selfish creatures driven by self-advancement and self-preservation.

The current state of government is not the creation of any individual. Cumulative fault can be assigned to many persons independent of party affiliations. The fault lies in the collective use of our government in ways in which it was never intended.

Our federal government was founded upon the concepts of natural and inalienable rights being possessed by the people and a collection of limited enumerated powers. The powers of government were derived from and surrendered by the people in the furtherance and protection of their inherent rights. The individual liberties and personal freedoms guaranteed by the Constitution were not bestowed by or derived from the government. Instead, the government was established to protect those preexisting rights.

The powers of government were intended to be a shield to protect those rights from infringement by others. Over time, the powers and scope of government have morphed to the point that government is now a sword, an implement through which to compel some action or prohibit some behavior in a manner consistent with the whims of whatever group, party, or consortium may have power at the moment.

As a society, we continue to feed the beast, and government is constantly poked and prodded by those, who would have it do their bidding. It should not surprise anyone that, in growing stronger and more powerful, the beast has cast its spell upon its guardians and now threatens to become unfettered.

Postscript -

As is my custom, I distributed the forgoing essay to several persons for comment prior to publication. One reader gave a well considered response, and he questioned whether it was appropriate that I chastise President Obama (and other administration officials) for "creating" an environment, which "fostered" and "condoned" abominable behaviors by and within government. He felt that I placed too much focus and blame on the current administration. The reader questioned whether it would have been appropriate to point out and acknowledge the shortcomings and failings of Obama's predecessor, George W. Bush, which may have "created" or at least exacerbated the problems faced by Obama. The piece above began with theme found in the Introduction. The reader concurred in that sentiment about government in general. The essay then grew and was fleshed out as contemporaneous events unfolded.

I entirely agree that Obama and (Hillary) Clinton did not give birth to Washington as we know it, but they are among the current "caretakers" of the Leviathan. Highlighting the actions of the current administration is the most timely and relevant means of analyzing the beast itself. The actions of prior administrations are fixed in history, and the resources, which may have been lost or wasted as a result of their policies, are unrecoverable sunk costs.

Complaining about Bush's (many) shortcomings does not justify continued bad acts by the current administration. Need it be said, "Two wrongs don't make a right"? Nearly all prior administrations were complicit, and each contributed it its own way to the current state of affairs. I would question whether Cincinnatus himself could tame the beast that is government in Washington today.

I intentionally removed many references to "creation," which may have been taken to imply that Obama single-handedly spawned the current beast; nevertheless, the inclusion of words like "fostered" and "condoned" was conscious and

88

deliberate. I continue to believe that those references are entirely appropriate, and administrative actions are replete with additional examples arising before and after the noted events. It should be clear from the piece that I do not assign any unique fault on Obama, but he is not free from blame.

Obama's proponents, included among them the fawning media, touted him as a political Messiah come to allow us to transcend partisanship and petty squabbles. He himself identified "change" from the intransigent *status quo* as his primary theme. My principal argument is that no "change" is likely in the inherent characteristics of big government (*e.g.* inefficiency, abuse of power, corruption, *etc.*).

Big Government is inconsistent with personal rights and individual liberties. Those things cannot live in harmony. Obama may be no worse than his predecessors, but he has proven himself to be no better. On the contrary, he has demonstrated absolute faith in the benevolence and efficacy of the Nanny State, as evidenced by his allegiance to "Obamacare." Nevertheless, I do endeavor to be "fair and balanced," and I hope that I demonstrate that trait better than Fox News, from whom I appropriated the tagline.

As an example, I direct attention to an essay, which I wrote back in 2007, "Oxymorons and the Republican Party." At the time, I sent that essay in letter form to the entire Congressional delegation from North Carolina. As expected, my words had no appreciable impact then, and I hold little hope for a substantially different result from this latest endeavor.

Government abuses are not new, but some things are "new:"

- The arrogance and blatancy, with which government erodes rights and liberties;
- The acceptance by the people of politicians and government agencies secretly spying on citizens;
- Government abuses and infringements of rights being seen as "normal," "legal," or "constitutional;" and
- Government's conscious and deliberate efforts to destroy any expectation of privacy in favor of the efficiency of the state.

The commenting reader identified what he believed to be the "problem" behind government today. In his mind, the problem was the relentless pursuit of self-interests, and he identified, as evidence in support of that claim, the "unlimited flow of money" used to finance campaigns, which face continuous election cycles. He felt that the pursuit of self interests delegitimizes government action. He sees government as being for sale to the highest bidder, and all sides are eager to feed at the government trough. However, this is a problem without a viable solution. Despite social ideals and moral arguments to the contrary, persons are entitled to act, and should be expected to act, in their own self-interests.

Government cannot create wealth. It can only impress wealth from those of its citizens, who are producers. However, wealth is to government a motivator of people and a principal source of its power. Money is the carrot, which complements the sticks of military might, bureaucratic regulation, and criminal enforcement. The fallacy is in the belief that there is some inherently "right" ratio of wealth to sustenance, which should be established and maintained by government action. Marx expressed it succinctly as, "From each according to his ability, and to each according to his needs." However, Marx's equation has a fatal flaw based upon unreasonable assumptions.

Producers are never going to produce exclusively for the benefit of others, particularly when they see the consumers as being capable of providing for themselves, and consumers will never be sated by having their sustenance needs fulfilled. So long as the wealth flows freely and unrestricted from the dispensaries of a coercive government, the definition of "need" (*i.e.* dictated standard of living) will increase. In the end, production decreases (either from lack of incentive to the producers or lack of motivation to the consumers), and there are insufficient resources to fill the continuing demands of consumers.

We are quickly and possibly inevitably approaching that point. America has a nearly $17 TRILLION national debt. No one is even hinting that federal budget deficits will be eliminated until at least 2035, which is nearly a generation away. Within a decade, the conservative estimate for the accumulated national debt is $25 TRILLION. The unfunded obligations of all governments (*i.e.* federal, state, and local) exceed $100 TRILLION, and that colossal amount does not even include the unmet needs for current and future infrastructure, which are interestingly among the few universally accepted tasks of government.

It is hard to ask, much less answer, the difficult questions:

- Should government allow "disproportionate" influence over its actions to those who ultimately will be responsible for paying the bills (*i.e.* the "Rich")? ... OR

- Should government give a non-contributing electoral majority unlimited access to the purse strings the treasury such that a dependent majority could effectively "rob from the 'rich' to give to the (ever increasing number of) 'poor'"?

That is the Hobson's Choice in Washington today:

Do you coddle the goose that lays the golden eggs in appreciation for her largesse, or do you beat her incessantly when she fails to deliver after one's demands exceeds her capacity to produce?

It is a matter of quantity (of votes) versus quality (of life):

- Should government pamper the numerical majority, as do the Democrats, with the hope and expectation that it can cajole, regulate, and threaten the producers to continue to produce in order to fulfill expanding benefits to the dependent populace? ... OR

- Should government recognize the necessary contributions of the producers and foster their successes, as do the Republicans (to a fault)?

Everyone, of course, would like to have their cake and eat it too, but I am skeptical that such a reality exists.

One can acknowledge that persons should be left to their own devices and accept that in doing so, social Darwinism will assure that many of them will fail and that there will be a disproportionate distribution of resources and wealth (just as there are disproportionate utilizations of talents and opportunities). Or, one can punish the producers by continuing to take more and more of the fruits of their ingenuity and labors in futile efforts to quell the insatiable appetites of those, who are dependent upon and beholding to government. The end result of this latter course is to reduce everyone toward the only attainable level of equality, the lowest common denominator.

The ultimate question is, "To whom do wealth, resources, and opportunity belong?" Rephrased, "Does property and the fruits of one's labors belong to individuals or to the collective (*i.e.* government)?"

If they belong to individuals, then the collective should have limited say in how such things are distributed and utilized. Government should only interfere in instances where some person or entity directly infringes upon the personal or property rights of another citizen. If such things belong to the collective, then there must also be faith in the collective to utilize that wealth more efficiently and to be better stewards of that wealth and resources than those who gave rise to it. Government has not proven itself to be that worthy steward.

Nearly all men can stand adversity,
but if you want to test a man's character,
give him power.

- President Abraham Lincoln

The poorest man may in his cottage bid defiance to all the forces of the Crown. It may be frail —

its roof may shake —

the wind may blow through it —

the storm may enter —

the rain may enter —

but the King of England cannot enter — all his force dares not cross the threshold of the ruined tenement!

- WILLIAM PITT
First Earl of Chatham
(1763).

Prisoners in Our Own Homes:
The Death of the Expectation of Privacy

Introduction -

The 5th Circuit U.S. Court of Appeals in New Orleans recently ruled that government agents are entitled to obtain cell phone call records without a judicially issued search warrant.[23]

The Government contends, and the court agreed, that citizens have no "expectation of privacy" in acts performed voluntarily without government compulsion. A similar holding likely would apply to the NSA's domestic surveillance dragnet and also to individual requests by law enforcement and government agencies, at least as to the states within by the 5th Circuit.[24, 25]

Judge Edith Brown Clement in writing the opinion of the divided court said that the use of cell phones is "entirely voluntarily;" therefore, individuals who use them have forfeited the right to constitutional protection for records showing where they have been used. Judge Clement reiterated:

> *The Government does not require a member of the public to own or carry a phone. ... Because a cell phone user makes a choice to get a phone, to select a particular service provider, and to make a call, and because he knows that call conveys cell site information ... he voluntarily conveys his cell site data* [to the government] *each time he makes a call.* [Emphasis added.]

---

[23] 5th Circuit Court of Appeals, Case No. 11-20884 (Decided July 30, 2013.)

[24] Contrast the ruling reported upon by Nakashima, Ellen and Ann E. Marimow, "Judge: NSA's collecting of phone records is probably unconstitutional," *Washington Post* (December 16, 2013).

[25] Another Federal Judge made a completely opposite ruling. Ultimately, SCOTUS will have to rule on these issues. *See* Horwitz, Sari, "NSA collection of phone data is lawful, federal judge rules," *Washington Post* (December 27, 2013).

A Government with Impunity -

Anyone who has ever "voluntarily" posted a letter is certainly aware that someone CAN rip open and read the contents of the mail, but that does not mean that the sender does not have an "EXPECTATION of privacy." Citizens of this country certainly should not EXPECT the government, which was established in support of personal freedom and individual liberties, to be the party blatantly infringing upon a protected right, such as privacy.

Then again, I realize that such a belief perhaps is naïve given that the Government has acknowledged reading, recording, and indexing the information contained on the face of all items passing through the U.S. Postal Service.

- What about those apparently toothless "Privacy Policies," which are required of companies by the same Federal Government, which wants to destroy any expectation of privacy?
- Do the policies themselves not give rise to an "Expectation of Privacy"?
- What about internet traffic and e-mail, which is encrypted?
- Does the act of encryption not evidence an "Expectation of Privacy"?

Some persons counter, "But, there is a process in place to assure that privacy is maintained" and that access to the information is limited on a need-to-know basis. Here is a summary of "the process:" *An individual, supposedly acting on behalf of a government agency (state or federal), asks, and the communications provider immediately replies with the requested information.* You are now privy to a complete understanding of "the process."

Such requests are nearly never denied by the communications companies. The companies have no incentive to protect the privacy of their customers because the federal government has said in legislation, "YOU HAVE NO LIABILITY for violating the customer's privacy (when responding to government demands and requests)."

Additionally, since many of the "requests" (read "commands") come with gag orders, the customers are unaware of the breach of privacy, and since there is no prior judicial review, those same customers have no way of protecting their own privacy interests. Government agencies, including the euphemistically entitled, Justice Department, have *carte blanche.* There is no effective judicial review or third-party oversight.

The government seems to have a conscious and deliberate objective of destroying any "expectation of privacy." Once citizens have no such expectations, then NOTHING is private. If nothing is private, then the restrictions and protections of the Bill of Rights become extraneous and meaningless: No Freedom of Speech, No Freedom from Searches and Seizures, No Right against Self-Incrimination, *etc. etc. etc.*

In the names of government efficiency and national security, our freedoms, rights, and liberties likely will become restricted to the confines of our own homes (assuming of course that such homes do not have telephone, cable, internet communications, or windows).

We are faced with a Catch-22. Either commit ourselves to being prisoners in our own homes or subject ourselves to the intrusions of government should we dare to venture outside.

We, as a people, are inviting the exact tyranny that our forefathers sacrificed to end, and we abandon too readily the constitutionally protected freedoms, which those same men and women died to defend.

Other persons may concede the loss of privacy but maintain hope and expectations that the extreme power, which comes from such vast amounts of information, will not be misused or abused by the government and its agents. Their concerns are not so much that the government has access to the information but in "how such information is used by government."

Consider the risks and ramifications should someone like former FBI Director, J. Edgar Hoover, or disgraced former President, Richard M. "Tricky Dick" Nixon, get access to such programs and information. Those corrupt historical figures are not so far removed from power, that we should think that such abuses are not a real and present danger. It is not a matter of if, but when and to what extent, domestic surveillance programs are going to be misused and abused.

Hundreds of thousands of "Top Secret" documents were "improperly accessed" and distributed worldwide (read "misused" and "abused") by a lowly army PFC, Bradley Manning, and by a contract computer technician, Eric Snowden.

Do you think that the government cares to guard YOUR privacy and personal secrets with any higher level of security than that government guarded its own? And, do you not expect that there certainly will be similar lapses in that security in the future?

These are just two (2) "abuses" about which we know, and we know about them ONLY because the whistleblowers themselves WANTED us to know about them.

How many persons within the government have "improperly accessed" the collective information of private citizens (either to satisfy their own curiosities or have done so at the behest of government officials)?

There is no way of answering that question because the domestic surveillance programs and the resulting information are deemed "Top Secret." All we hear is the familiar if vacuous refrain, "Just trust us."

I would not trust my mother with my diary. Why would I trust the government with voluminous telephone metadata and the contents of all of my internet communications (and those of every other U.S. citizen)? When you have the fox in charge of the henhouse, you are bound to lose more than a few hens. The only way to prevent abuses and corruption is to remove the temptation and to deny the government unfettered access to the private information of citizens.

The saying goes, "Government takes freedom and liberty at wholesale and sells it back to the people at retail." What we forget is that personal freedoms and individual liberties are "inalienable" rights. Such natural rights are not subject to being legitimately taken or doled out by the government.

Privacy is not something that government should "allow" its citizens. It is among those rights that we should demand not be intruded upon by government without due cause and circumspection. Any impairment that is allowed should occur only upon a clearly defensible need for specific information and upon demonstrated probable cause that a particular target has committed a crime. Additionally, government should not be allowed to warehouse information about its citizens, which could be mined and manipulated at some future date in order to build (or manufacture) a claim or case against such citizens.

Conclusion -

Have no doubt that the tyrannical actions of government already have had a chilling effect on our precious freedoms and liberties already. If you have not yet experienced that chill running down your spine, you undoubtedly will unless we rein in the actions of our government. Our liberties and freedom will continue to be eroded until and unless we shore up the foundations that protect those rights.

My hope is that we rebuild those foundations before our rights and freedoms crumble into oblivion. We should not have to "expect" government to look for ways to erode and curtail our freedoms and liberty. Such rights and freedoms were not the creations of government fiat, and their continuation should not depend upon nuance and legal niceties.

Our "home" should include the breadth and depth of the entire United States not just the area within the walls of our residences.

Within the bounds of civility and human decency, we should enjoy similar comforts, freedoms, and liberties walking the streets, meandering through the countryside, and traveling upon communications highways of this great nation, as we do inside our own homes. For quite some time now, I have been feeling the walls of freedom and liberty closing in upon me.

THE LIBERTY BELL.

It All Boils Down to ...
Of the People, By the People, For the People

Blog Entry - July 2, 2012

In the frequent debates with my more "liberal" friends, the arguments about the powers of government in addressing the supposed plights of the country's citizens generally boil down two (2) fundamental areas of disagreement:

(1)   Persons either believe that -

> i. essentially all "wealth" is derived from or belongs to the government, and it is the prerogative of that government to either take what it wants or to restrict that which any individual is entitled to retain; or

> ii. the right to retain (and yes, even hoard) one's wealth and the fruits of his labors is fundamental to freedom, and impingement upon that right should only be done in furtherance of some other fundamental RIGHT and not for the PRIVILEGE of redistributing those assets to others for the sake of some notion of "equality;" and

(2)   The opposing beliefs that -

> i. a government, which is believed to be perpetually benevolent, is the highest and best arbiter and determiner of what is simultaneously right and fair for more than 300 Million citizens, or

> ii. the collection of citizens making individual cost/benefit decisions about what is in their own best interests billions of times daily, in the long run,

will result in a fairer and more equitable distribution of privileges and resources.

These points present a distinction between a supposed "Right" to BE happy, based upon some fluid and subjective government mandated definition of the term, versus the more attainable Right of the individual to PURSUE happiness, however he may choose to define that idea for himself, but without any guarantee of success.

I do not mean to imply that social problems are trivial or that the solutions are easy. To the contrary, my point is intended to say that the problems are so complex that I do not believe there is a single "right" answer, which can be mandated and implemented by government fiat.

Not only is implementation of a "Nanny State" not a proper role of government, but no government is capable of defining and enforcing an ever increasing standard of living for its people. Instead, the most "value" can be achieved collectively by individuals assuming responsibility for their own well beings, and that of their families, even if their every want is not fulfilled.

"Necessity" will require most persons to apply their intellects and labors in "inventive" and productive ways. Those, who do not, will fail, and those failures will provide cautionary tales from which others may learn.

Yes, there is a role for government to assist those who cannot help themselves, but a proper definition of "need" in those cases would make the availability of government benefits the exception rather than a generally applicable rule. My greater faith is in the ability of the individual to overcome adversity in order to fulfill his own needs (and wants) rather than faith in a presumptively benevolent government, upon which the people will become increasingly more dependent.

After comments from a dyed-in-the-wool liberal friend, whose opinions I respect for their sincerity, if not for points of agreement, I noted a THIRD fundamental divergence.

He, like others of similar ilk, seems to be of the opinion that governments (as well as institutions in general) can have a moral compass. This seems to follow a similar belief among the more liberal minded that individuals will ultimately do good and succeed in life if given ample (if not unlimited) opportunities and resources. More to the point, such persons believe that governments should be moral (and ultimately will do the right things).

I will note that, if access to resources were a guarantee of a happy and care-free life, there should be no wasted opportunities, disappointments, chemical addictions, or bouts of depression among those more fortunate persons, who have ample means and resources. However, we know this not to be the case. Even privileged persons face challenges in life, and they make mistakes similar to all human beings.

Additional talents, means, and opportunities, which are afforded to some, may allow such persons to recover more quickly from a stumble or misstep. However, ultimate success is not entirely determined by the number of tools and amount of resources that one has. Successes are very much dependent upon whether one is motivated to utilize the tools, which are at hand, and whether he chooses to use his tools, talents, and opportunities in a positive manner.

I believe that only individuals have the capacity to be moral, and I wholeheartedly support high moral standards in individuals. However, I do not believe that institutions have an inherent morality (good or bad). Instead, institutions (and governments) mirror the collective moral compass of those in authority; therefore an institution's morality is fluid, and its moral direction is not fixed. Governments ideally should be morally apathetic or indifferent (but not amoral).

The proper role of government is to prevent harm from being inflicted upon its citizens by other persons, entities, or countries. In this case, "harm" is the improper taking or destruction of property, impairment of natural rights, or harm to the person. Actionable harm should NOT include being a social or economic impediment to one's success or happiness, nor should it include committing an offense against another's sensibilities.

Freedom and liberty necessarily lead to free enterprise, and in bidding for products and services, there are winners and losers. Some can acquire more than their proportional share and others will be left wanting or will make a bad bargain. The role of government should not be to guarantee equality or even some vague concept of fairness but to assure fluidity. Government should assure that the deal is administered as stricken but not choose winners and losers.

Far from my friend's belief that government ultimately will do good, I believe that government, like each individual who

106

comprises the political body, is inherently self-serving and ultimately corruptible. As it has been said, "Power corrupts and absolute power corrupts absolutely."

A unique feature of the U.S. government is that it was not founded as sovereign. The rights of the people were not bestowed by an all powerful state. Instead, the PEOPLE are sovereign, and the people voluntarily ceded to the government certain powers and vested in it limited authority. When government unilaterally expands those established roles and broadens the enumerated powers such that the government approaches sovereignty, government exponentially increases the risk of corruption.

Similarly, when the voluntary relationship between the government and the individual evolves into a compulsory one, this change undermines the foundation of the institution. When there is no consensus between those making requests of the government (the "have nots") and those from whom the government sequesters wealth or liberties (the "haves"), government programs ultimately will fail. There must be a general consensus that the actions of the government are in the best interests of ALL citizens. Where such a consensus cannot be reached, the government should resist the urge to act and intervene.

Regardless of whether one believes that he would be a better steward of the wealth of another, he has no right to take assets from that person by force (or coercion) and to convert those resources to his own use. This principle is no different when government acts as intermediary. In fact, I would argue

107

that it is worse because the "taker" is cloaked in some perceived right or entitlement, and the government (rather than the ultimate beneficiary) deals with the "giver" making the transaction more distant and impersonal (seemingly without cost, sacrifice, or detriment).

During the last presidential campaign, a great deal was made about Mitt Romney paying "only" fifteen percent (15%) of his income in taxes. It was rarely noted in media reports that Romney gave a nearly equal amount in charitable contributions.

The question that I have often posed without answer is, "What is enough?" There is little doubt that what Governor Romney paid was legal, and in fact, with the charitable contributions, I would contend that he far exceeded even any moral obligations regarding his contributions to society. Apparently, that was not enough.

It was not enough that he paid in one year more than the average citizen will pay toward the common good in his or her lifetime. It was not enough that he gave more in charitable contributions than the same citizen would give in that same lifetime.

Thirty percent (30%), or thereabouts, was not enough? Most religions promote the concept of a tithe (*i.e.* 10%) for the church and to benefit the poor. Is government a better judge of the quality of one's works for the poor and downtrodden than religion, which is guided by scripture?

Speaking of Scripture, God demonstrated that He had the power to bestow wealth and comfort, but He generally leaves mankind to its own devices. There are examples of God bestowing riches upon those whom he favored; Abraham and Job come to mind. Conversely, God has sometimes allowed his chosen ones to suffer the natural occurrences of death, loss, and famine.

Jesus Christ dwelt among the poor and downtrodden. He healed them. Christ taught and educated the common people (and religious leaders), but he did not bestow upon them luxuries. The truly poor, about whom Christ spoke, would be hardly identifiable among those within our present society that consider themselves "poor."

The poor in the U.S. are measured relative to our materialistic society, which collectively is the wealthiest in the history of civilization. Do I grieve for one who has no food, clothing or shelter through no fault of his or her own? Certainly, I do. But, for every such person, there are 100's, who have modern luxuries, and are "poor" only in relation to their neighbors. The vast majority of those falling on hard times or for whom the Fates seems to have dealt a bad hand, if honest, would identify within themselves, or through some personal act or omission, the primarily source(s) of their ills.

Should society feel a collective guilt because some "needy" persons do not have the comforts, trappings, or luxuries that other more productive or fortunate persons may have secured for themselves? No, it should not.

Yes, I feel a moral calling and personal obligation to help my fellow man, but each of us should be allowed to choose how best to apply our talents and resources toward that aid. One should choose the persons who are the beneficiaries of his charity. One should not feel obliged to pay homage to government in order for that government to expend his taxes for purposes and to transfer those dollars to persons that he would not feel obliged or inclined to pay directly.

It this harsh? Perhaps, it is. Nevertheless, it is in recognition that there is a cost to someone for every benefit that government bestows on another. That cost often is not felt or appreciated by persons receiving government benefits. It is as if such wealth comes from an infinite source. Disassociating the producer from the consumer distorts the value relationship in the transaction. Government only has such wealth as it takes from its citizens, and that resource is certainly finite.

Americans are not good students of history and experience. Social Security and Medicare are seen by most persons as "self-help" programs. Individuals, even if compelled, make contributions, which will be returned to them in old age when they no longer work. There are also some insurance components for persons with disabilities and children, who cannot work. Arguably, these are reasonable uses of the power of government.

However, when such programs are so underfunded from contributions that they amount to wealth transfer programs from one group to another, the efficacy and justification of the programs are diminished or lost. The same can be said of "Obamacare."

The Affordable Care Act ("ACA" a/k/a "Obamacare") was initially described as "insurance" for the uninsured. Medical Insurance is what most of us used to think of as "major medical." The objective of such insurance is to address an unexpected or extraordinary medical need by paying a premium that is a fraction of the actual potential cost, thereby avoiding financial hardship.

However, there is little, if any, insurance component to the Obamacare prescribed healthcare policies. Instead, these programs are intended to be prepayment plans, and many beneficiaries are likely to pay only a small fraction of the actual cost for services as a result of government subsidies. Many persons will get a windfall by the transfer of wealth occasioned by increased premiums and taxes from others, which will be necessary to fund this massive entitlement program.

It may be uncomfortable to consider whether one's elderly grandmother should undergo a six-figure medical procedure or treatment, which has a questionable efficacy or which offers limited extension of the duration or quality of life. Nevertheless, such a decision ultimately must be made either by the family or by some other company or agency responsible for payment.

It may be easy to say that "any" additional time with a loved one would be worth "any" price, but none of us is likely to say that a single day would be worth $1 Million. What is the tipping point? ... $100,000 for a year ... six (6) months ... thirty (30) days? Yes, life does have a price and quality of life has a value. We make cost-benefit decisions every day that recognize these facts (*e.g.* drive a car, fly in a plane, *etc.*).

The uncomfortable fact is that many persons squander innumerable opportunities to better themselves and to improve their situations in life. Such persons, before dying in old age, likely will squander many months if not years of life in idle pursuits, vice, and other activities, many of which provide little benefit beyond immediate gratification. The same persons in advanced age likely will assert that they are entitled to every treatment, medical device, medicine, and procedure, which may allow them to gain additional days on the earth in order to assuage internal guilt and feelings of loss for lives poorly lived.

Society should not be fined and penalized for the poor choices and bad decisions of its members. Those who make better life decisions should not be guilted into contributing to a pool, which essentially enables the continuation of poor decisions and bad behaviors.

I would happily be a bleeding heart liberal if someone could demonstrate to me realistically how new and existing social programs are going to be funded. Ideally, a person benefitting from government programs should contribute to his or her own well being, with the primary benefits coming from the collective efficiencies of scale.

Nevertheless, one, who advocates for a government benefit or program, also should advocate that any such program be fully funded and its costs honestly presented. If funding means that the government will take substantial portions of the wealth of the propertied classes, then so be it. Such is the power of a democracy: The tyranny of the majority.

But, be honest about the objectives both in scope and cost. Let the people make truly informed decisions rather than choices, which are based upon propaganda, and rather than relying upon alternatives, which are distorted by smoke and mirrors. It is unreasonable and disingenuous to tell half the country, "You can have all that you want," without simultaneously telling the other half, "We're going to take all that you have."

In the name of benevolence toward the "poor," I believe that government is entirely capable of using the wealth of others for the purpose of securing the political support (and votes) of the growing dependent class. Should this belief prove true, the result is a downward spiral that will continue to feed upon itself until the foundations of our society are entirely consumed.

We the People

114

A Cost-Benefit Analysis of War

Blog Entry - September 15, 2013

On 9/11, approximately 3,500 Americans died. There was approximately $30 BILLION in property damage and lost income (from those businesses, which were directly affected).

Post 9/11, America fought two (2) protracted wars in Afghanistan and Iraq. Those wars have cost the lives of more than 6,000 military personnel and another 2,000 military contractors (approximately 8,000+ in total).

Depending on whose counts and estimates that you use:

- The numbers of innocent civilians, who have been killed in these wars, total between 100,000 and 200,000;
- The out-of-pocket costs to date are approaching $2 TRILLION; and
- Total projected costs including long-term benefits and disabilities total $3-4 TRILLION.

What did we get for this massive additional loss of life and gargantuan expenditures?

Our government has created situations in which two (2) countries, which we "aided," are today just as much enemies as allies, and millions of civilians are arguably no better off than they were before U.S. involvement.

Here is an interesting factoid:

*Had the federal government taken the out-of-pocket war costs to date (without even giving consideration to future expenditures) and given those monies to the families of those, who died on 9/11 DIED ON 9/11, **EACH** family would have received more than **$500 MILLION**!*

Was this money well spent, and were the additional lives lost a fair price paid for political vanity?

"War is Hell"[26]

Introduction -

Anyone, who is trained in the use of and proper respect for firearms, is taught to never point any gun (whether presumed loaded or not) at anything that the potential shooter is not fully prepared to destroy. Similarly, the only proper objectives of war are unqualified victory or absolute surrender. The costs of war are too great for such efforts to be half-hearted.

We, as a society, are on a slippery ethical and moral slope when we try to make "war" relatively painless and to distance the average citizen from the true costs of war, as measured in losses of life, limb, materiel, and treasury.

A remote controlled drone war, in which alleged combatants are killed in a manner similar to playing a video game, opens up the very real potential for abuses and atrocities where the actual horrors of war are far removed from the soldiers, who "pull the trigger," and from citizens, who are being shielded from a supposedly greater harm.

It is hard to "justify" the deaths of hundreds of innocent civilians on foreign soil many thousands of miles away from

---

[26] Throughout this essay, I sometimes assume the role of "Devil's Advocate." I do this to challenge presumptions of historical fact so as to establish that such "facts" are not without detractors and that the foundations of history (and thus our present geopolitical situations) are worthy of energetic debate and close scrutiny. I do not claim any omniscience in resolving questions of historical accuracy. Where deemed appropriate, I have identified and/or cited the source of information, particularly when such information is likely to be controversial. I have endeavored to include only controversial information when it appears that the certainty of the presumed facts is legitimately challenged. Where attribution is uncertain or the information is likely apocryphal, I have attempted to identify it as such. My objective is to identify a process of critical analysis, which allows sincere debate when warranted, rather than blindly accepting versions of history or other events, which are likely skewed by prejudice and bias.

U.S. shores with the objective of assassinating individual terrorist leaders. We should never be so comfortable and calloused by war that the deaths of innocents are easily dismissed as acceptable collateral damage.

The inexorable purposes of a military are to break things and to kill people. Some persons argue that military might exists not necessarily to be used but that its mere presence acts as a deterrent to those, who may wish harm upon us. Like former General and then President, Dwight D. Eisenhower, I fear that, in feeding and fostering a burgeoning "Military Industrial Complex," there is a great temptation to use such might, which sits at the ready, in order to justify its continued existence and exorbitant cost.

Notwithstanding these issues, one who plays a "bluff" must be prepared to have that bluff called by a determined adversary; therefore, it is the actual threat of (mutually assured) death and destruction that makes such a "deterrent" effective. Regardless, war powers and military might are ill suited to enforcing the finer points of diplomacy or promoting social engineering.

With great power, comes great responsibility. Might in the defense of self or of the oppressed is a necessary and admirable trait of peoples. Military might used to exploit another's weakness in order to further one's own position and standing in the world is simply bullying on an international scale.

IF there is truly an "imminent threat to national security" (the point at which military action is warranted), then there should be a factual explanation and clearer understanding of that threat and a direct buy-in from the American people before instituting military action or exercising war powers.

All is Fair in War -

The Union General, William Tecumseh Sherman, advocated "Total War," in which an entire population (including civilians) rather than just its designated combatants may be viewed as adversaries. Sherman is infamous for burning Atlanta and other locales in his devastating "March to the Sea" during the U.S. Civil War. He is nearly as famous for his restatement of the seemingly obvious, "War is Hell."

An acquaintance noted the irony of having "Rules of War." He questioned the propriety of a sense of "civility" in an undertaking, which inevitably includes atrocities on both sides of the conflict. More specifically, he questioned whether "Weapons of Mass Destruction," including biological and chemical weapons, were any "less bad" than the large-scale use of conventional firearms and explosives. He asked, "Why do we establish 'red lines,' against the use of some weapons but not others?"

I appreciate the irony, and I have often considered the same concepts. I have "settled" on the explanation that there is no effective defense for general citizens against an attack using chemical or biological weapons. The killer is often silent and unseen until it is too late to flee. There is no building or safe room, which is likely to provide shelter. There is no readily available weapon or act of self defense that can provide effective protection.

As horrific as "conventional" war may be, there are few things as staggering as the abject devastation of an entire population dead in the streets where they stood or in their homes where they slept unaware of the approach of death. Such horrors are exceeded only by the total devastation of a nuclear detonation.

Rules of War do not exist to make war pleasant or to make it more palatable. I would also argue that such rules are hardly a deterrent to those who would be inclined to instigate war. Instead, such rules are for the benefit of combatants and political leaders, who detest war and who abhor the unreasonable costs of war, but who acknowledge that war and armed conflict are likely inevitable. The Rules of War remind such reluctant warriors that victory at all costs is unreasonable if those costs include the loss of a sense of civility or the loss of one's own humanity.

The Fallacy of a Noble War -

Recently, Steven Spielberg, the Director, whose multiple Oscars include "Best Director" and "Best Picture" for the World War II inspired movie, *Schindler's List*, released another wartime movie, *Lincoln*. This most recent cinema release focuses on the life of the 16th President of the United States, Abraham Lincoln, and the time span of the movie is closely centered around the adoption of the Thirteenth Amendment to the Constitution (1865), which abolished slavery.

The movie opened to rave reviews, and Daniel Day Lewis, who plays Lincoln, pays homage to the legendary President. The movie is a theatrical portrayal not a documentary. President

Lincoln deservedly comes off as an admirable figure, a hero who saved the Union. As art, the portrait is pleasing, but the man, who was Lincoln, was a multi-faceted product of his time.

Lincoln was a man, who was part of the machinery of politics, capitalism, and corporate America. It is rarely noted that Honest Abe, the man whose statue sits regally in the memorial, which bears his name, once had the tawdry position of Lobbyist in Washington for the benefit of the Illinois Central Railroad. At the time, his client/employer was one of the largest corporations in America. This established relationship with corporate America was as instrumental to Lincoln becoming President as were the now famous Lincoln-Douglas debates, which gave evidence of his intellect and political acumen.

I admire the man, who was Lincoln. I think that he did his damnedest to save the Union at a time when its survival was genuinely in question. Maintaining the Union assured the prominent role that the United States would play in the geopolitics of the Twentieth Century. Without that prominence and power, the outcomes of two World Wars and the "Communist Menace" may have been much different.

However, the American Civil War has been cast by many persons as a "noble war" with the promotion of basic human rights through the abolition of slavery as its singular objective. Admittedly, the abolition of slavery was the most notable and noble accomplishment of that war. However, the persons, who are often given credit for achieving that end, including Lincoln himself, were not the moral idealists, which history often paints them to be. Similarly, the motivations, which led the states of

121

the Confederacy and the persons therein to secede from the Union, cannot be summed up in the single world, "Slavery."

A Thousand Shades of Grey -

In early cinema lore, it was easy to distinguish the good guys from the bad guys. The bad guys all wore black hats and sported handlebar mustaches. The good guys all wore white hats and more often than not carried a badge. In reality, we have learned that some bad guys carry badges or operate under the auspices of "the law," and nearly all persons wear hats of varying shades of grey regardless of whether they are cast as heroes or villains.

As abhorrent and repugnant as the concepts of slavery and human bondage are to us today, slavery as an institution was an accepted part of the human condition for millennia. Slaves were among the trophies and spoils of wars. A trophy of battle, which could be sold into slavery, provided a much better return than did a casualty of war. Some of the early slave traders to America were African, and their wares were the victims of tribal warfare. The African country of Ghana and more recently chieftains of indigenous African tribes have acknowledged direct involvement in that slave trade.

Slavery was formerly such an accepted (if not integral) part of human society that not only is the *Holy Bible* replete with examples, but the scripture contains little in the way of rebuke or chastisement for those, who owned slaves. Admonishments were primarily reserved for those who would "abuse" or "mistreat" their slaves.

122

An entire, albeit short, book of the New Testament focuses on the relationship between a slave and his master, both of whom are identified as Christians. The much revered St. Paul (Saul of Tarsus) writes a letter to the slave owner, Philemon, to explain that Paul has encouraged his runaway slave, Onesimus, to return to Philemon. Paul does not insist that the slave be given his freedom but only that Philemon show mercy on him and afford him Christian grace.[27]

One of the motivating factors within the abolitionist movement in the United States was the description of slavery, as told in Harriet Beecher Stowe's novel, *Uncle Tom's Cabin*, which was published in book form in 1852. To many, the cruel slave owner character, Simon Legree, who interestingly was a Northerner by birth, came to epitomize not just slave owners but Southerners in general. The lingering image of those, who fought on behalf of the Confederacy, as domineering slave owners helps solidify the perception that the cause of the Confederacy was founded in ignorance and oppression.

That limited perspective ignores other realities of the time. While slavery was a defining issue for many persons on both sides of the war, there were multiple reasons and causes for secession. Ultimately, the driving factors related more to the concentration of power within the Union and to the respective economies and wealth of the North and South rather than any moral quest on the part of the Union political leaders.

---

[27] Some religious scholars debate the nature of the relationship between Philemon and Onesimus. Some persons have asserted that these persons may simply have been close friends or family members, who had become estranged. Nevertheless, the passage is most often interpreted as described above.

By way of example, one significant source of revenue for the United States (and thus the "Union") in the 19th century was from import tariffs on goods coming into the country. Many raw materials originated in the South (*e.g.* timber, cotton, *etc.*), and such materials were used in manufacturing activities, which were concentrated in the North. Completed manufactured goods were then returned to and sold within the Southern states. Northern manufacturers resisted the potential competition from foreign producers.

A large influx of foreign goods came into the country via the ports in the Southern states, and the Southern states accounted for the vast majority of exports out of the country. Other countries, including those in Europe, were eager to trade with the states of the Confederacy. Ready access to foreign manufactured goods, would have reduced the South's dependence on Northern industrialists, and revenues within the Confederate states would be increased if those revenues did not have to be shared with their Union neighbors.

Less than Twenty-five Percent (25%) of Southerners owned slaves, and most of those, who did own slaves, owned five or fewer.[28] Life on the "Plantation," which we think of today, was foreign to most whites and many slaves alike.

I can hardly believe that mothers within the Confederacy condemned 250,000 of their sons to die in battle in order to support an effort, which principally benefitted the landed gentry. Consider a war today in which persons willingly sacrifice

---

[28] See Williamson, Samuel H., and Louis P. Cain, "Measuring Slavery in 2011" – An analysis of wealth disparities between the North and South, www.measuringworth.com.

124

themselves in droves to protect the wealth of the infamous "One Percent." That concept would have been no less repugnant 150 years ago.

Rebels without a (Certain) Cause -

Many would paint the supporters of the Confederacy as traitors to the United States and to the ideals espoused by our founding fathers. Others would describe those, who led the Confederacy, as being the guardians of the concepts of self-reliance and self-determination, which were so integral to goals and objectives of those same founders. As always, a complex reality is much harder to understand and define than the adoption of a view originating from a singular perspective.

While arguably shortsighted, those who supported secession were confident that they were capable of forming a government, society, and economic system more beneficial to themselves than those which would be afforded to them by remaining in the Union.

Were their actions in furtherance of self-determination materially different from those persons, who less than a century before had risked their lives and fortunes in seeking independence from Great Britain? Were the successes, which had been derived from the establishment of that earlier democratic Republic, any more assured than the hoped-for successes of the Confederacy?

In hindsight, the survival of the Union paved the way for America to become a superpower and the world's leading economy. While such outcomes were hardly predestined, an internally competitive American likely would have been a less successful participant within the international community.

One Family's Legacy -

In challenging the ideas that Southerners had little appreciation for or connection to the "old" Union, I need only identify one Confederate General and briefly explore his family's intimate relationships to the Father of Our Country, George Washington.

General Robert E. Lee is well known as the military leader for the Confederate army. A native of Virginia, General Lee previously had served with distinction in the Union army. Before resigning his commission: Lee graduated with honors from West Point; He was decorated as a military commander; and prior to the outbreak of war, Lee had been offered the command of the Union army by none other than President Abraham Lincoln.

Lee's ultimate surrender to Union General, Ulysses S. Grant, at Appomattox Courthouse dominates history texts about the Civil War. What is less known is the family lineage of Lee's wife, Mary Custis.

Mary was the daughter of George Washington Parke Custis, who was himself the son of John Parke Custis. John's mother, Martha Dandridge Custis, was widowed, and she is better known by her later married name, Martha Washington. After his father's death, George Washington Parke Custis was adopted by President George Washington. Washington having no natural children of his own, Custis was among the children reared by George and Martha. Thus, Robert E. Lee's wife was the (great)grandchild of none other than George Washington.

Lest you think this connection tenuous, Robert E. Lee's father, Henry "Light Horse Harry" Lee, was the son of Mary Bland, who was a contemporary and early romantic interest of George Washington. At the death of George Washington in 1799, Henry Lee was serving in Congress, and his fellow Representatives selected Lee to give the Eulogy at Washington's funeral in Philadelphia. If any Southern family had access to information about the personalities and philosophies, which gave birth to the nation, the Lee family certainly did.

It is unlikely that Robert E. Lee casually abandoned and turned away from the hard won legacies of his family and of his wife's family. Like many others who fought in furtherance of the Confederacy, Lee likely believed that such actions were complimentary to the goals of independence and self-determination, which had been espoused by Washington and others, rather than making them traitors to their common cause.

Moralism vs. Pragmatism -

Just as there were Southerners for whom slavery was the controlling issue leading to secession, there was undoubtedly an active abolitionist movement within the country.

In 1859, the white abolitionist, John Brown, led an unsuccessful attack on the federal arsenal at Harpers Ferry in what would later become West Virginia. Brown believed that an armed slave revolt or insurrection was the only way to achieve freedom for the slaves.

Brown and his band were captured by U.S. marines, who were led by then Colonel Robert E. Lee. Brown was convicted and hanged for the murders of five (5) persons, who died in the attack, and for treason against the Commonwealth of Virginia, of which he was not a resident.

John Brown went to the gallows believing himself to be a martyr for the abolitionist cause and proclaiming himself an agent of God. The fear of continued revolt and insurrection were still fresh in the minds of Southerners when Lincoln, who previously had expressed his personal opposition to slavery, won the nomination of the Republican Party and ultimately the presidency in 1860.

In a race in which there were four (4) candidates vying for the office of President of the United States, Lincoln won the presidency with only Thirty-nine Percent (39%) of the popular vote (and with not a single vote having been cast for him in 10 of the 15 Southern states).

Lincoln's most able contender was the Democratic candidate, Stephen A. Douglas, who had beaten Lincoln for a U.S. Senate seat from the State of Illinois and who along with Lincoln participated in the famous Lincoln-Douglas debates in pursuit of that seat in 1858. Those debates were preceded by a speech given by Lincoln, which drew upon the biblical passage contained in *Mark* 3:25, when he said:

> *A house divided against itself cannot stand. I believe*
> *this government cannot endure permanently half slave*
> *and half free. I do not expect the Union to be*
> *dissolved—I do not expect the house to fall—but I do*

*expect it will cease to be divided. It will become all
one thing, or all the other.*

However, Lincoln was not a moralist or idealist. Instead,
Lincoln was more of a pragmatist, whose primary goal was the
solidification of the Union.

New York Tribune Editor, Horace Greely, wrote an editorial
purporting to speak for "20 Millions" in asking Lincoln to free
all of the slaves in Union held territory. On August 22, 1862,
Lincoln penned a letter in response:

> *I would save [the Union] the shortest way under the
> Constitution. The sooner the national authority can
> be restored the nearer the Union will be 'the Union as
> it was.' ... If there be those who would not save the
> Union unless they could at the same time destroy
> slavery, I do not agree with them — My paramount
> object in this struggle is to save the Union, and is not
> either to save or to destroy slavery. If I could save the
> Union without freeing any slave, I would do it, and if I
> could save it by freeing all the slaves I would do it;
> and if I could save it by freeing some and leaving
> others alone, I would also do that.*

Less than five (5) months later, Lincoln issued the
Emancipation Proclamation on January 1, 1863. However, that
proclamation did not free all slaves. It only freed slaves in the
rebelling states of the Confederacy. Slaves were not freed in
slave-owning Union states (*e.g.* Kentucky, Maryland and
Delaware). In making the proclamation, Lincoln hoped to turn
the tide of a Civil War in which victory for the Union was far
from guaranteed.

At that time, the United States did not maintain a large
standing army. In the event of national emergency, the

President, in his capacity as Commander-in-Chief, would put out a call to Governors of the various states seeking volunteers for military service. During the Civil War, initial enlistments were for a mere ninety (90) days, but enlistment periods were later extended to three (3) years.

Career military officers often were tasked with organizing and training these green troops into fighting units. It was a role similar to that played today by the legendary Green Berets, who organize and direct indigenous fighters in foreign conflicts. In such cases, leadership is imperative. After all, men were being asked to risk their lives and to leave their homes, families, and occupations in order to serve and pursue a cause, which may not have been entirely their own. Political fracturing in the North was the result of varying degrees of support for the war, and recruitment efforts were greatly hindered in some locales.

Despite early recruitment successes, the Union found it difficult later in the war to muster troops at levels, which were necessary to defend the nation from the more motivated Confederate forces. The issuance of the Emancipation Proclamation came through the exercise of Lincoln's war powers. The President hoped that the freed Southern slaves would be encouraged to serve in the Union army and to take up arms against those, who formerly confined them in servitude.

Members of Lincoln's own Republican Party deplored the limited scope of the proclamation. His Secretary of State, William Seward, verbalized the hypocrisy:

We show our sympathy with slavery by emancipating slaves where we cannot reach them and holding them in bondage where we can set them free.

The boarding, maintenance, and retention of slave labor were costly undertakings.[29] In addition to the costs, it is difficult for obvious reasons to maximize the productivity and efficiency of forced labor.

These costs and inefficiencies fueled an economic trend, which combined with an inherent sense of immorality regarding slavery and human bondage. These things led to slavery being abolished throughout much of the industrialized world during the 18th and 19th centuries. The move to abolish slavery in the United States was primarily an acknowledgment that the Industrial Revolution had made slavery inefficient and no longer viable as economic system, at least as far as the North was concerned.

In an ironic twist of fate, the same revolution, which allowed the Northern states to leverage human resources and to increase productivity through manufacturing, fostered the continuation of slavery in the South.

In 1794, Eli Whitney invented the Cotton Gin, and the advent of the mechanical ginning (*i.e.* separating cotton from its seeds) encouraged cotton production and made the South economically dependent upon that single crop. By 1860, the South provided roughly two-thirds of the world's supply of cotton.

---

[29] Some more "humane" slave owners, George Washington among them, provided for a "pension" from which to pay slaves' expenses in old age. Washington also provided in his Will for the release of his slaves within five (5) years of his death.

Southern economic and political leaders feared that a concentration of power in Washington would destroy the autonomy of the southern states and which would threaten the vast accumulation of wealth among propertied classes. As it was, the differing economies between the North and the South created a rift, which expanded into an unbridgeable chasm.

While the institution of slavery was dying even before the Civil War, had the owning of slaves still been integral to the economy of the country as a whole, abolition likely would have had only nominal support and little chance of success.

"Never let a Crisis go to Waste" -

In times of war, governments in general and Presidents in particular cloak themselves as the protectors of the people, and they often assume powers and usurp authority, which under normal circumstances would clearly be identified as abusive and tyrannical. The brush of history often glosses over these abuses and focuses on the more noble accomplishments brought about during or after the conflict. This is true even if such accomplishments were only incidental rather than instrumental to the outbreak of war.

As President, Abraham Lincoln suspended *Habeas Corpus*, the right to seek relief from unlawful imprisonment, in direct contravention of the U.S. Constitution (*a la* Guantanamo Bay). Furthermore, Lincoln's military officers and his Attorney General blatantly ignored a ruling by the Chief Justice of the Supreme Court, Roger B. Taney. That ruling confirmed that only Congress, not the President, possessed the constitutional authority to suspend *habeas corpus,* and Chief Justice Taney had commanded that political prisoners be brought before the court for a hearing.

President Lincoln, by and through agents of his administration and general officers under his command, also suppressed free speech by censuring the press and by punishing newspaper editors, who criticized Union war efforts or who were sympathetic to the causes of the Confederacy.[30] Finally, Lincoln was at least complicit in allowing General Sherman to wage Total War against Confederate cities.

The reasons for the Civil War (and ultimately abolishing slavery) were more pragmatic than noble. The Civil War was in its origins just like all other wars. It was about the concentration of power and the accumulation of wealth. The story of the Civil War, told as a means to those ignoble ends, does not shine with the same glimmer as a fight to free the oppressed slaves. History is written by the victors. Thus, it can hardly be said to be "unbiased."

A Common Trait -

One might argue that my portrait of Lincoln and the Civil War tarnishes the image of a great President. Lincoln's greatness is indisputable; however, his image and that of his presidency should not be viewed through rose colored glasses. We do ourselves a disservice when we evaluate others and our present actions in reference to legend rather than fact. It should be obvious that truth and liberty are early casualties of war, and

---

[30] See Bulla, David W., *Lincoln's Censor: Milo Hascall and Freedom of the Press in Civil War Indiana*, Purdue University Press (2008).

such abuses certainly are not limited to Abraham Lincoln or the Civil War.

Misplaced Faith -

One of the most intelligent and educated among American Presidents was Woodrow Wilson. He held a Ph.D. in History, and he came to the Presidency following his service as President of Princeton University. As a leader in the Progressive Movement, Wilson's expansion of government and his legislative accomplishments were likely exceeded only by the "New Deal" programs, which were later begun by Franklin D. Roosevelt and further implemented by FDR's successor Harry Truman.

Wilson had faith in the powers of government and in the strength of his own intellect. That faith (some would say hubris) was evidenced by his expansive legislative agenda and in fashioning the League of Nations after World War I.[31]

President Wilson was not forthright in pushing the country into the "Great War." Leading into his second term, Wilson campaigned on the slogan, "He kept us out of war." By that time, however, Wilson was well aware that U.S. involvement in World War I was all but assured. Even with the perceived successes of his first term, Wilson barely won reelection against his Republican opponent, Charles Evans Hughes. Thereafter, Wilson plunged the U.S. into WWI, which was optimistically described as the war "War to End All Wars."

---

[31] Despite Wilson's efforts in establishing the League of Nations, Republican opposition assured that the U.S. did not join.

Societal evolution, as evidenced or prompted by legislative and political reforms, encourages those, who view government as primarily a productive and benevolent force. I am certain that Wilson foresaw the dawning of what he believed would be a Golden Age for diplomatic powers and institutional efficiencies, but the lasting peace and unceasing prosperity, which he would have identified as the certain byproducts of these things, never came to fruition. Just as the catastrophic losses of the Great War failed to deter future wars, the growth and expansion of government failed to rid the country of want and perceived inequities.

Instead of acknowledging the intractability of base human traits and the limitations of institutions, some parties choose to double down betting that bigger government can unilaterally raise humanity beyond its natural state. While government may provide an impetus toward change, such change can only be complete and effective if individuals are receptive to it.

Truth vs. "Need to Know" -

Franklin D. Roosevelt had a confidence in government at least equal to that of Wilson, and FDR had a similar propensity for deception and expansion of power in order to achieve government's ends.

Preceding the U.S. entry into World War II, FDR made a vow similar to Wilson's:

> *I have said this before, but I shall say it again and again: Your boys are not going to be sent into any foreign wars.*

Like Wilson before him, FDR knew that he was making false promises. He explained to an aide: "If someone attacks us, it isn't a foreign war, is it?"[32] Documents from that period and subsequent revelations, implicate FDR and those in his inner circle for consciously goading the Japanese into an attack on Pearl Harbor in order to justify America's entry into the war.

Although members of the "Greatest Generation"[33] are properly credited with turning the tide of the war, the voting public, in whose minds the horrors of WWI were still fresh, was initially reluctant to join what was still viewed by many as a European conflict. A majority of Americans were decidedly against the U.S. entering WWII prior to the Japanese attack on Pear Harbor.

From grade school, I recall learning of the "deceit" of the Japanese diplomatic delegation in Washington, D.C., which continued to feign peace negotiations even as Japanese ships were steaming toward Pearl Harbor.

Most often omitted from this narrative is the fact that the United States had deciphered the encryption keys, which the Japanese believed allowed their government to communicate secretly with Ambassadors and Embassies overseas. As early as 1939, the U.S. regularly intercepted and decoded these messages. The attack on Pearl Harbor, while not forecasted to or by local military commanders, hardly came as a surprise to those, who were better informed in Washington.

---

[32] Jones, Howard, *Crucible of Power: A History of U.S. Foreign Relations Since 1897*, p. 170 (2001).

[33] A term for the cohort of persons, who were born from 1911-1924, and being the generation which gave birth to the "Baby Boomers." The term was coined by Tom Brokaw for his book of the same title (1998).

After a meeting of the War Cabinet on November 25, 1941, Secretary of War, Henry L. Stimson, wrote in his diary:

The question was how we should maneuver [the Japanese] into firing the first shot without allowing too much danger to ourselves.[34]

Following the attack on Pearl Harbor, Stimson stated:

[M]y first feeling was of relief ... that a crisis had come in a way which would unite all our people.[35]

When his own son questioned his honesty, FDR replied:

If I don't say I hate war, then people are going to think I don't hate war. ... If I don't say I won't send our sons to fight on foreign battlefields, then people will think I want to send them. ... So you play the game the way it has been played over the years, and you play to win.[36]

Some persons (particularly those who may be fairly described as Utilitarian) would argue that the U.S. entries into WWII and the preceding WWI were inevitable and that FDR and Wilson before him were just being pragmatic. If entry into the war was inevitable and thousands of U.S. servicemen were going to die regardless, then hastening the start of the war (and the concomitant deaths of roughly 2,400 Americans at Pearl Harbor) was arguably rational decision with an acceptable outcome.

---

[34] Stimson had apparently become calloused and jaded during his time in government. In 1929, as Secretary of State under President Herbert Hoover, Stimson had discontinued funding for the Army's secretive "Black Chamber" program, a precursor to the NSA. In explaining and justifying this decision, Stimson famously said, "Gentlemen do not read each other's mail."

[35] Morgenstern, George, "The Actual Road to Pearl Harbor," in *Perpetual War for Perpetual Peace* edited by Harry Elmer Barnes, pp. 343 and 384 (1953).

[36] Excerpts taken from Goldberg, Jonah, "Obama's Big Lie," *National Review Online* (October 30, 2013).

In pursuit of the Greater Good -

FDR's purported (in)actions might be compared to the legendary decision, which was attributed to Winston Churchill, not to sound air raid sirens to warn residents of Coventry, England about the approach of German bombers. Those bombers inflicted a level of destruction, which would have been almost unimaginable previously.

Before the bombardment, Britain had obtained the "Enigma Codes," which allowed the British and U.S. military to decipher "secret" German communications. However, the story goes that military commanders feared that advanced warnings of the German attack would alert the Luftwaffe that their secret code had been broken, and British commanders feared that the ability of the Allies to successfully intercept and read later encrypted messages would be compromised.

The story is likely apocryphal, but if true, military leaders could have saved the lives of many residents of Coventry had those persons been given timely warnings and afforded an opportunity to seek cover. Instead, the explanation goes that the greater good was furthered by sacrificing the lives of the residents of Coventry and potentially saving more lives by shortening the length of the war.

Even if this specific incident cannot be verified, similar, "cold" calculations are among the inescapable challenges, which are faced during armed conflict and war. One such challenging decision by President Truman[37] led to the U.S. dropping Atomic Bombs on the Japanese cities of Hiroshima and Nagasaki.

Given the tenacity and ferocity with which the Japanese had fought other Pacific battles, the prevailing thought was that a direct assault on the Japanese homeland would result in tremendous Allied casualties. Therefore, the strategy was to unleash unfathomable devastation on certain Japanese cities in order to motivate unconditional surrender without significant loss of life among Allied forces.

Allowing for the possibility that FDR knew about (or even facilitated) the impending attack on Pearl Harbor and consciously chose not to warn or remove those in harm's way, more cynical persons might describe FDR as complicit in the deaths of U.S. servicemen. Even if one would argue that a similar number of deaths were inevitable, what right or privilege should be presumed by FDR and commanders today to determine that any particular persons on a specific day should be sacrificed for the cause of war?

Could it be that those Americans, who died and were wounded at Pearl Harbor, served a role similar to that of the Roman Infantry?

"Infantry" has as its root the word "infant" or youth. Historically, the infantry was made up of persons who were too young or inexperienced (or poor) to be among the more senior ranks or the cavalry.

---

[37] Vice President Harry S Truman succeeded FDR as President after FDR's death on April 12, 1945.

In battle formations, the infantry was the first to face the opposing enemy force. It was expected that this first line would be sacrificed to the opposing force. The hope was that the infantry would inflict some damage; slow the enemy's advance; effect chaos among the enemy force; and give a better opportunity for the more seasoned forces to achieve ultimate victory.

Sacrifice for a Cause that is Worthy -

I certainly do not envy decisions, which have to be made by political leaders in times of war or which are made by commanders on fields of battle. Irrespective of the "justifiable" deaths of enemy combatants or even foreign civilians, military commanders historically have had to face and consider the reality that their decisions would inevitably lead to the deaths of persons within their command. As evident by the statements of Wilson and FDR, it was this potential loss of "mothers' sons," which assured that war would be undertaken infrequently and with great prudence.

What happens when the war is not to repel an aggressor, which threatens our borders? What happens if the threat is not to our physical safety but to our "way of life" or our lifestyles? Are extraordinary measures, which are likely to result in loss of life as well as losses of liberties and freedoms of citizens still warranted and justified?

Undoubtedly, there were men at Pearl Harbor, who were prepared to sacrifice themselves for home and country. There were likely those, who would have been prepared to make that sacrifice even if they had been fully apprised of the complete circumstances surrounding the Japanese attack. Other men may have been reluctant to die had they believed that they served as sacrificial pawns. Regardless of the decisions, which might have been made by particular individuals, should it not be the right of every man to know the true nature of the cause for which he sacrifices life, limb, and liberty?

There are certainly causes worthy of war and for which the costs of war, including the resulting death and destruction, are justified. Nevertheless, such horrific costs, as measured partially in the deaths of young sons and daughters, should never be undertaken based upon a lie. Those who risk sacrificing life and liberty for the sake of home and country deserve to know the true nature of the cause for which they are asked to sacrifice and the true cost of that sacrifice.

No matter how much government and its agents may deem their ends noble, unscrupulous means should never be utilized toward those ends. Not even a caretaker government possesses authority legitimately, which would allow that government to keep its wards in the dark about acts that are being undertaken on behalf of such citizens, and such citizens should not be unwittingly used as pawns in the pursuit of the questionable aims of government.

Conclusion –

The existence of internally established and internationally adopted Rules of War may seem irrational. How can there be limitations and rules when victory over your enemy is the ultimate objective?

Such rules are not in place to negate the inescapable death and destruction of war. Instead, they are in place to protect the humanity of those who believe that civility, while perhaps not a natural state of man, is the only state in which our species can survive. Without respect for our fellow man, even those who would be considered enemies, we risk winning costly battles only to ultimately lose an internal war for our own humanity.

If accepted defenses to mankind's misdeeds are, "My higher reason couldn't control my baser instincts," or "I was only following orders," then we deserve to fail as a species. Instead, we should strive to excel and succeed even under the most trying of circumstances. We should want to better ourselves and humankind. Contentment with the bestial state of man is a recipe for our ultimate destruction. Yes, "War is hell," but in the defense of one's home and family, we should expect some deference to the more humane attributes of our seemingly fleeting humanity.

Politicians often are blinded by power. Once "war powers" are in the grasp of politicians, such powers are rarely ceded completely and released voluntarily following the cessation of hostilities. Instead, those who would wield such powers often become enamored and addicted.

Politicians seek to justify the retention of those powers for the sake of government efficiencies and for the supposed protection of the people from some future threat. Since conflicts of some description are inevitable (especially if actively sought in order to justify increased strength and retained powers), the more tragic and most likely threat is that the resulting losses of freedoms and liberties will be permanent.

Even more troubling is the extent to which repeated uses of extraordinary powers have become commonplace and routine. Calling some conflict or government action a "war" seemingly justifies many otherwise impermissible acts and supposedly excuses a host of evils undertaken in pursuit of that war. Today, government seemingly is waging "Total War," in which the Constitutionally protected rights of citizens are being sacrificed in self-declared wars with political aims.

What happens when there is no identifiable foe, whose defeat will mark the end of war and the culmination of victory? What happens when the "war" is being fought against a philosophy, religion, or idea, or it is pursued to promote a personal concept of proper behavior or to further a lifestyle? How much leeway should government be afforded?

Our government in recent years has fought supposed "wars" on multiple fronts: "War on Drugs" ... "War on Poverty" ... "War on Crime" ... and the ubiquitous "War on Terror."

What is the end game in fighting such "wars"? Is it reasonable to expect near-term ends to the use of illicit drugs, poverty, crime, and terror? Is it reasonable to expect a wholesale change in human nature?

What is the exit strategy? When, if ever, will we know that victory has been achieved? Or, do we accept that government resources (and that of its citizens) will be expended incessantly in pursuit of ends, which are almost certainly unattainable?

Do we accept that, in pursuit of such "wars," the liberties and freedoms, which our government was established to protect, must be sacrificed for our own safety and protection?

Independent of abuses of power on the battlefield, extraordinary powers, which legitimately may be usurped by or surrendered to government in defense against an attacking foreign foe, are now being argued to be necessary in the pursuit of some nebulous concept of "National Security." Rather than being involved in a finite war with identifiable objectives and determinable end, government seems to have involved itself in an indeterminate "War on Terror," with ill-defined objectives against an amorphous collection of adversaries.

In the pursuit of such a "war," we are told that the losses of privacy, personal freedoms, and individual liberties, are the necessary and reasonable costs for supposed safety and security. If we surrender our rights and liberties, either to a foreign adversary under threat of terrorist acts or to the government in the pursuit of perceived safety and security, the more important war has already been lost.

A Pox on Both Houses:[38]
The Problems with Politics Today

Form and Function –

I have different views of the functions, scope, and roles of "governments" depending on the level. The higher and broader the government the much more "Republican" versus "Democratic" government should be (in the form of representation and scope not necessarily by way of party platform).

I believe that the FEDERAL government should be one of specific limited powers, consistent with the originally mandate within the Constitution of the United States. The broader "police powers" fall to the STATES (also as contemplated by the Constitution). By necessity, LOCAL governments must take on a much more "Democratic" slant.

At the local levels, a *quid-pro-quo*[39] government is much more easily implemented. The actual costs and benefits of programs and services are better appreciated and more closely administered at the local level, and there is less of a chance for disconnect between those who fund government and those who most directly enjoy the benefits from government.

Also, local governments are able to serve as microcosms of trial-and-error rather than attempting to apply a universal one-size-fits-all product. Good policies can be expanded and bad

---

[38] Paraphrased from Shakespeare's play, *Romeo and Juliet*. As Mercutio approaches death, he curses the feuding houses of Capulet and Montague by saying, "A plague on both your houses."

[39] Meaning: "This for that," one thing given in return for another, or a substitute. In this context, I am not referring to bribery or corrupt activities but rather an acknowledgment and recognition of the series of interrelated social contracts among all persons and institutions.

policies can be more readily abandoned rather than having programs, which are imposed top down from the federal government and which turn into inefficient entitlements and inalterable birthrights.

This also means that one has a higher likelihood of directly effecting change in local government when necessary, or in the worst case scenario, moving out of the sphere of influence and control, which may be established by an oppressive or inefficient local government. These latter options are not practically available to individuals when nearly all laws of any substance are mandated at the federal level.

Besides the scope and functions of government, two additional problems with government today are that the decisions of politicians often result in them spending OTHER persons' money and result in disrupting the lives and liberties of OTHER persons.

It is easy to tell someone that you can spend his money more effectively and with a better purpose than he can himself. Similarly, it is easy for someone to say that he knows best about someone else's life despite never having experienced that life or its challenges.

Politicians on both ends of the political spectrum claim the moral high ground and attempt to govern based upon fixed ideologies. They claim that their actions (or inaction) are governed by principle.

They would do well to remember that principle is expensive, and actions taken on behalf of one's principles should not be funded with someone else's wealth. Additionally, the sacrifices made to promote one's principles should be shared by those, who benefit from the application of the principle. It would be most appropriate for those asserting a moral imperative to put THEIR money and THEIR actions where their mouths are.

The give-and-take of politics has been replaced with fixed ideologies and acerbic rhetoric. Principles may guide personal behaviors, and ideologies may even be the starting points for legislation. Nevertheless, efficiency and efficacy should be the end results of good government.

Humility versus Hubris –

In the first debate between President Barak Obama and the Republican challenger, former Governor Mitt Romney of Massachusetts [10/03/2012], the overwhelming consensus was that Romney was the surprising winner.

I cannot say that I "liked" the fact that Obama did not have a good showing in that first debate. What I did like was that Obama finally was being seen as more human than Messianic. Had he brought some humility into the job of President rather than unmet promises of "Hope and Change," perhaps, then we would not have the major political parties standing on opposite sides of a fiscal abyss pointing fingers at each other while the ground beneath their feet crumbles. Unfortunately, Obama succumb to his own hype. As he has acknowledged before, "I believe my own [B.S.]."

After all, Obama was awarded the Nobel Peace Prize having served less than a year in office without any notable accomplishment other than his historic election to the presidency. He seemingly expected that all persons would bow to his supposed greatness. He chose to ignore the reality that the tools, energies, and resources, which are integral to and necessary for the implementation of his ideas, come from others.

Obama saw the support and concurrence of the private sector and wealth generators as unnecessary. He saw any opposition to his aims as being based upon irrational stubbornness and entrenched ignorance. His has been a difficult and costly lesson for the American people; however, I am not sure that Obama's arrogance will allow him to take that lesson to heart. Hubris is likely his fatal flaw.[40]

Some would argue that the fault falls not upon the President but upon those, who have failed to take up his banner. Faulting the troops for not following a leader into battle is placing the blame on the wrong parties. If a leader expects citizens to sacrifice for a cause, it is the leader's obligation to convince those citizens that the cause is worthy and that the sacrifice is reasonable.

Obama promises new and continued benefits to some without requiring adequate contributions or concurrent sacrifice. He fails to acknowledge openly that with certainty of outcome comes loss of liberty and freedom. He fails to appreciate that for every benefit bestowed there is a price to be paid. Where benefits flow to persons other than those who pay the price, there will almost certainly be resistance and resentment. For many from whom such sacrifice and contributions will be

---

[40] Hubris is a negative trait held by numerous politicians on both sides of the political aisle. Cincinnatus definitely would feel out of place among such "leaders."

required, he has identified no benefit beyond forced altruism. No matter how supposedly noble the effort, Obama has failed to sell his vision to those upon whom the burdens of that vision will fall. Regardless of the shortcomings of the citizens, the buck stops with the President.

Proponents of Obama's style of government argue that it is supported by a majority of the country's citizens. However, Obama's selling of his programs and positions to the "majority" is hardly an accomplishment when the numbers of those, who are increasingly dependent on the government, continue to swell. Of course, he has no trouble preaching to the choir. Instead, Obama should deliver his message to the supposed hoarding wealth mongers.

Yes, he DOES have an obligation to say what is in it for them. Wealth is finite, and it is mobile. It is not a resource that can be mined recklessly without exhaustion. The Leviathan could hardly be restrained and controlled before Obama. Rather than grapple with the monster and tame it, Obama has sought to force feed it and unleash it from its fetters.

I think that Obama is basically a good well meaning person. I believe that he is thoughtful and intelligent. I also believe that he had a naïve and ego-centric view of his presidency and of his ability to impose by fiat his view of society and politics upon the country and the rest of humanity.

Obamacare was a prime example of the sales pitch, "Trust me ... I know better than you what you need, and you'll eventually appreciate the medicine that I'm giving to you."

It does not matter if you are the smartest person in the room if you cannot convince others, who initially disagree with you, about the rightness of your positions.

My biggest qualm with Obama is this lack of demonstrated leadership. He is Commander in Chief, and he commands the respect afforded to his office. However, he has done very little to demonstrate his leadership and earn requisite respect. Leaders lead from the front by instilling confidence in those, who follow the blazed path.

Obama's "leadership" is a lot more like pointing and giving directions. He points toward a supposed destination, gives instructions to follow, and says, "Trust me, I know the way; although, I've never been there myself." Obama entered his presidency blaming George W. Bush. He continues to blame the "obstructionist" Republicans. After five (5) years in office, does Obama shoulder no blame for the *status quo*?

In the Vice Presidential Debate, the incumbent, Joe Biden, chided the challenger, Congressman Paul Ryan, and thus Ryan's running mate Mitt Romney, about not fully outlining the policy proposals, which Governor Romney would implement as a first-term President.

After that debate, the Obama administration was similarly chided by the formerly reverent and lenient mainstream media. In a *Washington Post* op-ed [10/13/2012] entitled, "Show Me a Policy," the editors of the Post finally asked Obama to relate to the American public what would be his desired policy objectives in a second term. In the movie, *Jerry McGuire*, the character

Rod Tidwell famously tells the movie's namesake, who is played by Tom Cruise, "Show me the money!"

In sketching out second term policies, the President would have to acknowledge that there is no money to show and that there is not a lot of show for the money which has already been spent. Obama is not the only guilty party, but he believes himself to be bigger and better than nearly everyone else. He certainly has not demonstrated himself worthy of that high opinion of himself.

A Case in Point -

The decision to take military action in Syria (or some other foreign land) costs real dollars, which are paid by American taxpayers, and such actions almost inevitably result in "collateral damage," which can be measured by human lives ruined or lost.

Is the measure of that loss really that much different depending upon whether the mothers of the dead are American or from a foreign land? This is not a board game where you move pieces around and simply reset the board when someone loses.

If attacking a foreign land is of such grave national interest to the U.S., then why does President Obama not don a uniform and personally lead troops into battle like George Washington, U.S. Grant, Teddy Roosevelt, John F. Kennedy, and Dwight D. Eisenhower?

If it is not important enough for the President to get his hands dirty with the blood of fallen enemies, maybe it is not important enough to spend someone else's money or to kill someone else's children.

If one does not possess sufficient leadership skills so as to inspire confidence in those, who must follow and implement plans and programs, then one's goals and objectives likely should be amended or adjusted. Have we learned nothing from recent history?

Instead of a reasoned answer or explanation, we hear the incessant refrain, "Just trust us." However, these words do not provide a comforting reassurance from politicians, who obviously do not "trust" their own citizens. Do domestic spy programs elicit "trust" from the people?

As was famously said during the Cold War, "Trust, but Verify." If the information and government positions cannot be subjected to critique and verification, then trust is unjustified. Government has hardly proven itself trustworthy of late.

The President lost the benefit of the doubt when he unabashedly retained and expanded secret spy programs on the American people. His actions, which were undertaken supposedly in our best interests, are unconscionable and obscene. How do we trust anything that he says?

Obama has failed to prove himself to be materially different than the other power mongers, who occupy Washington and other world capitals. A little genuine humility is undoubtedly too much to ask of one who enjoyed a messianic rise to office.

The President's mantra is "Forward!" However, forward on the current course is fraught with perils, and the ship of state very likely could be dashed upon the rocks. Instead of "Leading from behind," it is time for Obama (and politicians in general) to get out in front of an issue for a change.

Examples Unfollowed -

Most of us first learn of George Washington through recitation of the legendary story about him chopping down a cherry tree and replying when confronted, "I cannot tell a lie."

Similarly, the legendary stories of the Roman statesman, Cincinnatus, may be more apocryphal than fact. Nevertheless, we like to believe that our political leaders hold positions of authority out of a sense of service to the people rather than as a means to fulfill aspirations of power.

As the first President of the fledgling United States, George Washington certainly knew the story of Cincinnatus, and Washington personified the ideals of that Roman Statesman when Washington said:

I had rather be in my grave than in my present situation, I had rather be on my farm than be emperor of the world; and yet they charge me with wanting to be a king.

King George, III inquired of Benjamin West, the American painter commissioned to paint the portrait of the British monarch, what would become of his foe and adversary, General George Washington, after America prevailed in the Revolutionary War. When West replied, "They say he will return to his farm," the King with great deference to General Washington purportedly said, "If he does that, he will be the greatest man in the world."

George Washington was the military commander of the Colonial armies and civilian militias during the Revolutionary War. He was a reluctant statesman, but he willingly surrendered his comfortable life in Virginia to lead armies of men for nearly a decade in the American war for independence. Washington, having helped to mold and forge America, had available to him the reins of the government and the opportunity of unfettered power. Nevertheless, he was a true servant of the people, and he repeatedly refused the powers offered to him or even thrust upon him.

Can any of us imagine President Obama, or nearly any other politician today, pushing aside vanity long enough waive off such offices and accolades?

Unfortunately, government amasses politicians not leaders. What would a more modern leader look like? He would look like Senator Daniel K. Inouye (D–HI).

Inouye was a leader and hero by any definitions of those words. He died December 17, 2012 after a lifetime of service to his state and to his country. He served as a Japanese-American in World War II, when many like persons were shunned and placed in confinement camps by the federal government. In nearly six (6) decades, he never lost an election. He served in Congress from 1959 until his death, achieving the position of Senate *Pro Tempore* (third in line of succession to the Presidency). His exemplary example, as a man not just a politician, should be a model for persons, who aspire to be leaders:

In April 1945, [Inouye] led an assault on a heavily defended hill near San Terenzo, Italy. Three German machine guns pinned his unit, and one bullet pierced his abdomen and went out his back, barely missing his spine. Still, he fought, subduing two machine gun nests with grenades. Crawling toward the third, a German rifle grenade shattered his right arm, leaving his final grenade "clenched in a fist that suddenly didn't belong to me anymore." Waving his unit back, he pried it loose, tossed it left-handed and destroyed the third bunker. He fought on until a bullet in his leg left him unconscious. ... The Army awarded him a Distinguished Service Cross, the second-highest award for valor — not until 2000 was it upgraded to the Medal of Honor — along with the Bronze Star, a Purple Heart with cluster and 12 other medals and citations.[41]

A Case for LESS Transparency -

There are very real and serious differences between the [most recent] Presidential Candidates and the major Political Parties. However, instead of addressing and dealing with those issues and finding areas of agreement or compromise, most persons seem content to be entertained by the concerted efforts to engage in politics for sport.

Proponents and opponents of various positions, and often the supposedly objective news media, rip phrases out of context and distort statements for effect. The desired effects may be self-promotion, the denigration of one's opponent, or sensationalism.

Many times, the statements are not even examples of those infamous gaffes, which occasionally spew from the mouths of politicians and give momentary insight into their true thinking.

---

[41] *Dallas Morning News* - Op-Ed (December 18, 2012).

Often when one listens to the reported statement in full context, it hardly has any resemblance to the distorted caricature. Political debate and media reporting should not cloud the real issues or obstruct honest discussion and sincere discourse.

Contrary to the current popular but misguided beliefs in the supposed virtues of unlimited "transparency" and "full disclosure," all persons, including politicians, need a forum and venue within which to express openly and without a public filter (unconventional or even bad) ideas and matters of opinion so that those ideas and opinions can be fully expressed and ultimately vetted. It has been said, "The making of laws is like the making of sausages - the less you know about the process the more you respect the result."[42]

One of the overriding problems with Washington today (and politics in general) is the need for politicians to perform constantly for the C-SPAN cameras and to avoid a 24/7 media blitzkrieg. Frankness and sincerity have been replaced by rhetoric and deception. The current state of affairs does not eliminate bad politics; it just makes bad acts more covert. So long as beliefs are held privately (rather than expressed openly in a protected setting), those beliefs are allowed to fester and seethe. There is no means to tame the acerbic rhetoric and no mechanism to allow balance from opposing and better reasoned points of view.

---

[42] This quote, or some derivation thereof, is often misattributed to the German aristocrat and former Prime Minister of Prussia, Otto von Bismark. The earliest known attribution is to John Godfrey Saxe, *University Chronicle*, University of Michigan (March 27, 1869). Nevertheless, the statement has been around for more than a century, and that staying power should give it credence.

The recent Congressional budget deal, which provides an outline for federal spending over two (2) years, is an example of how less disclosure yielded a positive result. Given a polarized Congress, the deal was brokered almost exclusively in private meetings between House Budget Committee Chairman, Congressman Paul Ryan (R-WI), and Senate Budget Committee Chairperson, Senator Patricia L. "Patty" Murray (D-WA). In interviews, both legislators commented that the difficult compromises, which were reached much to the consternation of members of their respective parties, would not have been possible without the mutual trust that their negotiating positions would not be disclosed for competitive advantage prior to a final agreement having been reached. [43]

There is a difference between clandestine closed door deals and frank communication giving rise to productive debate and effective governance. If someone is not allowed or does not feel free to speak his mind, his thoughts are going to be constrained and his actions are going to be timid. Timidity should not be a trait that we cultivate in (political) leaders.

Conclusion –

Some persons believe in a benevolent government. I do not. Those same persons likely believe that the ends reached by government will ultimately be right and that the means, which government uses to effect those ends, always will be just. I do not. I believe that government should provide a shield against oppression and abuse (both internal and external ... both foreign

---

[43] *Meet the Press*, NBC News (December 15, 2013).

and domestic). I believe that the power of government should be used only as a weapon of last resort, even if the "war" is against acknowledged enemies such as sickness, ignorance, hunger, or poverty. I believe that a government wielding unlimited power is more apt to crush innovation, freedom, and liberty, than it is to bestow harmony and plenty among its peoples.

Even when well reasoned persons can agree on the ends, if not the means, we seemingly debate candidates and political positions not for the good of the whole, but for the thrill of the hunt. We define success not by the efficiency and effectiveness of the resulting policies and programs, but from the inanimate trophy that results from the kill.

As long as our debates are couched as "us" versus "them," each of us is an enemy of another. As long as government tells a group of its constituents that some other ill-defined group has too much of some right or commodity, there will inevitably be envy and strife. As long as politicians tell voters that favored groups are entitled to take from a trove of scarce resources or "hoarded" wealth whatever their whims may dictate (via taxes or other means), there will undoubtedly be resistance and rebellion, open or covert. As long as we ignore the fact that that "personal responsibility" applies not only to one caring for himself and his family but also extends to each of us caring for our fellow man, we will continue to fuel strife and resentment.

Without change, I would proffer that we are barely one generation removed from riots in the streets. Should that happen, it will hardly matter whose fault it was.[44]

---

[44] Portions of the text, which is contained in the "Conclusion," were previously published as a Letter to the Editor in the *Star-News* (August 23, 2012).

159

Democracy and the Tyranny of Mob Rule

Blog Entry - June 27, 2013

In a meme, which was recently posted on FaceBook, the caption that accompanied the picture indicated that, if we ONLY raised the Social Security income cap from its current base limit of $110,000 to $250,000, then Social Security ("SS") would be solvent for seventy-five (75) more years.

One should understand, that those paying as much as $21,000.00 more in taxes annually would get no additional benefit for their extra payments, and those who receive benefits effectively would receive a direct transfer of wealth from one citizen to another at the behest of government.

I understand the math, but I proffer the following questions:

- Is the taxing system a proper mechanism for direct transfers in order to effect redistribution of wealth among free citizens?

- And, if the answer to that question is, "Yes," then where does it stop?

- Is the government then empowered to decide what is the "fairest" and most productive use of all assets of its citizens?

- Does that then not diminish, if not destroy, the rights of citizens to have personal property?

- Would the democratic majority thereafter be empowered to take all that it wants from the propertied minority and redistribute that wealth for the self-defined "common good"?

Democratic mob rule is no less tyrannical than an oppressive monarch or dictator. In such a system, citizens do not "own" anything. Instead, they are only licensed to use and be stewards of the property of the state. This is no different than a sovereign King granting lands for true and faithful service of his subjects.

However, we are not subjects of the state. To the contrary, all of the power and authority of these United States must be voluntarily ceded to it by the people. Personally, I do not see wealth redistribution as a proper use of the taxing power of the state, no matter how "fair" and "equitable" it may seem to those on the receiving end of the equation.

Greed may be a deadly sin, and the hoarding of wealth may be an issue for moral philosophers. Nevertheless, establishing a "fair" (and fluid) minimal standard of living for a consumer class of the population to the detriment of a producing class should not be within the purview of government's power and authority.

Is this not institutionalized "theft"? The government plays the role of the legendary bandit, Robin Hood, who stole from the rich to give to the poor. While the sentiment may have populist appeal, theft for a seemingly noble cause is no less theft and no less contemptuous. There exists within a pure Democracy the possibility of tyranny by mob rule.

Such tyranny of the majority relates not only to reaching in the wallets of the privileged classes. Overreach and abuse of the powers of government power can also affect more personal rights and privileges.

Fortunately, our federal government is NOT a "true" democracy. A bare majority of fifty percent plus one (50% + 1) cannot terrorize and oppress with impunity a nearly equal minority of fifty percent minus one (50% - 1). Such would be the "right" of a democratic majority without our constitutional guarantees of personal rights and individual liberties.

Around the time that the Supreme Court of the United States ("SCOTUS") ruled in *Loving v. Virginia*[45] that interracial marriage would be allowed throughout the land, opinion polls showed that 73% of Americans opposed such marriages, and only 20% were in favor.

Many of the same arguments used today to oppose same-sex marriage (*e.g.* Religious prohibition, societal decay, protecting the sanctity of marriage, *etc.*) previously were used by a similarly adamant but equally misguided majority, which opposed interracial marriages.

Religious and moral convictions aside, recognition by the state of same-sex marriage is a legal issue based upon two persons exercising their respective contractual capacities to undertake a personal commitment to a mutual loving relationship. Government is incapable of identifying a

---

[45] 388 U.S. 1 (1967).

legitimate state interest, which can be advanced by overt discrimination against this defined class of citizens.

Yet again, those vested in the tyranny of the *status quo* will ultimately find themselves on the wrong side of history. It is fortunate that, as Americans, our inalienable personal rights and immutable individual liberties are not dependent upon the grace and consent of the majority. Unfortunately, the issue of whether a tyrannical majority can command unfettered access to the collective wealth of propertied classes is less settled.

Americans must awaken the Sleeping Giant[46]

Introduction -

In discussing geopolitics with a friend of Middle-Eastern descent, he offered that the current state of world affairs, if not inevitable, should be seen as the natural byproduct of reckless missteps, some would say intentional overreach, by the United States and other nations around the world.

In essence, his argument was that the machine of geopolitical relations has been in motion for some time and that redirecting its momentum is certainly a Herculean task.

Knowing him, I did not take his words as evidence of a fatalist position. Instead, I took them as challenge to explain my own frustrations and positions:

- Man is basically selfish at his core, and man must utilize his rational mind to overcome his bestial nature;

- Government, which was seen by our forefathers as a necessary evil, is a Leviathan, which is eager to break its fetters;

- Politicians are generally more interested in the accumulation of power, which is brought about by the dissemination of the wealth of others, than they are in objectively examining and reining in the role of government in the lives of citizens; and

---

[46] Paraphrased from the quote, "I fear all we have done is to awaken a sleeping giant and fill him with a terrible resolve," which is attributed to Japanese Admiral Isoroku Yamamoto regarding the 1941 attack on Pearl Harbor.

- Absent intervention by citizens, governmental assaults on personal rights and individual liberties will likely continue undeterred until eventually there are no appreciable distinctions among America, socialist nations, and even members of the old Communist bloc.

My friend responded that the current geopolitical environment represents a failure of SYNCRETISM. Resorting to my dictionary, I discovered the word to mean:

The attempted reconciliation or union of different or opposing principles, practices, or parties, as in philosophy or religion.

In Search of Greener Grass -

In recent years we have been inundated with words like "multiculturalism" and "diversity." Such concepts are deeply rooted in philosophies embracing Political Correctness. The intended effect is to remove any qualitative judgment about persons or peoples, and to treat all persons and peoples as "equal."

While it is entirely appropriate that individuals should be "equal" under the law and that government should not favor one individual, group, or class over another, it is entirely unreasonable to believe that all Six Billon persons on earth are the same in every respect, to treat every person the same as every other person in all respects, and to treat every culture and political philosophy as equally desirable:

- In the interest of "equality," do we give the same treatment and benefit of the doubt to persons, who may be fairly described as willfully ignorant, habitually reckless, criminally inclined, and/or sociopathic?

- In the interest of some perverse sense of "fairness," do we treat Nazism, Fascism, and Communism as equally desirable political systems?

- In the interest of not offending anyone, do we accept as innocuous the (often adulterated) religious dogma of various faiths, which gave rise to the Inquisition, Salem Witch Trials and which is currently cited in support of misogyny, jihad, and the continuing persecutions of persons of differing races, religions, sexual orientation, *etc.*?

Yes, we should have open minds, but we should also be willing to engage in candid and frank communications. In an effort to distill truth, debate should be energetic and passionate. Obfuscation through insincere debate and disingenuous communications should not be tolerated.

We should be driven by a conscious desire to actively pursue truth. Success in that endeavor means a willingness to acknowledge uncertainty and mistake, to admit fault and wrongdoing, and to embrace better opportunities and new ideas even if they are not our own.

Germans call the prevailing thought of a given time, "zeitgeist." Movement toward a social or political philosophy merely because it is currently in vogue is hardly defensible.

There seems to be a current mindset that anything new and different from the past is necessarily better. However, a move toward doing things just like everyone else assures a race toward mediocrity.

The difference between incremental growth by the inclusion of proven traits and ideas from other sources versus diversity merely for the sake of diversity is vast. If we, as a species, devolve into tribal warfare, which dominated the relationships of mankind for millennia, and neglect the intellectual and social tools developed just in the last few centuries, then humanity is destined to return to the Dark Ages. One does not defeat barbarians by making and proving oneself to be the social and intellectual equal of the uncivilized.

On September 16, 2013, Alexei Pushkov, Chairman of the foreign affairs committee in the lower house of Russia's Parliament, sent a gloating tweet immediately after the shooting in the D.C. Naval Yard:

> *The USA should part with the notion of American exceptionalism. It contradicts the principles of equal rights and smells of political racism.*

I would like to argue with his position, but I would have to admit that our government has been anything but "exceptional" of late. With secret domestic surveillance, our federal government likely has much more in common with the former Communist Russians than anyone cares to admit.

On September 11, 2013, Russian President Vladimir Putin also criticized the notion of "American Exceptionalism" in an op-ed article published in the *New York Times*:

It is extremely dangerous to encourage people to see themselves as exceptional, whatever the motivation.[47]

If exceptionalism is no longer our goal as a nation, then there is little incentive to grow as a people. There is little challenge to being just like everyone else. If America does not set a higher example for others to follow, then it is unlikely that any other country will serve as standard-bearer. If Survival of the Fittest ignores humanity's exclusive traits of rational thought and self-determination and instead focuses on our baser instincts and brute force, then our species is doomed.

A Challenge to All -

In recent years, the U.S. has begun to lose its stature as a "giant" among the nations of the world. Do we, as a country, have the resolve to face the daunting tasks, which confront us, or do we sit back and await the approaching calamities (internal and external)? Are we willing to make the necessary changes to once again be great or do we steam headlong toward an increasingly inevitable fate, which will likely be shared by all peoples?

The "Giant," which Japanese Admiral Yamamoto feared was not then President, Franklin D. Roosevelt ("FDR"), or even the extensive collection the New Deal bureaucracies, which FDR established to bolster his administration.

At best, government plays the role of a puppeteer or flawed "Wizard," whose fragile powers as well as the wonder and esteem in which it is held rely entirely upon politicians being

---

[47] "A Plea for Caution From Russia: What Putin Has to Say to Americans About Syria," *New York Times* (September 11, 2013).

able to pull the strings of the country and of its people from behind curtains of secrecy and deception. It is the people's (misplaced) faith in government's prowess, which gives government any power whatsoever.

The true potential and power of the United States comes not from the institution of government but from its people. It is the people acting in concert, who give life to the "Giant." Collectively, the people provide the brains, heart, and courage to succeed. If they have confidence and faith in themselves, then there is no obstacle or foe that cannot be faced and overcome.[48]

FDR may have set the machine in motion, but WWII was won by the 16 Million GI's, who fought with courage, honor, and distinction on foreign fields of battle, as well as "Rosy the Riveter" and the millions, who sacrificed, worked, rationed, scrimped, and saved in support of the collective war effort.

Presidents and governments, before and since, have sought to harness and mobilize this vast power. However, they miss the point that such power cannot be contained and harnessed except with the consent of those, who produce the power. Only when individuals are personally committed to the task at hand can the power be put to productive use. The power cannot be harnessed through lies, deception, and subterfuge. Unless the people affirmatively adopt the cause as their own, they cannot be impressed or guilted into indentured servitude.

Viewing the mosaic that composes our current reality does not mean that our perspective is necessarily fixed. Our view of

---

[48] I offer my apologies to the author, L. Frank Baum, for the extended analogy to his novel, *The Wonderful Wizard of Oz* (1900).

that reality can be changed and expanded. We do not have to accept the current state of affairs without objection, even if certain outcomes seem inevitable.

A Legacy of Liberty and Opportunity -

Previously, the difference between "us" versus "them" was founded upon dogged independence and fostered by concepts of self-determination, self-reliance, and personal responsibility. That independence cannot exist without personal rights and individual liberties. More recently, our government has begun to curtail those rights in order to foster its own expansion. We are told that such losses of freedoms are in our best interests.

The voluntary coming together of a people expressly to form a government for the protection of our natural inalienable rights is among the distinctions, which define what it is to be American. Such rights and liberties were neither conceived nor awarded by government, and government is incapable of usurping the same unless they are heedlessly ceded by the people.

The recognition of and respect given to these rights are part of the heritage and legacy, which were handed down to us by our forefathers. In asserting and protecting these rights, our forefathers risked their lives and their fortunes. We must always remember that these personal rights and individual liberties are worth whatever fight may be necessary to retain them. It is in that fight that we earn the right to call ourselves, "American."

The Giant is once again sleeping. Just as Gulliver of *Gulliver's Travels* fame awoke shipwrecked on the shores of Lilliput to find himself captive of the tiny Lilliputians, might and power can be overcome not only by superior strength but also from the concerted efforts of weaker forces. Similarly, terminating actions need not be swift and overwhelming. Death can come slowly from a thousand small cuts.

Today, our country and its citizens bleed profusely from the initially innocuous cuts of bureaucratic red tape and from crisp new currency streaming off the presses to pay our country's wasteful expenditures and mounting debts. Our strength, creativity, and motivations are being sapped by an oppressive government, economic waste, excess regulations, and micromanagement of citizens' lives.

We do not face an overwhelming foreign force, but we are debilitated by an internal cancer that is slowly eating away at the rights and liberties, which define us as Americans. Invasions of privacy, the chilling of the press and speech, unreasonable searches and seizures (of information), and the wholesale erosion of the Bill of Rights are blows which combine to bring our punch drunk country nearly to its knees.

Conclusion -

America cannot bask in the glow of its past accomplishments. America cannot be content to rest on its laurels. The United States is capable of retaining its role as a world leader, and the world needs the U.S. as a standard bearer for freedom and individual liberties. However, leaders need not be imposing figures. Yet, by their actions, leaders must inspire confidence and trust in those, who might be inclined to follow.

As a people, our goal should not be to make other countries and peoples in our own image. Instead, we should strive to set an example so distinct and successful that those, who see it, are drawn to emulate it. In doing so, we can be a beacon of hope for the world. In doing so, the Giant will awaken to put its great strength to good use.

SCENE FROM "TRIAL BY JURY," AT THE ROYALTY THEATRE.

II. LAWS & CRIMES

The High Costs of Safety: *Freedom and Liberty*

© 2012

Introduction -

On December 14, 2012, Adam Lanza, a troubled twenty (20) year-old, killed his mother in the home, which they shared, before traveling five (5) miles to Sandy Hook Elementary School in Newtown, Connecticut. After arriving at the school, he found the exterior doors locked (the result of a newly enacted safety measure). Using one of the three (3) guns, which he carried, Lanza shot out a window and entered the school. Hearing the shots, members of the school's faculty, including the principal, quickly confronted the gunman.

Lanza killed the approaching adults before entering into multiple classrooms and killing persons inside. The results of autopsies revealed that each person killed had been shot multiple times with an assault rifle, and that rifle was fed with multiple high capacity clips. In the end, twenty-eight (28) persons were dead: Twenty (20) first-graders, six (6) adult faculty members, the shooter's mother, Nancy Lanza, and finally the shooter himself, by a self-inflicted gunshot wound to the head.

Expectedly, there are those who, instead of placing blame squarely on the actor, propose greater limitations on access to guns as a means to curtail gun violence. If someone has done nothing to threaten or cause harm to anyone else, there is no reason or justification to curtail his rights.

Instead, go after the perpetrators and enforce laws, which are already on the books. Definitively deal with the mentally ill rather than dumping those with extreme mental illness onto the streets to fend for themselves. Most importantly, when we, as a society, fail to address these causative issues affirmatively, we should resist the urge to lay the blame on law abiding citizens.

Second (2nd) Amendment: *Right vs. Privilege* -

Absolute safety is illusory, and incremental increases in perceived levels of safety often come with high costs. Those costs are not only in the form of increased "gun control" regulations, but there are additional costs through increased limitations on personal rights and individual liberties.

At his photo op regarding "gun control" [01/16/2013], President Obama stated, "If we can save just one life, we owe it to them to try." The President paraded grieving parents around as "human shields" to fend off those, who might oppose his policies.

The President, however, is not in a position to be the arbiter on the value of human life. He has implemented systematic executions with the use of unmanned drones throughout the Middle East, which have resulted in the killings of at least [four (4)] U.S. Citizens either without the benefit of trial or without full due process under the law.[49]

The President's "Drone War" has been deemed "legal" as an exercise of his powers as Commander in Chief and in the furtherance of some nebulous and undeclared War on Terror.[50] Many would argue that such actions are "necessary" to assure

---

[49] Van Dyk, Jere, "Who were the 4 U.S. citizens killed in drone strikes?," www.cbsnews.com (May 23, 2013).

[50] The Constitution precludes "Bills of Attainder:" *A special legislative enactment that imposes a death sentence without a judicial trial upon a particular person or class of persons suspected of committing serious offenses, such as Treason.* A power explicitly withheld from the legislative body certainly should not be presumed by the Executive.

the safety of U.S. Citizens (other than those, who may be deemed by the administration deserving of summary execution).

Yet, how many innocent persons (including children) have died as collateral damage in the furtherance of the President's drone program? I would dare say more than twenty-six (26).[51]

Nevertheless, the "one life saved" rhetorical device is absurd. Thousands of lives could be saved by outlawing automobiles and airplanes. Nevertheless, we choose to ride in cars, and nearly everyone takes advantage of flying, despite the dangers.

Life is a series of balancing tests of risks versus rewards. We continuously make decisions about whether perceived "risks" are outweighed by the anticipated "rewards." Let us recognize that persons apply those balancing tests differently with varying weights and priorities placed on each element.

After the Sandy Hook massacre, there was a push to increase the frequency and depth of "background checks," which would be required for the purchase of firearms. However, the proposed changes would have done little or nothing to prevent the Sandy Hook massacre itself.

According to reports, all of the guns, which were used in the Connecticut shooting, were legally purchased by the mother of the shooter (in a state with relatively "tough" gun laws), and those purchases likely would not have been stopped by the additional checks, which were included within the proposed federal legislation.

---

[51] Subsequent reports by international Human Rights agencies estimate civilian deaths from U.S. drone attacks to be between 100-200 persons.

For weeks, I incredulously listened to the repeated recitation of the statistic, "Ninety-two (92%) of Americans favor background checks for the purchase of guns." I say "incredulously" because I can hardly believe that 92% of Americans can agree upon what day of the week it is much less any element of an issue as divisive as Gun Control.

Nevertheless, I knew that the strength or weakness of that statistic was to be found in the question being asked, and after some effort, I located the specific poll question:

Do you support or oppose requiring background checks for all gun buyers?

That naked question without detail or explanation is like asking, "Do you support or oppose everyone eating three square meals a day?" Of course, the answer will be in the affirmative the vast majority of the time.

However, the devil is in the details:

- What if some persons do not wish to eat three meals a day?
- What if eating three meals, in fact, would be detrimental to some persons? ... OR
- What if in answering in the affirmative the respondent would thereafter be obligated to furnish such meals to all persons not having access to the same?

Where the respondent does not have a complete frame of reference or does not have a vested interest in the question or the potential outcomes, little consideration is likely given to the answer, and little weight should be given to quality of that answer. Ask the question a different way, including all of the potential effects and requirements, and the answers will likely differ dramatically.

It is impossible to make an informed decision without all of the information. It is similarly impossible to encapsulate public opinion so simplistically. As Mark Twain one stated, "There are lies, damned lies and statistics."

When the Senate refused to take up the issue of gun control [04/17/2013], Obama chided the Senators (several of whom were from his own party) calling their inaction "shameful." Obama had all but promised the parents of the Sandy Hook shooting victims that Congress would fall in line to his drumbeat and would further restrict access to guns.

However, making criminals of otherwise law abiding citizens does nothing to address the underlying issues of violence and senseless murder. Rather than demeaning himself to be a successful "salesman," Obama wanted his policies implemented simply in deference to his will. Instead of sincerely engaging those with opposing points of view, he demonizes them and prefers to preach the choir.

The efficacy of proposed regulations is further diminished by the lack of enforcement activity relating to EXISTING laws. In 2010, there were roughly 76,000 rejected gun applications. Of those, ONLY FORTY-FOUR (44) cases were prosecuted. Having been allowed to remain at large, how many of those persons thereafter went out and purchased a gun illegally?

Making new laws, which will go unenforced just like existing laws, does nothing to address the real problems. A law, being a species of social contract, is only as good as a party's willingness and ability to actively enforce it. Having unsupported and unenforced laws or regulations is an impediment to the efficacy and enforcement of all laws.

Too often, those responsible for enforcing laws fail to do so because they personally disagree with the effect of such laws or because it is determined that the cost of enforcement exceeds the perceived damage or threat (*e.g.* Immigration). If a law is not important enough to be enforced actively, then it should not be on the books.

It is naïve and reckless to assume that those, who flagrantly violate laws, later will adhere voluntarily to other seemingly "more important" laws absent an appreciable threat of enforcement. Similarly, it is naïve to believe that persons, who vehemently oppose governmental micromanagement of citizens' lives, will accept government intrusions without significant opposition or without imposition of harsh penalties by government for noncompliance.

I am not saying that there are not things that could and should be done to address societal issues, but the gun control regulations, which were proposed, represent an emotional façade obscuring much deeper unaddressed problems (*e.g.* Disintegration of the family unit, lack of respect for human life, gratuitous violence, an ineffective mental health system, *etc.*).

As the Boston Marathon Bombing and Ricin-laced Letters to Obama and members of Congress demonstrate, violence and terror have unlimited instrumentalities. The "shame" is not having the fortitude to admit that one does not have the tools or political will to address the real problems. The "shame" is in

182

giving false hope, while not taking any responsibility for the *status quo*.

The primary effect of the proposed legislation is that of a placebo. It is feel-good legislation meant to salve the emotional wounds of the nation. The more practical and lasting effect would be opening the door to increasingly more restrictive measures, which would be pursued and implemented when these ineffective and misguided measures inevitably fail to "protect the public."

Let us also recognize that the Second Amendment protects a political right not a recreational privilege. The right to bear arms has nothing to do with deer hunting. Our founding fathers believed, as I continue to believe, that such a right is integral to the furtherance of liberty and intended as a defense from government tyranny. With those as the objectives, the debate takes on a different tenor. Yes, things should be done to protect the public, but removing firearms (of any type or description) from responsible law abiding citizens does little to further that goal.

The National Rifle Association (NRA) has been castigated for protecting the liberties and freedoms guaranteed by the Second Amendment to the Constitution. Why is it that the NRA has been so adamant to hold the line? ... Because, total prohibition is the preferred resolution of many gun opponents:

> *Owning a gun should be a privilege, not a right. Declare the NRA a terrorist organization and make membership illegal. ... [T]he NRA has led to the deaths of more of us than American Commies ever did. (I would also raze the organization's headquarters,*

clear the rubble, and salt the earth, but that's optional.) Make ownership of unlicensed assault rifles a felony. If some people refused to give up their guns, that "prying the guns from their cold, dead hands" thing works for me. Then I would tie Mitch McConnell and John Boehner, our esteemed Republican leaders, to the back of a Chevy pickup and drag them around a parking lot until they saw the light on gun control. And if that didn't work, I'd adopt radical measures.[52]

I would like to believe that "reasonable restrictions" could be implemented, but I cannot in good conscious give government the benefit of the doubt as to whether it can act reasonably and demonstrate reasoned self-restraint. Instead, I would expect, as it has proven to be true, that if you give an inch government will take a mile. What government can regulate, government can tax. What government can tax, government can proscribe.[53]

Thomas Jefferson said, "No free man shall ever be debarred the use of arms."[54] Termination of any Constitutional Right is not likely to occur through a violent coup. Instead, our liberty and freedom are more likely to erode away. Rather than summary execution, our constitutionally guaranteed rights are more likely to die as a result of neglect or suffer a slow agonizing death by a thousand cuts.

---

[52] This was not taken from a knee-jerk "Letter to the Editor." It was an opinion piece written by the columnist, Donald Kaul, and published in the Op-Ed section of *The Register Citizen* [CT] – (December 21, 2012). Mr. Kaul was previously nominated for the Pulitzer Prize for Commentary in 1987 and 1999.

[53] In 1819, Chief Justice John Marshall writing for the Supreme Court of the United States in *McCulloch v. Maryland* stated that the Constitution exempts the Federal Government from state taxation by the States. In *dictum* Marshall stated, "[T]he power to tax involves the power to destroy."

[54] 1 *Thomas Jefferson Papers*, p. 334.

The main arguments that I have heard in support of curtailing or infringing upon the Constitutional Right guaranteed by the Second Amendment are:

(1) The right to bear arms applies only to a "well regulated militia," and we have the government to protect us;

(2) At the time the amendment was written, guns were single shot muskets; and

(3) Today's firepower is too dangerous to be in civilian hands.

For those who believe that the government is ready, willing, and able to defend all citizens against any threat, both foreign and domestic, then consideration and debate regarding the possession and use of guns will likely be short among such persons. Nevertheless, one may want to consider the experiences of the citizens of modern-day Egypt, Libya, and Syria, who are faced with defending themselves against oppressive governments. Such governments impose their wills with military might.

Consider the example of our founding fathers. As individuals, they successfully took up arms against the British army, arguably the most formidable fighting force of the day, but their resistance would have been futile had those civilians not had weaponry, which would have been considered "advanced" for their time.

Ask any oppressed peoples whether they believe their weapons are "too advanced" or "too dangerous." A war prosecuted by a malevolent government against its own people

185

is not won necessarily by the people successfully combating the overwhelming forces of that government. Instead, victory can be had by citizens demonstrating themselves victims of an unconscionable abuse of power. The inability of an oppressive government to quickly stomp out the embers of insurrection, revolt, and revolution assures an opportunity for the cleansing flames of change and rebirth to take hold.

Defense against Tyranny -

I believe that there is a beneficial and legitimate role for the Second Amendment to assure that government is aware that its authority is derived from the people and that such authority, should its abuse rise to the level of tyranny, can be removed, or at least subverted by the people, using the power and force available to them.

One may counter, "That could never happen here, in the United States!" Our founding fathers were not nearly so certain:

> *Before a standing army can rule, the people must be disarmed; as they are in almost every kingdom of Europe. The supreme power in America cannot enforce unjust laws by the sword; because the whole body of the people are armed, and constitute a force superior to any bands of regular troops that can be, on any pretense, raised in the United States.*
>
> *— Noah Webster*

And, Thomas Jefferson noted:

> *Laws that forbid the carrying of arms ... disarm only those who are neither inclined nor determined to commit crimes.... Such laws make things worse for the assaulted and better for the assailants; they serve rather to encourage than to prevent homicides, for an*

unarmed man may be attacked with greater confidence than an armed man.[55]

If one is so confident in his safety and freedoms so as to trust government to guarantee the same, then by all means he may put himself at the mercy of that government and others, who would welcome his vulnerability. Nevertheless, the way in which we assure that our government does not devolve into tyranny is to zealously protect the freedoms, which we, as Americans, have, even if such freedoms are foreign to the rest of the world.

Most of us can recall Patrick Henry's famous admonition, "Give me liberty or give me death!" He also questioned:

> *Are we at last brought to such a humiliating and debasing degradation, that we cannot be trusted with arms for our own defense?*

What was so "tyrannical" about the British rule of the American Colonies? The British were not enslaving the people; they were not burning towns and salting the earth; and they were not randomly imprisoning and killing innocent persons.

Tyranny came from depriving a people of self rule and self determination. It was tyranny to take disproportionately the wealth of the colonies in the form of taxes for the benefit of Britain without a corresponding benefit being bestowed upon the colonists, who paid those taxes. In short, the "Social Contract" broke down. There was a failure of the consideration within the transaction between the British government and the American colonists.

---

[55] Thomas Jefferson's *Commonplace Book*, 1774-1776, quoting from *On Crimes and Punishment*, by criminologist Cesare Beccaria (1764).

Rather than colonies and a foreign monarch, apply those concepts to a country and its citizens. Is our current government infringing upon basic rights and individual liberties of certain citizens for the benefit of some other segment of society (or arguably the society as a collective)? Is one class being taxed disproportionately for the benefit of another group without a vote or say proportionate to the size of their contributions?

Tyranny is not the destruction of a people, but rather it is an unjust abuse of power. Determining what is just and what constitutes abuse is quite subjective. Some would argue adamantly, "WE HAVE NO DANGER OF TYRANNY." More dangerous and naïve words have never been spoken. In contrast, many persons would argue that tyranny is upon us (or nearly so).

If one were part of the newly infamous "one percent" and paying twenty percent (20%) of the funding for government with even more were being demanded and with fifty percent of the populace (50%) contributing nothing (or nearly so) to the general funding of that government, that would likely seem: "Arbitrary," "unrestrained," "oppressive," "unjust," "unduly severe," or "harsh." Those are all badges of tyranny.

In the "Virginia Statute for Religious Freedom," Thomas Jefferson wrote:

[T]o compel a man to furnish contributions of money for the propagation of opinions which he disbelieves and abhors, is sinful and tyrannical.

Others would argue that additional examples of increasing tyranny include:

- The concentration of Executive Powers in the Office of the President;
- The unrestrained growth of government Bureaucracies (particularly with and following the implementation of Franklin D. Roosevelt's "New Deal"); and
- The abdication of Congress in assuming its proper roles of maintaining fiscal control over the government and passing laws.

Human nature is highly resistant to change. It is the ultimate hubris and delusion to believe that we are, at heart, any different or better than those who came before us. Some would point to the abolition of slavery, women's suffrage, and expansion of gay rights as evidence that we have evolved as a species. Social Constructs change ... Laws change ... Economies change, but not the basic rules and underlying concepts, and not human nature.

Slavery was abolished because it was no longer integral to the economy after the Industrial Revolution. That change had little to do with society, as a whole, having a moral epiphany. Women's right to vote stemmed also from industrialization and urbanization, as well as compulsory education. With changes to the traditional gender roles and freer flow of information, expansion of the voter base became feasible. The same applies to gay rights. With knowledge and understanding, comes broader acceptance.

However, NONE of those things detract from the original statement that HUMAN NATURE, which is generally selfish, shortsighted, and self-serving, has not changed. In fact, the continued reluctance by government to implement and address what some would consider basic human rights supports that proposition.

I am of the opinion that unfettered expansion of the role of government and decreasing the rights and freedoms of the people will have greater long-term detriment than continued access to guns.

Again, quoting Thomas Jefferson:

> *Experience hath shewn, that even under the best forms of government those entrusted with power have, in time, and by slow operations, perverted it into tyranny.*

Means, Motive, and Opportunity -

In committing the first murder, Cain killed Able while living in near perfect environs, at a time of little strife, with no appreciable want, and without an example to follow. He did not require a motive any more sinister than envy and jealousy. He did not use a gun. He created the method and means without guidance or assistance.

I see no reason to expect that surrendering additional individual rights on the pretext of safety is a worthy trade. I am willing to risk some comforts and safety for the opportunity to live my life as I see fit, and yes, that includes carrying a gun.

I was asked by an acquaintance, "What would you personally do or change that would have assured that those first graders were alive today?" To which I replied, "Probably nothing." Innocent people die every day, whether it is on the highways with a family member or loved one at the wheel of an automobile, or at the homicidal hands of a stranger.

I do not know enough about the gunman to speculate about his specific mental state, his personal history, or his commitment to undertake this heinous act. I am not arrogant so as to say that I could have stopped the shooting, and anyone who says that he could have stopped it is likely deluding himself. I take responsibility for my own life. I participate in the lives of my family, friends, and those within my sphere of influence. I endeavor to stay out of the lives of other people. I do not expect the government to be involved in, much less fix, all of life's problems.

If other persons spent more time focusing on living their own lives, rather than comparing themselves to the Joneses and riffraff of the world, so that they are simultaneously dissatisfied with their own lives and content that they are better persons than those, who cling to the lowest rung of the evolutionary ladder, then we would all be better off.

If the gunman's mother, who by all indications was well educated and had access to resources, did not see the danger or could not stop her own son, then I do not know what would have likely stopped this or another tragedy on some scale.

I was chastised vehemently for my response. I was told that "I" personally should feel some responsibility and that "I" should personally do more to assure that a similar event never happens again.

191

I empathize with the family members, who lost loved ones, particularly the parents of small children. I sympathize with everyone over the senseless loss of life. But, why should I feel guilt or personal responsibility for the act of a madman?

There are more than SIX (6) BILLION persons on earth. It is utterly unreasonable for me to mourn for each death or to correct every injustice. The levels hubris and/or delusion required to believe and expect that anyone can accomplish such a Herculean task are great contributors to the problems at hand.

Some persons believe that there is a direct correlation between removing guns from the hands of law-abiding citizens and a decrease in deaths. I believe that those, who are intent upon killing, will find the means and opportunity to do so (*e.g.* Unibomber, Timothy McVey, 9-11 attackers, Boston Bombers, *etc.*). I also believe that the continued curtailing of individual liberties and personal rights will ultimately undermine and destroy the America that this country was intended to be.

What Can be Done? -

Is there a perfect answer? No, there is not.[56] Some persons have much more faith in government and put more trust in humanity in general than I am able to muster. I am too much of a cynic to believe that mankind will ever change basic human nature. If ever mankind faces the demise of our species, one can rest assured that mankind itself will be the source of our ultimate destruction.

---

[56] Dedman, Bill, "Newtown anniversary: US schools keep trying wrong fixes to deter school shootings, experts say," www.nbcnews.com (December 11, 2013).

The only thing that anyone can do realistically is to live the best life possible and to contribute wherever an opportunity arises. However, no one should feel guilt for not stopping the criminal acts of madmen or others persons, who may be intent upon doing harm.

We can have compassion for the less fortunate. We can offer care to the needy. We can empathize with those, who suffer loss. Nevertheless, those, who face challenges and loss, ultimately must work and take responsibility to fulfill their own needs. They must look to themselves in order to overcome those challenges and losses. No amount of resources can pave a path without obstacles, and no amount of effort can carry each person through life unscathed.

We should anticipate that persons will fail. We should anticipate pain and loss, but I do not believe that suffering and loss can ever be removed completely from our lives. That is not to say that I propose doing nothing, but to think that there are "easy fixes" to problems such as this is ludicrous.

Evil acts cannot be outlawed by government fiat. A blanket federal regulation is unlikely to put an end to such "senseless killings." The changes which need to be made are on the micro- rather than macro- level.

Let us consider some not-so-easy "fixes:"

- Encourage and foster marriages (or other relationships, which are likely to result in the births of children) that are more than matters of convenience – *i.e.* Marriages that have commitment and lasting power;

- Work to assure that children are born into such marriages (or relationships) rather than to single parent mothers and "baby daddies" and that parental commitment exist so that both parents act in the best interests of all children, who are brought into this world, rather accepting benign neglect and broken homes as the norm;

- Instill a sense of hope and opportunity in persons who are outcast or feel removed from society; and

- Identify the causes and contributing factors for mental illness and provide treatment for those with pronounced mental illness.

It Starts at Home -

In 1965, Daniel Patrick Moynihan, who was a sociologist by training, served as an Assistant Secretary in the U.S. Department of Labor. Later, Mr. Moynihan served four (4) terms as a U.S. Senator (D-NY). He retired in 2000, and was succeeded by Hillary Clinton.

In his capacity as Asst. Secretary for Policy, Planning and Research, Mr. Moynihan prepared a much vilified report.[57] In that report, Moynihan cited that 23.6% of African American children were born out of wedlock, compared to just 3.07% of white children, and he postulated that a deterioration within the family unit was (at least partially) responsible for cycles of poverty among blacks.

In other studies, poverty is often cited as a contributing factor to high levels of crime in certain locales and within

---

[57] Moynihan, Daniel Patrick, "The Negro Family: A Case for National Action," U.S. Department of Labor (1965).

194

designated segments of the population. The dynamics of poverty and crime combine to exacerbate an already vicious cycle, and the resulting downward spiral is one, from which it is extremely difficult to recover.

When the "Moynihan Report" was leaked publically, both Moynihan and the report were branded as "racist," and the report was criticized as "victim blaming."[58] While cause-and-effect certainly can be debated, the report does seem somewhat prophetic in bringing to light continuing cycles of poverty and the continuing deterioration of the nuclear family (not just among blacks).

Nearly fifty (50) years after the Moynihan Report, 41% of American children are born today to unmarried women, including: Nearly half of first births, 29% of non-Hispanic white children, 53% of Hispanic children, and 72% of African American children.[59] Today, the out-of-wedlock births of white children exceed the level of similar black births in 1965, and while there has been a nearly three-fold increase among blacks, the rate among whites has increased by more than 800%.

There are millions of children being brought in to this world to ill-prepared parents, and many of those children are unplanned, unappreciated, or even unwanted. How can anyone realistically expect government, or society in general, to "fix" the associated problems (*e.g.* poverty, poor social development,

---

[58] See – Will, George, "For Santorum, the fight goes on," *Washington Post* (October 25, 2013).
[59] Centers for Disease Control and Prevention (CDC), "National Vital Statistics Report," Vol. 62, No. 1 (June 28, 2013).

inadequate nurturing, educational challenges, poor employment skills, *etc.*)?

Should government step in and license births and (further) regulate child rearing? I do not see anyone clamoring for a literal "Nanny State." Nevertheless, the associated problems are not likely to change in the near term without concerted efforts by parents and others who can have a direct positive impact on the children, who face these challenges.

Let us start with the basics, and the "hard stuff" probably would not be so hard. The key is personal responsibility and self-reliance. If you cannot fix the foundation, the building will inevitably crumble regardless of the beautiful façade.

The Individual vs. Institutions -

Our routes through life are based upon a constant series of choices and decisions, which are undertaken by each of us daily. The varied courses of our lives cannot be dictated from the Oval Office. These courses cannot be designated by legislation from the halls of Congress, and we should not be led leashed and bridled with the red tape of government Bureaucracies. Through the hundreds of choices that each of us makes daily, the hope is that an individual makes considerably more good choices than bad.

It is my belief that, in those billions of collective choices made every day, most persons will make cumulative choices, which overall are more beneficial to themselves and to society at large than any plan or script that could be dictated to them by some governing authority.

196

Each person has within himself the innate intelligence and ability to make right and good decisions on his own behalf. Those who regularly make bad decisions, poor choices, and blatant mistakes should expect to suffer the consequences of those actions (or inactions). However, no amount of intervention by government or any number of well meaning individuals can overcome or offset a lifetime of indifference, ignorance, and neglect.

There have been debates about the potential role of religion in averting the Newtown massacre. Others have countered that religion is unlikely to have had an effect on a deranged mind. What is often missing in the lives of such perpetrators is HOPE. Those, who act out in violence, often feel isolated, frustrated, and powerless. Their horrendous acts (and self destruction) are often last grasps at taking control and asserting power.

Religion provides hope to believers; although, some would describe religion as an irrational panacea or even the "opiate of the masses." Whatever the source of our hope, be it religion or human will, we must provide each other with opportunities, comfort, and support. We must live together as a civil society, and we must all have hope that love will overcome evil.

Violence and destruction are often the end results of the perpetrator's desire to acquire or assert power over his own life or to take retribution against another individual or against society at large. Violence is rarely, if ever, a demonstration of a naturally evil heart. Instead, it is most often a manifestation of all too common human shortcomings and frailties.

Only the truly deranged undertake evil acts purely for the sake of evil. The individual may lash out to combat loneliness and despair. The object of the violence may be the perceived source of the despair, or the targets may be innocents, who are the victims of misdirected anger and rage.

On a larger scale, the actor may crave power to feed his greed or hubris. Toward that end, he may seek to oppress and subjugate entire peoples through demonstrations of terror and acts of violence.

It is important that we acknowledge and understand the root causes of such horrific acts. Rarely, are they the acts of "rational" men. Painting them as simply "evil" does nothing to address the issues and circumstances that precede and give rise to the violence. Until and unless we are willing to acknowledge, understand, and address the root causes of such violence, we will have little hope of ending or curtailing it.

Hope and change can be fostered by government or other institutions. However, the heavy lifting will have to come from individuals reaching out and lending helping hands to family, friends, and neighbors.

Conclusion -

Ann Curry, a NBC News Anchor, proposed in one segment about the Sandy Hook Massacre that persons adopt a commitment to do an act of charity or kindness to commemorate each of the individuals killed. This proposal was picked up via social media and became a movement originally known by the hash tag "#20Acts" [for the children killed] and later expanded to "#26 Acts" [for all those killed]. The campaign went viral and thousands of persons committed to participating.

While such a campaign cannot solve all of the underlying problems, it is important to realize that simple acts of kindness have ripple effects. The benefits are received not only by those, who were the subjects of the original acts, but benefits also flow to those, who witness and are inspired by such acts, and for others, who are downstream and who benefit from future acts of kindness.

It is important that we recognize the opportunities for such acts of kindness. Those opportunities may be obvious to address a specific need or loss (*e.g.* poverty, loss of a loved one, natural disaster, *etc.*), or the opportunity may be more subtle and more difficult to address directly (*e.g.* depression or mental illness).

It is time that we seize upon opportunities to serve and to force ourselves to recognize, appreciate, and work to address the needs of our family members, friends, and neighbors. With a genuine sense of inclusion, community, and belonging, we can instill in each other hope for the future. Such individual acts of compassion and kindness can never be abdicated in favor of government intervention.

I do not know what, if anything, the shooter's mother, Nancy Lanza, could have done to prevent this tragedy. One may question why her legally acquired guns were not stored safely out of reach of her now obviously unstable son. I cannot know if, prior to being her son's first victim, she truly was aware of the violence of which he was capable. One has to think that she was aware of the seeds of that violence, even if she did not anticipate its fruition.

If she did not know, how can we assure that others in her situation become aware when such a danger is imminent? If she was aware and did not know how and to whom to reach out for help, what can we as a society (in the interest of self-preservation if not compassion) do to provide resources for counseling and therapy for those psychologically ill persons for whom the massacre of innocents seems like a viable option to their present existence?

Those are questions, which need answering. The easy out is to blame someone else. The easy action is to curtail someone else's liberty in the pursuit of perceptions of safety. The hope is that the ends will justify the means.

Taking guns out of the hands of law abiding citizens will not remove the instrumentalities of violence from those with criminal intent or a deranged mind. Such persons will simply substitute one instrumentality for another. Unless and until we get to the root causes through identification of and intervention with individuals, who may inclined toward violence, such persons will always find a means through which to do harm.

Those, who are now proposing to curtail broad classes of liberties as the price for deluded perceptions of safety, will eventually have to address the real issues or be prepared to pay even higher prices in the future.

What does it mean to "Stand your Ground"?

Blog Entry – April 12, 2012

A Florida judge said in a written opinion that a Miami man, who chased a thief and stabbed that thief to death, cannot be prosecuted because the defense, which is allowed by that state's Stand Your Ground Law, precludes prosecution for any crime.

"Stand your ground" can be interpreted as meaning: "Being, going upon, or entry into any place or area not otherwise prohibited." Under this rather expansive definition, "giving chase" as in the instant case or "following" as in the case of George Zimmerman and Trayvon Martin would not disqualify the actor from asserting the defense.[60] The "Stand Your Ground" provisions were deliberate extensions of traditional "Self Defense" and the previously existing "Castle Doctrine."

The Right of Self Defense was well established in the common law, and that right has been incorporated into criminal statutes. One has a right to defend himself (and others) from death or the threat of serious bodily harm, which is imminent, even if in defense of one's self he kills another person.

The defense may be available even if the actor is mistaken regarding the timing and nature of the perceived threat so long as a reasonable person may have responded similarly. In the event that the action is not reasonably justified or the force used in defense of one's self is deemed excessive, the actor may be guilty of homicide (generally voluntary manslaughter).

---

[60] Although Florida's Pattern Jury Instructions were amended to accommodate the "Stand Your Ground" provisions, Zimmerman's legal defense team relied primarily on traditional notions of "Self-Defense" at trial, and they did not base their defense strategy upon the more novel and recently implemented provisions.

Traditionally, the actor asserting that he acted in self-defense had a duty to retreat from the situation giving rise to the threat if he could do so without risking harm to himself. The "Castle Doctrine" negates the obligation to retreat from one's own residence or place of abode with the idea being that a person is entitled to defend his home from an intruder even with the use of lethal force.

The reasonableness of the newer "Stand Your Ground" provisions will likely depend on one's perspective. Some would argue that the thief above and Trayvon Martin (assuming that he, in fact, did physically assault Zimmerman first) brought about (or significantly contributed to) the situations, which led to their own deaths.

If one knowingly goes into a "high risk" area or intentionally mingles among persons known to be unfriendly to him, but without making threatening overtures against anyone, should he be deprived of a defense, which would be readily available while standing in front of his own home, if he is thereafter the victim of an attack? Or restated, "Should the events leading up to the initial act of violence be relevant to the availability of the defense?"

If one's answer to the latter question is, "No," then that person would likely answer that the Stand Your Ground Laws are reasonable. If one answers, "Yes," then he would probably assert that there was no justification for expanding traditional self-defense, which would require the actor to avoid confrontation, if reasonably possible.

Vigilance in Defense of Freedom and Liberty:
A Marathon not a Sprint

Blog Entry – Original Post: April 16, 2013

Introduction -

On April 15, 2013, some person or group detonated two (2) bombs near the finish line of the Boston Marathon while the race was still in progress. The perpetrator(s) have not been caught.[61] So, their specific reasons and motives are not yet known. Nevertheless, their underlying objective is certain: To instill fear and terror into the people of Boston and America.

That is the essence of any act of terrorism. The scope of the damage is not limited to horrific injuries and loss of life, but it can also be measured in the emotional and psychological toll that it takes on other citizens, who may be far removed from the blast zone.

In the wake of the Boston Marathon bombings, members of the infamous Westboro Baptist Church announced their intentions to protest at memorials and funerals for the victims. While church members did not set the bombs or cause the blasts, such persons are no less "terrorists" in that their power, such as it is, arises from bullying and intimidation.

Of late, similar church-sponsored "protests" have been little more than a handful of parishioners holding signs and spouting derisive rhetoric. These hatemongers are often vastly outnumbered by counter-protestors. With such small numbers,

---

[61] The original post was written after the initial reports of the bombings. The Tsarnaev brothers were later identified as the bombers. The older brother, Tamerlan Tsarnaev, was killed in a shootout with police days after the bombing. The younger brother, Dzhokhar Tsarnaev, escaped during the firefight, but he was taken into custody on April 19, 2013 after an area-wide manhunt

the Westboro cult members have no hope in successfully spreading their hate-filled message by themselves. What they crave is the free publicity, which they do not deserve. They feed on it. If everyone, including the enabling and complicit media, would ignore them and refuse to report and republish their actions, the beast would starve to death.

In the days following the Boston Marathon Bombings, coverage of the bombing and its aftermath ran nearly continuously on all major news outlets. Initial news reports saturated the collective consciousness of the nation. There is no question that the initial bombing was newsworthy. However, when new facts and significant developments were slow to materialize, the "news" turned to speculation, rumor, and innuendo. The media reports took on the tenor and credibility of an internet chat room.

We, as a society, have become information obsessed. We have implemented a 24/7 news cycle, which must be filled to avoid disconcerting dead air. Even with technologies, which allow almost unlimited recall of information, we seem afraid that we will miss that one integral tidbit of information, which will be uttered but once. Rather than focusing on living our respective lives, we become obsessed with some event thousands of miles away, over which we have no control.

Making Sense of the Noise -

What passes as news today is often little more than incessant noise. Most of us have no way to filter the plethora of conflicting information in order to make sense of it. Media outlets, which are tasked with disseminating information that is truly "newsworthy," often manipulate and sensationalize the news for the sake of higher ratings and profits.

Are we actually better served by twenty-four (24) hours of constant innuendo and speculation following a newsworthy event rather than a timely and well crafted piece of journalism, which includes truly relevant information that is supported by established facts and detached reason?

The events in Boston (and elsewhere around the world) should give us pause. Those events should make us appreciate life and should cause us to redouble our commitment to living our lives to the fullest. However, rather than applying that focus and commitment to our own lives, we risk continuous distraction by measuring and evaluating our lives vicariously. Such transference is a disservice to ourselves and to the memories of those, who were injured and lost.

Let us pray for those injured in Boston and for those, who mourn the loss of a loved one. Let us commit ourselves to bringing to justice those, whose actions call into question the humaneness of humanity. But, most of all, let us commit ourselves to living each life in such a way as to honor the memories of the victims and as positive examples for others to follow.

We need not recklessly ignore the potential dangers around us, but we should not be consumed by them either. If we demean our lives in deference to terrorists, we surrender ultimate victory to them.

Dignity in the Face of Fear -

How should we respond when faced with senseless tragedy or any act of terrorism, bullying, or intimidation?

The citizens of South Korea give us an example to follow. They live in the shadow of a nuclear armed North Korea, which has unpredictable, if not delusional, leaders. Those leaders use the threat of annihilation to extort wealth and goods from those, who fear that such calculated threats may one day be acted upon.

Despite repeated threats, the South Koreans continue to go about daily activities without giving their juvenile northern neighbors the satisfaction of disrupting their lives. On this issue, America should take its lead from the South Korea.

"We were in the wrong place, at the wrong time, but did the right things," this was the response of a waiter at the Forum Restaurant, which was the site of the second Boston Marathon explosion. The waiter was responding to reports, in which members of the restaurant staff were being called "heroes." Immediately after the bombings, he and his co-workers assisted patrons and bystanders, who were seriously injured.

There were many brave persons in Boston on that day, and they exemplified the adage:

Bravery is not the absence of fear, but the ability to respond and act with dignity despite the presence of fear.

Split Allegiances -

On September 11, 2012, the younger Boston Marathon bomber, Dzhokhar Tsarnaev, took the Oath of Citizenship and became a U.S. Citizen. He became a citizen after living more than a decade in and around Massachusetts. In taking that Oath, he said the following words:

> *I hereby declare, on oath, that I absolutely and entirely renounce and abjure all allegiance and fidelity to any foreign prince, potentate, state or sovereignty, of whom or which I have heretofore been a subject or citizen....*

Obviously, his allegiances and those of his now deceased brother and co-conspirator, Tamerlan Tsarnaev, were somewhere other than with the United States.

President Obama has said, "Words mean something." The words spoken in a vow or oath should be taken to heart by the person making the promise, and such acts should represent the most solemn promise that one can make to another human being or legal authority.

The Oath of Citizenship does not allow for split allegiances. "Absolutely" and "entirely" do not allow for qualification. While "abjure" is not a word in common use today, its meaning in this instance is quite telling and significant:

> *1. to renounce, repudiate, or retract, especially with formal solemnity; recant. 2. to renounce or give up under oath; forswear: to abjure allegiance. 3. to avoid or shun.*

Citizens by birth should also consider where our allegiances lie. Increasingly, citizens of the U.S. describe themselves not as simply, "Americans," but as: African-Americans, Mexican-Americans, Arab-Americans, Asian-American, *etc.*

Many would argue that such descriptors are merely acknowledgements to heritage and represent cultural pride. I would argue that if you are not "American" first and foremost, then such pride is misplaced.

Some may question, "What about 'dual-citizenship'?" ... Generally, "dual citizenship" arises by birth or marriage not through naturalization. The U.S. cannot "revoke" citizenship granted by another country, but U.S. citizenship may be lost when one affirmatively adopts citizenship in another country. U.S. law does not have provisions for dual citizenship, and the Oath of Citizenship for naturalized citizens would tend to exclude dual allegiances.

As stated above, my position is that either you are an American or not. If someone wishes to keep political or citizenship ties to a home country, that is certainly his or her prerogative. However, swearing allegiance to America severs those ties. Otherwise, the oath and the act of naturalization mean nothing.

Split allegiances are generally no allegiance at all. This whole, "We are all citizens of the world," concept is naïve. It is like an attorney representing opposing parties in the same action. It is impossible to address the resulting conflicts of interest and to zealously represent the interests of both parties simultaneously. Ultimately, an advocate is forced to pick sides, and the interests of one party (or all parties) suffer as a direct consequence of ignoring the existence of such conflicts.

If one takes the above Oath of Citizenship as a naturalized citizen, the words themselves do not allow for sitting on the fence. If one does not want to give up his citizenship to one country, then he should not swear allegiance to another. But, much like the marriage vow of "'till death do us part," oaths do not carry the same weight that they used to.

Be Afraid, Be very Afraid -

The administration and members of the GOP overtly and eagerly advocated the denial of constitutionally guaranteed rights (*e.g.* Miranda) to the surviving bomber (and U.S. citizen), Dzhokhar Tsarnaev, in order to advance perceived judicial efficiencies and illusory safety. Tsarnaev is almost certainly guilty, and he likely will be convicted for his heinous crimes regardless of the complexity of the procedures employed. The danger is not in his ever again being a free man. The danger is in chipping away at the rights and protections afforded to the rest of us.

In a speech on February 21, 2013 regarding the topic of Gun Control, Vice President Biden said:

No law-abiding citizen in the United States has any fear that their Constitutional Rights will be infringed upon.

Consider Biden's statement in light of an administration and representatives in Congress, which have openly advocated infringing upon the Constitutional Rights of the surviving Boston Bomber.

Consider the statement when "law abiding" is often determined not so much by *mens rea* (*i.e.* "criminal intent") but by what government (and specifically the executive branch) says a crime is on any given day.

Consider the statement in light of the book, *Three Felonies a Day*, by Harvey A. Silverglate, in which the premise is that professionals and business persons unwittingly commit three (3) potential federal felonies a day in just doing their jobs.

Only then, should you determine how much comfort that you take in Biden's empty words. If our rights and liberties are curtailed to promote illusions of safety, the bombers and similar terrorists succeed not just in killing Americans. America potentially suffers a slow and agonizing death as the country bleeds out from the loss of fundamental rights and liberties.

Our individual rights, which are enshrined in and guaranteed by the Constitution, are not for the protection of criminals. Those rights are for the protection of the innocent. Infringing on the surviving bomber's rights will have little practical effect on him. Still, our government ventures onto a slippery slope.

No Nobility among Savages -

The surviving perpetrator, Dzhokhar Tsarnaev, reportedly told investigators that the two (2) Boston Marathon bombers acted alone and were defending Islam after the American-led wars in Iraq and Afghanistan. The brothers waged this personal vendetta despite taking refuge in the U.S. and voluntarily living in the U.S. for a decade (and the younger brother actually becoming a citizen).

America as a "melting pot" does not mean being a mini-United Nations ("U.N.") with disparate factions bickering and engaging in incessant infighting. Assimilation necessarily means losing much of a political and cultural identity in order to

210

"be American." If persons are not willing to make that change and transition, then they have no reason to be United States citizens.

"Diversity" should mean taking the best traits of all citizens and peoples and incorporating those positive traits into an evolving culture and society. A misguided push for diversity for its own sake may mean losing positive traits: Inclusion, acceptance, cooperation, personal responsibility, and self-sufficiency. Those losses may be part of the price paid to avoid offending someone's unreasonably delicate sensibilities or to avoid potential conflicts with persons, who may not want to be American in the first place.

There are persons, who do not deserve to live among civil society. They are barbarians, and there is no nobility among such savages. We should feel no obligation to "diversify" our culture and society to allow such persons to infiltrate our midst. Similarly, we should not demean ourselves by opening our borders to such miscreants.

This is a lesson that the Brits will likely take to heart as well. On May 22, 2013, machete-wielding radical Muslims of Nigerian descent viciously attached and nearly decapitated a British soldier, Lee Rigby, without provocation. This barbaric attack occurred in broad daylight on the streets of London.

It is hard to believe that persons inclined to such actions fail to raise "red flags." Unfortunately, warning signs are too often overlooked or ignored by immigration authorities or other government officials. It was reported that both London attackers were known to British security forces prior to the senseless murder. Model citizens do not haul off one day out of the blue and start hacking off an innocent man's limbs with a machete and meat cleaver! And, they do not kill three (3) persons and injure nearly three hundred (300) others by exploding bombs in public places.

There are times when the realities of life justify closer scrutiny of individuals, and there are circumstances, which do not justify a willful ignorance of those realities in extending the "benefit of the doubt" beyond all reason. Authorities had repeated and ample evidence that one of the Boston Bombers was one of those "bad apples."

In 2011, the Russian Federal Security Service ("FSB") informed the FBI that Tamerlan Tsarnaev was a follower of radical Islam. After the Boston bombings, it was reported that Tamerlan was also a party to another Boston-area triple murder, which occurred on September 11, 2011. Regarding that earlier incident, news reports at the time reported that the victims' throats had been slashed nearly to the point of decapitation.

Yet, the United States provided asylum to Tamerlan Tsarnaev and allowed him to stay well after his "welcome" should have been exhausted.

Conclusion -

If political correctness means that Americans open our boarders to the enemies of our country, our culture, and our way of life, then on some level, it is time to be unwelcoming.

If a person enters and resides in the United States legally and that individual demonstrates civility, productivity, and respect for others, then he should be welcomed and integrated into society. His or her race, ethnicity, religion, gender, *etc.* should not matter. Such persons should not be measured by our expectations of them but by their personal abilities and their contributions to society.

In contrast, we should be critical of those persons who refuse to integrate, assimilate, and participate productively within civil society regardless of whether their origins are foreign or domestic. No one should get a "pass" in the name of privilege or political correctness. The same criteria should apply to "christians" of the Westboro Baptist Church variety and to machete wielding Muslims. Persons deserve to be called out for their bad acts, and society should not be expected to tolerate the intolerance of such persons.

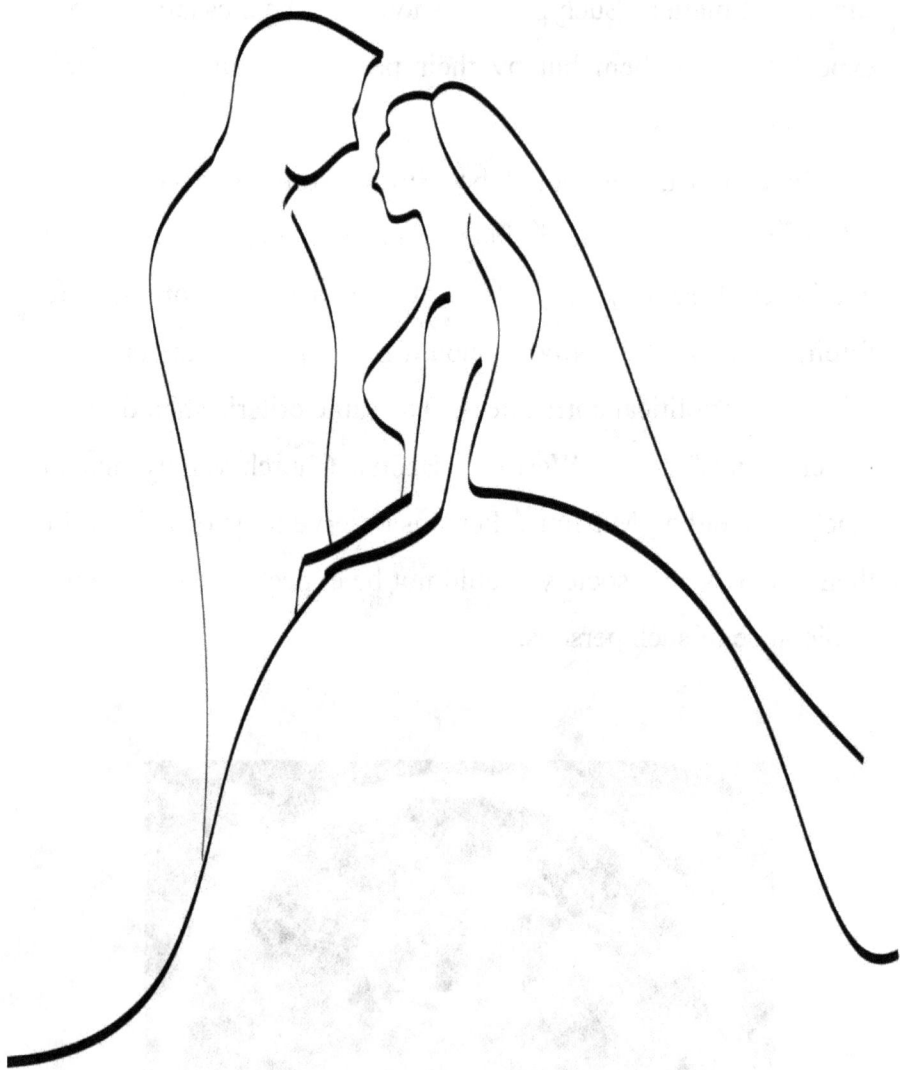

For Better or Worse, and We Mean It

Blog Entry – April 14, 2013

Newly emboldened, GOP legislators in North Carolina think that divorce after one-year separation is "too easy." Proponents of a new bill want to require a two (2) year waiting period (even in cases of domestic violence and spousal abuse), AND the spouses must undergo a series of counseling sessions on communications, conflict resolution, and child rearing while they wait. Do not worry. Your "Big Brother" has your best interests at heart.

While the establishment of a marriage requires the sanction of government in order to have legal effect, the continuity of a mutually beneficial marriage has nothing to do with the blessing of government or its admonishment. If the commitment does not exist between the spouses themselves, no amount of government coercion or religious chastisement is going to hold the union together.

Notwithstanding the Kardashians and Britney Spears, most people do not lightly enter into or frivolously dissolve a marriage. Forcing a bad marriage to continue for the sake of improving North Carolina's divorce rate is an invitation to disaster.

I agree that some persons fail to give marriage the level of commitment and respect that it deserves. I also agree that individuals may take the "easy" way out on occasion. However, the threat of eternal damnation was not sufficient to promote the moral ideals of marriage and to eliminate availability of divorce.

215

I doubt that government regulations would prove more successful.

Government established laws should be the floor below which human behavior is entirely unacceptable. Such laws are ill-suited to codify and mandate adherence to moral ideals.

Government is not a proper mechanism for saving the souls and micromanaging the lives of millions of disparate citizens. If the individual does not have a moral and ethical foundation based upon family nurturing or influence of a religious authority, it is unlikely that government disapproval will lead to a change in behaviors no matter how socially beneficial such a change may be.

Government can hardly establish itself as a moral arbiter. As flawed as human beings may be, they should still be the masters of their own imperfect lives without unnecessary intrusions by government.

"Give me Liberty, or Give me Death!"

Introduction -

The NYC Police Commissioner was on NBC's *Meet the Press* [08/18/2013] arguing in support of the city's "Stop-and-Frisk" program. Under that program, officers from the NYPD were given the power to stop anyone upon a self-defined and often poorly articulated determination of "reasonable (articulable) suspicion."

In practice, nearly ninety percent (90%) of such stops resulted in "no further police action," and approximately ninety percent (90%) of the persons stopped were either Black or Hispanic (*i.e.* non-white). After concerns were raised by some citizens, a federal judge ordered that the program be terminated finding that it was unconstitutional.

Statistically Validated Stereotypes -

The Commissioner argued that the disproportionate race mix should not be a factor in invalidating the program because the "universe" of those persons identified as perpetrators of violent crimes in NYC has a similar racial proportionality. The phrase, which the Commissioner struggled to avoid saying was, "Statistically Validated Stereotypes."

It may be beneficial and efficient to classify individuals by common group attributes and to associate with such classes or groups sets of behaviors, which are presumed consistent within the group. However, the classifications of the individual as a member of the group may be arbitrary, and the relationship between the identifying group attribute and the alleged behaviors may be weak or entirely nonexistent. If not closely monitored, a tool originally developed for effective law enforcement could easily be converted in to a weapon to be used against a disliked individual or to persecute a class of persons.[62]

I will not argue that "profiling" cannot be an effective law enforcement tool, but those in law enforcement should acknowledge that is what they are doing. It is entirely unreasonable to ignore objective history and a lifetime of experience in evaluating a potentially volatile environment and in making split-second decisions about a potential perpetrator's propensity for criminal behavior. Nevertheless, the Bill of Rights was not adopted to aid in the efficiency of law enforcement. Instead, it was adopted for the protection of individual rights and specifically to limit the police powers of government.

Safety at any Costs -

The Commissioner then adopts the refrain, which is now familiar from his federal counterparts at the FBI and NSA, when he argues that people will be "safer" if their personal freedoms and individual liberties are infringed upon. This may, in fact, be true, but increased safety does not make such police actions constitutional.

Citizens do not have a duty to aid law enforcement and to make it easy to apprehend persons merely because government has determined that the mere presence of such "miscreants" or

---

[62] On November 13, 2013, a Government Services Administration ("GSA") report recommended discontinuing a TSA Behavioral Profiling program being used in commercial airports. To date, implementation of the program has cost more than $1 Billion. The GSA found that Behavioral Profiling was ineffective and no more effective than chance in identifying dangerous persons.

the threat of some action upsetting to the current state of affairs makes it more difficult or less efficient for government to operate.

"Safety" should not be the supreme objective of government. There is no perfect safety, and incremental safety can have extremely high costs. Those costs likely include losses of liberty and freedom, and illusions of safety may encourage persons to undertake unreasonable risks or to act recklessly. The resulting actions may be more dangerous than the evils from which the government seeks to protect the public.

In promoting safety, government must acknowledge its limitations. Persons must be reasonable in their expectations of government, and individuals should be prudent in protecting themselves and promoting their own safety. Finally, the true cost and reasonable benefits should be made known so that people can determine if the cost is worth the benefit (whether those costs are measured in dollars or losses of freedom and liberty).

A Price too High -

During the "Red Scare," it certainly could not be said that all persons, who were labeled "Communists," represented clear and present dangers to the United States. In the name of protecting the U.S. from the scourges of Communism, Senator Joseph McCarthy (R-WI) systematically undertook a series of hearings with the end result being accusations of subversion, disloyalty, and treason against thousands of Americans without due consideration being give to actual proof or evidence.

Persons were subjected to "conviction" by conjecture and innuendo.

McCarthyism was the result of good intentions run amuck. In that case, the treatment was nearly bad as the supposed disease. In trying to "save" America from an external foe, the designated protectors of our rights unnecessarily tarnished those rights and abused the powers entrusted to them by the people. Are we seeing similar actions today in the treatment of persons of Middle Eastern decent and adherents of Islam?

Some would argue that Singapore is "safer" because of its infamous use of caning as a punishment. Should we reinstitute public lashings because they may be effective in curtailing petty crime? Or, do we as a society believe ourselves to have progressed beyond such barbaric punishments and retributions (some would say torture) in favor of more constructive reformation and rehabilitation? Law enforcement and the penal system should be a defense against harm to the populace not a tool of government to effect conformity and to socially engineer society.

On the whole, Iraq was less violent (*i.e.* "safer") under its dictator, Saddam Hussein. Egypt was a venue of perpetual unrest but it was less likely to erupt into civil war under the despot, Hosni Mubarak. Such governments promote safety through conformity, and they assure conformity by oppressing any dissent and opposition, which may upset the *status quo* of governments. Oppressive regimes may be "safer" but they are not FREE. There is no true freedom of speech, freedom of religion, and freedom of association.

The United States is unique in the sacrosanct nature of our personal freedoms and in the protections of our individual rights, which are enshrined within the Constitution. America does not become safer by destroying the freedoms, rights, and protections, which collectively define what it is to be American.

Conclusion -

No one questions the role of the government in protecting the safety of its citizens. However, the nature and extent of that role can be the subject of legitimate debate. There must be sincere and open debates about the extent to which innocent individuals are having their rights imposed upon without demonstrable and material increases in safety. Only with honest debates can we as a society make informed decisions as to whether such intrusions and impairments of constitutionally protected rights and freedoms are warranted and whether those impositions should be accepted by the people.

Such programs, which purport to be for the safety of the people, cannot be mandated by government fiat without input from those persons, who are both directly benefitted and adversely affected. Such programs should not be implemented in secrecy, and they must be subject to independent scrutiny by the courts. In this case, the court has spoken.

Future decisions must include considerations regarding the high costs, which arise from the collective losses of freedom and liberties. Consideration cannot be limited to whether such programs increase the efficiency and effectiveness of law enforcement. Many unjust and unconstitutional actions and programs would be extremely effective. The Bill of Rights is filled with provisions, which, if eliminated, would make the jobs of law enforcement officials exceedingly easier, but such changes would make the lives of citizens correspondingly less free. Our Founding Fathers erred on the side of caution in limiting the powers of government so as to prevent abuse, oppression, and tyranny.

Are we prepared to surrender liberty and freedom for illusions of safety?

I echo the words of Patrick Henry:

Is life so dear or peace so sweet as to be purchased at the price of chains and slavery? Forbid it, Almighty God! I know not what course others may take, but as for me, GIVE ME LIBERTY, OR GIVE ME DEATH!"

DONT TREAD ON ME

The Immorality of Unjust Laws

Blog Entry - September 29, 2013

It was reported [09/29/13] that conservative Muslim Clerics have argued that women, who drive, risk damaging their ovaries, and thereby presumably threaten a fundamental role of the woman in bearing children. This "religious" ruling was undertaken to support the political prohibition in Saudi Arabia against women driving automobiles.

This is yet another example of what happens when you mistake religion for moral right and you intermingle misguided religious ideals with political might. Government should not be an instrument to assure moral purity because morality is an individual trait, and the institutionalization of morality ultimately results in corruption, adulteration, and perversion of religious ideals. Religion and government are often the implements of power mongers, and only in recognizing the sanctity of the individual and the power of personal liberties can either institution be sufficiently tempered and controlled.

Most of us in the West cannot understand the bases for government actions such as prohibitions against women drivers or prescribing specific dress and attire. There remains some semblance of a belief that individual liberties should trump government powers, except where there is a clearly defined and legitimate state interest, which is superior to the individual right.

Government moralism seems irrational and foreign to most persons, but such prohibitions demonstrate the expectations of government and of the church that persons submit to the will of the institution and forgo personal judgment and rationality.

Governments, including our own, increasingly discount individual liberties in furtherance of tenuous state interests, illusions of comfort, and perceptions of safely.

Like the cleric's fatwa regarding women drivers, government's expectation seems to be that the people will abide by the established law just because government "says so." Worse even, those within government, who are responsible for legislation and enforcement of laws, are often seen as saying, "Do as I say, not as I do."

Morals, however, cannot be legislated. They cannot even be "taught." They can be exemplified, and they can be discussed. Furthermore, it is almost certainly true that, in an ethical vacuum and without an example to follow, an individual may never achieve moral enlightenment. Nevertheless, one most often becomes a "moral" person by internalizing and adopting that which is being rationally explained or exemplified by others.

Governments can define "crimes" (*i.e.* the standards of behavior below which SOCIETY will punish an actor for conduct against society as a whole or against an individual member), and government can PROSCRIBE criminal behavior. However, to be successful in curtailing (or dictating) any specific behavior, individuals (including potential actors and potential "victims") must agree that the behavior is inherently wrong (or desirable) and that the potential harm or loss is sufficient to justify restricting (or commanding) the specific behavior (and punishing the nonconforming actor).

Governments are much less effective in PRESCRIBING "moral behaviors" where such behaviors are not universally accepted or where the supposed public harm from noncompliance is minimal and the collective costs to individual actors and to society by way of enforcement are high.

Just as "rightness" cannot be determined by government fiat or institutional mandate, it similarly cannot be determined by majority rule. An erroneous statement of fact or the undertaking of an immoral act, even one which is (nearly) universally accepted, is no less abhorrent or reprehensible because it represents the concerted voice of a controlling group or majority.

Similarly, an act is not inherently "wrong," and therefore should not be a crime, merely because government (or some other institution, including the "church") defines it as such. "Crimes" or other prohibitions, which serve no legitimate aim other than to assure continued control and increased power to those in positions of authority, do not deserve the respect and submission of the people.

There must be a rational basis underlying the "rule of law." Where reason and intellect are inconsistent with the means and ends of a given law, persons are entitled, if not obliged, to oppose that rule. There is no shame or moral wrong in opposing an unjust law.

It is a poverty to decide that a child must die so that you may live as you wish.

— Mother Teresa

"Legitimate Rape" versus Illegitimate Laws

Politician's and political parties tend to take definitive positions on the issue of abortion. They often identify themselves as either being "Pro Choice," in favor of a woman's right to choose what happens to "her own body," or "Pro Life," in favor of protecting the burgeoning life of the fetus.

The fine distinctions in deciding, "What is life?," and the interplay between the rights of the mother and the life of the child, make legislating on this issue problematic and troublesome.

I abhor the concept of abortion. Putting aside the philosophical debate about when life begins, abortion takes a tremendous negative toll on the women involved. I say this, of course, as a man, but my perspective is fashioned from the experiences of the few women, who I have known well enough to have discussed with them this very personal topic. Each one of these women looks upon the experience with apprehension and regret, and these feelings are consistent even if she were certain, at the time, that abortion was her only option.

I do not know that any woman could ever be "happy" about having had an abortion; although, I have heard the procedure described with calloused indifference. It is described by some as the equivalent of removing an inflamed appendix or worrisome wart. I wonder how the handful of survivors of botched abortions take to being described as, and having been treated in a manner similar to, cancerous growths on the uterine wall?

I personally find it reprehensible that some persons would use abortion casually as a means of convenient birth control, and yes, I know some women that have had multiple abortions.[63] It is this lack of personal responsibility (on the part of men and women) that those who oppose abortion most often highlight.

However, one may ask, "How is personal responsibility advanced if government were to deny access to abortion to a woman that has been raped?" Is requiring her to bear the child of her rapist going to provide a positive incentive in her future behavior? Can any of us know the horrors of carrying that child for nine (9) months and then giving birth, and the impact that such a thing would have on the mother and her family?

In such situations, I may grieve the loss of the aborted fetus, but I am not arrogant so as to say that I know what is best for that woman. I defer that difficult decision to the woman, and any moral quandaries thereafter are between her and her Maker. No man (or other woman) should be entitled to pass judgment.

Most people would concede the extreme positions. Few in the Pro Choice camp would argue that abortion should be available on demand up until the moment that the fetus can survive unassisted outside of the mother's womb. Similarly, all but the most ardent Pro Life supporter would have to admit the existence of some scenario in which he would likely acquiesce, even if reluctantly, in the decision to abort (*e.g.* rape, incest, life of the mother, *etc.*).

---

[63] In 2008, there were approximately 1 Million abortions in the U.S., and roughly one-half (½) of those women getting abortions had had one previously. - Jegtvig, Shereen, "Offer Women IUD's," *Reuters Health* (November 15, 2013).

Government must be empowered to impose some rule of law and to establish reasonable standards of behavior for its citizens. The antithesis of the rule of law is anarchy. A problem arises when you attempt to make policy based upon the concepts of "always" and "never." When you govern from the extremes, any exception to the rule destroys the rationale behind it.

It was this trap into which Congressman Todd Akin (R-MO) fell when he made his unfortunate and misguided comment about "Legitimate Rape" rarely resulting in pregnancy. In trying to defend an indefensible position, Akin not only lost the instant debate on that issue, but he also jeopardized the credibility of the prevailing position within his party (and that of all persons similarly inclined).

To those for whom abortion is an issue, which turns on morality or a belief that the unborn fetus is worthy of government protection, any retreat from the absolutes may be disconcerting, but such are the realities of government and laws. Laws are intended to conform behaviors to some generally accepted standard of "right" and "wrong" not to assure adherence to a moral ideal.

This should have been the answer given by Congressman Akin:

When any law fails to advance the desired behavior and instead traps victims of heinous acts and exacerbates their pain, such a law is unjust.

As Demographics go, So goes the Nation

Blog Entry – November 10, 2012

Immediately after the 2012 presidential election, there was a theme prevalent in political commentary, "A voting bloc consisting primarily of angry middle-aged white men is unlikely to be successful base in future elections." However, I would note that it was just such a group that laid the foundations of this country and to whom we owe the time-honored right of political discourse and debate.

Were our founding fathers, and the leaders who followed, great persons BECAUSE of their gender, race, age, education, or religious affiliation? No, they were not. Accidents of birth or fate should not be the ultimate determiners of one's successes or failures in life. The overall measure of success or failure should be in reference to the cumulative acts or omissions throughout a person's life. I say "cumulative" because no person is perfect, and no life is without challenges.

We all have shortcomings and failings, but it is important to note that failure and success are not mutually exclusive. Learning through trial and error often produces the most well learned lessons. Thomas Edison realized that his 1,000's of prior attempts to invent the light bulb were necessary to his eventual success. Edison said, "I have not failed. I've just found 10,000 ways that won't work." It is also important to note that successes in one area of our lives may be accompanied by failures or shortcomings in other areas.

In hindsight, history has identified foibles, flaws, and weaknesses in our leaders and heroes: Jefferson's illegitimate children, Lincoln's bouts of depression, Kennedy's affairs, and then there are the likes of General Patton, who today would likely be seen as just plain crazy.[64] Such aspects of personality and character do not detract from the greatness of the deeds and works of such persons. We should not judge the quality of the act by the shortcomings of the actor.

There seems to be a growing consensus that there is nothing to be learned from the past and that whatever is new and different must be better. Any person, thing, or institution can be improved upon, but that does not mean that we go back to square one upon the discovery of a flaw or upon identifying an opportunity for improvement.

Yes, we should embrace lifelong learning (as individuals and as a culture), but we should not attempt to reinvent the wheel simply because we have a flat tire. Change merely for the sake of change is not necessarily productive. As a people, we must embrace the inevitability of change, but we should not abandon the principles, lessons learned from, and foundations provided by our collective past.

There is no doubt that the demographics of the United States are changing. Our population is aging; our middle class is shrinking, and the groups and institution that have been important in defining who we are as a country are waning in importance and influence.

Does "change" mean abandoning the lessons learned and examples provided by those who have come before us? Or, is

---

[64] Patton is said to have believed that he was the reincarnation of the Roman Emperor, Julius Caesar.

the most productive change, that which adapts the lessons learned from the past with opportunities and practical application to the modern world?

There have been repeated news reports recently about how both national parties must embrace Hispanics, as the fastest growing minority group in the country. I do not disagree with the significance of that growth. However, I believe that there should be an acknowledgement by the government that "illegal immigration" over the past decades was the result of a conscious decision by agencies of the federal government to ignore laws and regulations in favor a failed social experiment.

In deference to cheap labor and population growth (both supposedly in support of the economy), agencies of government in effect artificially suppressed wages and fostered the exponential growth of a segment of the electorate that openly disdains our laws and our institutions.

Now, we are being told that such persons are the "hope of democracy." Please forgive me if my "hope" is somewhat lackluster.

Nearly thirty (30) years ago, President Ronald Reagan oversaw one amnesty program. Now, we are told that another such program necessary "for the good of the nation." Yet, due consideration is not being given to thwarting a covert invasion and stemming the erosion of the many of the positive traits and characteristics that have historically defined America. What is best in the long run is not necessarily what is easy or convenient in the short term.

NOTE: Castle Garden.[65]

---

[65] The pictures above include elements of "Castle Garden" (a/k/a "Fort Clinton" or "Castle Clinton"). Many of us are familiar with Ellis Island; however, Castle Garden was the first immigration station in New York. Eight Million people entered the U.S. through this point of entry between 1855 and 1890.

Immigration Reform: *What's in It for Americans?*

Blog Entry - July 3, 2013

I am fully aware and understand (even if I disagree with) the arguments in support of "Immigration Reform:"

- "Indigenous" U.S. citizens supposedly do not breed enough children to maintain a sufficient population growth, and some branch of voodoo economics says that, without such growth, the U.S. economy, which is the world's largest, is going to drift into a death spiral.

- Low-skill (translated "low-wage") labor is needed for jobs that "Americans won't do;" however, this oft repeated explanation usually omits the parenthetical, "... at that wage level."

  You can always find someone to do any job (no matter how filthy or menial) at some price. The influx of low-wage (often illegal) labor floods the pool of labor (market) thereby artificially depressing wages for those, who would otherwise be competing for those jobs. It seems that human resources may be one commodity that domestic employers want to disassociate from the "supply/demand" curves, which are so integral to understanding free enterprise.

- There are more than 11 Million illegal aliens in the country already. So, we have to do SOMETHING. Either in this or some future generation, they or their offspring will have sufficient critical mass to affect the political process. (You mean like the 2012 Presidential Election?)

I would expect that, like many Americans, such newly minted citizens would gleefully sell their votes to whomever offers support for a pet cause or promises the biggest pot of gold at the end of the rainbow. Therefore, any political party not wishing to condemn itself to irrelevance (*i.e.* Republicans) must vote to allow a path to citizenship in order to assure access to this voting bloc and thereby protect its own viability.

As I said, I understand the arguments, but I vehemently disagree with most of them for the reasons indicated above. I welcome debates of any of these issues on the merits. Ultimately, the views of others may prevail among the political class. However, I have a real problem when the issue is framed in such a way so as to completely ignore the existence of a material factor, which should itself be integral to (if not determinative of) the debate.

Recently, the Associated Press ("AP") updated its style guide to discourage the use of the term, "Illegal Immigrant." That term relatively recently replaced the term, "Illegal Alien." The prior change was adopted despite the fact that the latter term accurately described the nature and status of such individuals in this country and likely had been in accepted use for more than two centuries.

Nevertheless, it was deemed "offensive" to those who were, in fact, "alien" to this country and here "illegally." "Illegal

Alien" connotes behavior that is improper and inconsistent with established law, similar to the terms: "Criminal" and "felon." That characterization, which implies improper behavior, is factually accurate, intentional, and entirely appropriate.

The more pleasing and euphemistic (if less succinct) phrase now being used is, "Immigrants, who are here without papers," or some derivation thereof. This was the phraseology used by the Columnist, Eugene Robinson, in a recent article in which he argued that:

> [T]he Senate did the sensible thing [when it] passed a bill allowing _law-abiding_ immigrants who are here without papers to stay - and eventually become citizens.[66] [Emphasis added.]

Mr. Robinson, however, merely glosses over and completely ignores the fact that such persons ARE NOT LAW-ABIDING IMMIGRANTS. "Law-abiding immigrants" follow U.S. Immigration Laws rather than flaunting such laws. "Law-abiding immigrants" waited their turns in line rather than jumping that line with the expectation of special dispensation.

Americans are being told that the currently proposed Immigration Reform bill will "fix" immigration. Does that mean "fix" immigration like the 1986 "reform" bill, which itself granted amnesty to 3 Million illegal aliens?

It is also argued that there are provisions to "secure the border" in order to stem the future flows. Does that mean "secure" in the same manner as the 2006 "Secure Fence Act,"

---

[66] Robinson, Eugene, "How Boehner gets a Win-Win," _Star-News_ (July 3, 2013).

237

which itself mandated increased border security and which to this date has only been partially implemented?

Why do we not simply implement and enforce the laws, which are already on the books?

It is ridiculous and ludicrous to believe that amnesty and a path to citizenship will do anything but fuel the torrent of illegal immigration. I would argue that there has never been an "inability" to police and secure the borders so as to greatly curtail, if not stop, illegal immigration. Illegal immigration is seen by government, at worst, as a "necessary evil."

In fact, I would argue that government has been complicit in fostering illegal immigration. Government policies, whether express or implied, are the means to an end that is defined and gauged by the profitability of powerful special interests.

If immigration reform is, in fact, good for the country as a whole, then let us have an honest and sincere debate rather than hiding behind semantics and some misplaced moral platitudes. Tell Americans what is in it for them rather than trying to convince citizens that they "owe" something to Illegal Aliens.

The Costs of Immigration Reform

Following the most recent national election [2012], in which the Democratic Party secured seventy percent (70%) of the Hispanic vote, a bipartisan consensus quickly developed that political success, or even survival, requires pandering to this quickly expanding demographic group.

Following the election, a bi-partisan group of Senators representing the predominant parties proposed a "path to citizenship" for the more than 11 Million illegal aliens, who flouted our immigration laws and entered the country (or extended their stays) illegally. This opening offer was quickly bettered by President Obama in what is likely to become a bidding war to purchase the votes and support of this increasingly important voting bloc.

Allow me to ask one question, "How is immigration reform, which includes a 'path to citizenship,' good for the United States (not the individual illegal aliens but the country as a whole)?"

The public explanations given as to why these steps are "necessary" generally exclude the obvious self-preservation efforts of politicians. Instead, proponents argue that we, as a society, "owe" this privilege to those, who came to the country illegally. This argument presumes the need for national "penance" for the actions of those, who chose to employ illegal aliens.

Rhetorically, employment conditions for illegal aliens have been described by some as "slave-like" and even "inhuman."

Apparently, those using such descriptors have little knowledge and appreciation of the conditions of slavery or even the conditions of human existence throughout much of the world even today.

More broadly, there is a line of thought that the United States must provide an avenue for the populations of the world to better themselves through an improved standard of living. We also are told that there is some nebulous good furthered by "diversity" without due consideration being given to quality over quantity. Americans are goaded into feelings of guilt and obligation to open our borders in furtherance of some misguided Utopian ideal.

The final argument in support of open borders is that "we are all immigrants" to this land, and once again, there is an undertone that we owe penance for the "displacement of indigenous peoples."

Many desperately poor families around the world subsist on less than $5 per day. That representative family of four spends less in total than many Americans spend on their daily cup of coffee. It is futile to attempt to raise the standards of living experienced by the billions of such persons to that which we enjoy as Americans.

As for "slave like" and "inhuman" conditions for which penance is demanded, if the living and working conditions in this country were not a marked improvement over the situations, in which most of those laborers found themselves before coming to the United States, then the tide over the borders would not be constantly rising.

We, as Americans, often view the situations of other persons throughout the world through the limited perspective of our own experiences. We attribute our perceived needs, wants, aspirations, and moral foundations to all other occupants of earth. Not only is such a singular perspective severely limited, but it is entirely unrepresentative when considering the disparate peoples of the earth and their individual circumstances and situations. We cannot make all residents of earth (like) Americans.

It is unrealistic to expect that "equality" can be achieved by bestowing upon all peoples of earth a lifestyle or standard of living substantially similar to Americans. Instead, any semblance of equality could be achieved only by Americans sacrificing our established lifestyles and standards of living and distributing our collective wealth to the other peoples of the world (with no appreciable return beyond intrinsic rewards).

If lowering the collective standard of living of the United States is the cost of being "fair and open," we may want to ask, "Just how far are we prepared to go?"

There are too many desperately poor in the world to make appreciable changes in their lives even if we were to roll back by many decades or even a century the collective standard of living within the United States. Instead of promoting a genuine appreciation of privilege and encouraging self-sufficiency and self-development (both externally among other peoples and internally among our own citizens), we are led to feel shame for accidents of birth and to shun individual successes.

Had government not turned a blind eye to rampant illegal immigration, then the "abused" laborers would not have been subjected to alleged abuses on U.S. soil, and the employers would have become more efficient and fairer to employees out of necessity (with the employment of domestic, or at least legal, replacements).

As for the "indigenous peoples," no human being is indigenous to this continent. Furthermore, it is a fact of life that either a people utilizes and defends resources or that people risks losing the land and its resources to other persons, who would zealously guard, cultivate, and develop the same.

Is this "right" in the cosmic scheme of things? Perhaps, it is not. However, it is unreasonable and impossible to Monday-morning-quarterback 10,000 years of human history and societal development.

There are no easy answers. Most persons propose (self-serving) answers without serious consideration of the underlying issues or offer superficial resolutions as knee-jerk reactions to some limited (self-serving) goal or to address some perceived slight.

I do not give Congress and the President credit for being smart enough to have all of the right answers to such a complicated issue. Similarly, I do not give them credit for objectivity and selflessness in divining those answers.

What should (have) be(en) done to address illegal immigration? Government should enforce the laws that are already on the books rather than advancing laws only for the sake of political expediency and ignoring valid laws that are politically difficult. If there had been active enforcement of existing laws thereby giving rise to a legitimate fear of breaking those laws, then there would not have been an open invitation to flout immigration laws for more than twenty-five (25) years.

Now, we are poised to reward illegal aliens by granting them citizenship. Such actions are certain to encourage a THIRD (and fourth and fifth) wave of illegal immigration because the federal government is unlikely to make and implement the hard choices, which will effectively regulate the borders and control immigration.

The temptations will be too strong to bring additional new voters into the fold. Favored employers will continue to crave and demand access to cheap labor. Politicians can hardly be expected and trusted to cut off the flow of below-market labor and newly minted voters. As modern indentured servants, the expectation is that such persons, being indebted and beholding to politicians, will dutifully vote and support the aims of those same politicians.

I have no qualm at all with regulated legal immigration. I have no issue with adding the best and brightest to the melting pot that is the United States. Nevertheless, open borders and unrestrained immigration would turn our shining seas into cesspools. The fields containing amber waves of grain would be decimated, and urban sprawl would supplant the formerly fruited plains.

Reform of federal immigration laws is certainly needed. The process is inefficient, cumbersome, and not well understood. Equally urgent, is the need to close our porous borders. We must develop a respect for laws and actively promote personal responsibility (rather than disdain for the rule of law). Building a "path to citizenship" without installing a valve to stem the flow of illegal immigrants does nothing but reward bad behavior and encourages it to flourish.

How much is a Day of Life Worth?

Blog Entry – July 8, 2012

The story of Ms. Althlee Williams, late of St. Louis, Missouri, was reprinted on the front page of the Sunday Edition of the Wilmington *Star-News* [07/18/12]. The story presents a real-life illustration of the hypothetical situation, which I have been arguing against and which likely will become even more common with Obamacare, particularly should the program morph into a single-payor healthcare system:

> *Their mother, Althlee Williams, 89, had fallen into a coma. Her eyes were shut. She couldn't speak. A machine pumped her lungs. It was time, the doctor told them. They should let their mother die. For months, they had watched her suffer through rashes and bedsores, heart stoppages and breathing problems. Her weight fluctuated by 100 pounds. Williams' two daughters agonized, but seemed ready. Their brother ... refused. "Don't take her off. ... Do whatever you can," he said, before bolting out of the room. ... For months, ... their mother navigate[d] a maze of hospitalizations, blood transfusions, drugs, side effects, infections and dialysis. ... Their mother's health only got worse during the repeated hospitalizations, and she often suffered despite extraordinary measures to comfort and save her. "It was not a comfortable or peaceful death," said Williams' younger daughter[;] "It was just prolonged." ... Cost never appeared to enter into the decisions about Williams' care; the hospital billed Medicare and a supplemental insurance plan.*

The article notes, "In the final six months of her life, Williams' care totaled about $1.2 Million...." Each one of those agonizing and excruciating days likely cost taxpayers more than Six Thousand Dollars ($6,000.00).

Medicare beneficiaries often argue that they have "earned" those entitlement benefits. For the sake of illustration, we can ignore the fact that Medicare was not begun until 1966, and that Ms. Williams likely contributed into the system for less than twenty-five (25) years. Instead, let us assume that Ms. Williams began working at age twenty (20) and continued to work until the standard retirement age of sixty-five (65). She would have worked a total of forty-five (45) years.

Assuming that she grossed $27,500 / yr. (just under $14 / hr. - likely a very generous assumption), the medical bills during the last six (6) months of life would have equated to her entire earnings during her lifetime, much less the meager Three Percent (3%) paid from those presumed wages toward Medicare ($1.25 million versus less than $37,500).

Spending an amount equal to the entire lifetime earnings of a then eighty-nine (89) year old woman to extend her life by six (6) months is irresponsible by any measure. When you consider that the quality of that life was poor, by even the accounts of her children, the decision is unconscionable.

Whether we like it or not, COSTS of care and QUALITY of life MUST be factors in making end-of-life decisions. It is ludicrous to spend millions to extend life just because it is technologically possible.

Sometimes, we demonstrate more compassion for a pet in deciding to take it out of its misery than we do for our elders, who may be allowed to linger and suffer needlessly when a dignified death would be a better alternative.

I do not have a problem acknowledging the potential role of the so-called "Death Panels" if we are moving toward a single-payor system of healthcare (as President Obama has repeatedly indicated would be his preference). Such review panels are "necessary evils" if government is going to provide universal healthcare. Ultimately, someone has to make cost-benefit decisions.

Persons want to believe that life is easy, and we often hope that the difficult choices and necessary sacrifices will be made by someone else. Persons want to believe that they will not ever have to consider "pulling the plug" on Grandma. It is hard to accept that, eventually, it is time to allow Grandma to die (even if that decision comes with the realization that persons more fortunate, lucky, or even richer may receive services or treatment that could have extended a particular patient's life).

The key is to live life well so as not regret the time that we do not have. Taxpayers should not be burdened with the fruitless attempt to extend life by a matter of days in order to make up for a lifetime squandered.

Listening to President Obama's own words, it seems clear that Obamacare is intended by the President and his party as a stepping stone toward a single-payer health system. There are no significant cost savings provisions in Obamacare; therefore, the cost projections are unreasonably conservative. Obamacare likely will end up being a bottomless money pit, and the program will fail almost certainly to be replaced with the desired single-payer system. With nationalized healthcare, everyone will expect the "highest and best" healthcare without any consideration of the costs; however, those expectations almost certainly will be met with disappointment.

I do support insurance reform, including: High risk pools for individuals with preexisting conditions, cost transparency, and interstate marketing of policies. However, Americans in the end want much more government (benefits) than taxpayers are willing (and able) to pay for. It is easy to be charitable with other people's money, but it is said that, "Charity begins at home."

Each of us must answer the question, "What are we willing to give up or sacrifice in order to better ourselves or to benefit our loved ones?" There is a price and consequence to every benefit. In the long run, however, it is fiscally impossible to spend millions of dollars for short-term extensions of life and to expect that any insurance company or government program can remain solvent.

This point is consistent with government experience. It is demonstrated by both Social Security and Medicare, which are both steaming headlong toward insolvency.

If one wants government provided healthcare, then the patient gets the healthcare, which the government wants the patient to have. After all, "He, who writes the checks, makes the rules."

To believe that you, or a loved one, are entitled to millions of dollars in healthcare just because someone else received the same or similar treatment and to believe that such benefits will always be available to everyone without consideration of cost is unreasonable. THE MATH DOES NOT WORK!

Whether one likes the debate or not, the issues will have to be considered either now or later. Now, being a time far enough in advance that we can do something proactive. Later, being a time when our collective backs will be against the wall, and we will be fighting for our fiscal lives.

There are lessons to be learned from insolvent European nations, if only we are willing to take those lessons to heart. I fear that the arrogance of the American political system will lead politicians down the same perilous road, from which our country is unlikely to emerge unscathed.

My view of healthcare is that you get what you pay for, and you pay for what you can afford. Healthcare is a privilege not a right, and as with all privileges, healthcare services are not equally distributed. Healthcare is a limited commodity, and as such, its availability cannot be guaranteed in equal shares to all.

Yes, that means that some persons will die under circumstances where more advanced medical treatment may have saved them. But, how many of the roughly 160,000 persons, who die daily around the world could be saved with even basic medical treatment? Are their lives not also worthy of saving? Why do we, as a country, not make the commitment to prevent each one of those premature deaths as well?

To me, the biggest shame is not the fact that a nearly ninety (90) year old grandmother may not have an extra six (6) months spent struggling to hold onto to her fragile life. The much bigger shame relates to the tens of millions of lives poorly lived.

Such wasted lives lead to individuals clinging to the hope for one more fruitless day rather than celebrating the accomplishments of a life well lived (no matter how short). Death should not be feared by a man, who has lived, and no greater wealth can be squandered than a day wasted through self destruction and idle pursuits.

Thou Shalt Not Covet Thy Neighbor's Doctor

© 2012

One of the least quoted, and perhaps least appreciated of the Ten Commandments, is contained in *Deuteronomy* 5:17:

> *Thou shalt not covet thy neighbor's house, thou shalt not covet thy neighbor's wife, nor his manservant, nor his maidservant, nor his ox, nor his ass, nor any thing that is thy neighbor's.*

"Covet" means: "To desire wrongfully, inordinately, or without due regard for the rights of others." It is easy to be charitable with someone else's money, and it is easy to think, "I deserve 'that' more than him."

It is fair to say that healthcare is an "inelastic" commodity. Patients cannot always make an equally viable "yes" or "no" purchase decision because an emergent need may create a compulsive act. That is not to say that there cannot (and need not) be cost/benefit analyses in healthcare. However, patients (or family members) do not want to be placed in the position of choosing between forgoing a medical procedure and parting with substantial personal assets.

No one likes the idea of telling a ninety (90) year old grandmother that she is not eligible for a $250,000 procedure or telling the parents of severely premature infant that $1 Million in intensive prenatal care is unreasonable when the prognosis in each case is marginal.

These are tough decisions, but ultimately, these decisions are ones that likely will have to be made by someone. Many persons actively avoid uncomfortable situations and conflict, and such persons prefer transferring responsibility and burden for such difficult decisions to others.

Many persons believe that Insurance Companies or the Government should provide the highest and best medical treatment at all times regardless of the cost or circumstances. This belief avoids uncomfortable decisions and those pesky cost issues ... supposedly.

However, government has hardly proven itself a good administrator of healthcare:

- The Pentagon was forced to close its flagship hospital, Walter Reed, due to mismanagement and poor care.
- Government has proven itself similarly ineffective of reining in healthcare costs.
  - o The scheduled cut in physician billing rates under Medicare has been postponed so many times that it is financially inconceivable that the original legislation will ever be implemented.
  - o Despite the inevitable requirement of oversight, treatment recommendations are ignored, because they are unpopular. When a qualified review board recommended that breast exams be decreased or delayed due to limited efficacy, a hue and cry was heard. This was true despite the fact that few questioned the science or methodologies by which the initial recommendation was made.
  - o Medicare approved a drug for prostate cancer that costs nearly **$100,000** per course of treatment and

extends the life of the average patient by a mere four (4) months (from 22 to 26 months).

o The FDA insisted on designating a single source provider for a tried and true formulary for preventing premature labor. In doing so, the cost of a course of treatment was projected to go from **$300 to $30,000**.

Government is not likely to be an effective tool for fixing these and other problems. People must become more involved in managing their own health(care). The majority of chronic illness is directly related to diet and lifestyle, both of which are entirely within the control of the patient without significant cost. Patients also have to become more involved in the purchase decisions for medical services, and there should be more transparency in the costs of those services. Finally, we should look upon healthcare as a privilege and not a right.

Yes, I know the latter concept is uncomfortable and unpopular, but if I cannot covet my neighbor's house, then I should not covet his doctor either.

A "Right" is something that attaches merely by reason of birth and existence. It is not contingent upon location, class, familial relations, or the efforts of third parties. Rights are inalienable. That is, it is not subject to being transferred, taken, or repudiated. They just "are."

That is why we have the Right to PURSUE happiness rather than a guarantee of achieving it. Where something, even if protected by law, is subject to contributions by others and varies according to one's ability and willingness to secure it, that thing is a privilege not a right. To be free from want and need is never a "Right." While the platitude may sound reassuring, it is impractical and cannot be guaranteed by government.

Healthcare as a Right would remove any expectation or obligation from citizens to do anything at all in order to qualify for or to receive medical services. There would be no requirement of contribution or expectation of personal responsibility. Is that really appropriate?

When you remove the "Rights" argument, the debate turns on the questions:

- What are the appropriate costs of healthcare, which may be contracted for or received by a patient?;
- On whom does the legal responsibility fall for payment of those products and services?; and
- What portions are to be paid by the various parties, who contribute to payment (*i.e.* patient, insurance, government)?

These are legitimate questions to be addressed, and they allow a reasoned debate on the subject. Many persons may not like the resulting answers, and there is no guarantee that every person will receive the health services that he or she may need or want. Nevertheless, such difficult questions must be discussed and ultimately answered.

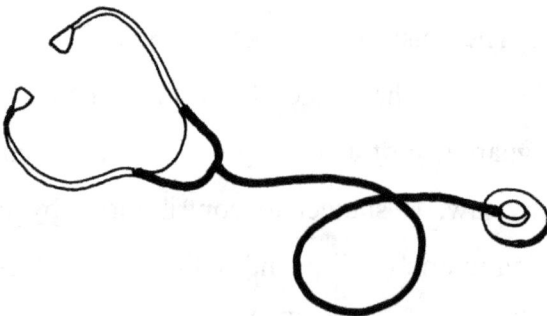

One Cynic's View of Obamacare

Blog Entry - September 25, 2013

A race toward mediocrity is not one that I think America should strive to win. In a society, which rewards excellence, creativity, and initiative (or that should strive to do so), one who does not excel or who lacks creativity and initiative should not expect the same rewards afforded to persons, who do possess such traits.

If one's primary objective in fostering society is the mere "sustenance" of its people, then so be it. However, reduction to similar levels of suffering and misery is likely the only "equality" that can be achieved. In America, citizens will never be content with subsistence or mere sustenance (obvious from the fact citizens in the richest country in the world seem so "needy").

There long have been poverty programs, like Welfare, Food Stamps, and Medicaid. However, the definition of "poverty" continues to expand, and those, who constitute the "needy," now encompass nearly the entire populace. We are quickly becoming wards subject to the Guardian of Government. Wards cannot dictate the behaviors of the master, and in becoming subservient, the people surrender sovereignty to an ever expanding and more powerful government.

Many have argued that the published exchange premiums under Obamacare are "lower than projected." However, many "premium" estimates INCLUDE government subsidies, which SOMEONE has to pay. Welfare is still welfare so long as someone else pays your bills.

Nevertheless, currently inexpensive premiums do not mean "long-term" viability. Obamacare will be a bottomless money pit for both insurance companies and government. There are no significant cost containment provisions, and there will not be the will to properly fund its provisions or the single-payor system, which will likely follow.

I will offer as my cases in point the increasingly insolvent Social Security and Medicare programs. They work in theory but not in practice. Of course, nationalized healthcare will be "cheap" for those not tasked with paying the unlimited government tab.

Obamacare provides government subsidies (i.e. WELFARE) to persons whose compensation is several MULTIPLES of the poverty level. So, programs, which supposedly start off to address a dire "need," quickly expand to pacify "wants." The idea being that people should not have to make difficult decisions for themselves. People should not have to prioritize their lives. Every want, need, and whim should be satisfied (by government) without sacrifice, loss, or disappointment.

So, the "minimum accepted standard of living" which is to be mandated by the government will continue to grow and expand. First, it was *"self-funded"* retirement benefits for the elderly (*i.e.* Social Security). Then, it was medical benefits for retirees (*i.e.* Medicare), and let's throw on an unfunded drug subsidy for kicks and giggles. Because of poor planning and bad management, both Social Security and Medicare are running headlong into insolvency.

Obamacare (or the eventual single-payor system that replaces it) will be similarly mismanaged and underfunded, and as with other entitlement programs, the people will become hopelessly dependent upon failing programs with no viable alternatives.

Obamacare passed both Houses of Congress without a single Republican vote. Healthcare represents nearly Twenty Percent (20%) of the Gross Domestic Product ("GDP") of the United States. Obamacare represents the largest expansion of entitlement benefits in fifty (50) years, but it was passed without even token support from the opposition party.[67]

"Bipartisan" means consensus support from two factions. It does not mean a token Republican (or four), who have been goaded into voting in favor of a piece of legislation. Nearly everything in Washington (and government in general) has become a moral imperative. All significant legislation is debated in terms of cosmic right and wrong. Debates are no longer expressed as matters of differing opinion, which at the outset nearly all such positions are.

No one can guarantee the immediate efficacy and ultimate success of any specific law or program. There is no longer an effort to sway opinion based upon reason and logic, not to mention give-and-take. Neither side is willing to admit to mistakes (individual or collective), and in refusing to acknowledge such mistakes, it is impossible to learn from them. BOTH sides are self absorbed and self-righteous.

---

[67] Republican Representative Joseph Cao (2nd District – Louisiana) voted for an early version of the ACA. He did not vote for the final version, which ultimately passed Congress. Cao lost his reelection bid following his vote.

Some have argued, "Obamacare is now the law." This statement would seem to imply that the continuing and future costs of the program should not be considered and that whatever funds are required to continue the program should be paid without objection. Such a position is ludicrous. If a patient is bleeding out, a physician does not continue to transfuse blood indiscriminately. He first stops the bleeding.

Like Social Security and Medicare, the continued existence of Obamacare is not decided by a single "yes" or "no" vote. Each year, votes on continued government funding (*i.e.* budgets) must take place, and such votes include consideration of whether to fund respective government programs, including Obamacare. Each such vote represents a vote of confidence on the efficacy of the program.

Nearly four (4) years after passage, public opposition to Obamacare stands at nearly Sixty Percent (60%).[68] The administration cites great challenges, which led to a bungled roll-out of the insurance exchanges, on which Obamacare is entirely dependent. Administration officials argue that time was short and that Republicans repeatedly obstructed implementation.

In response to those self-serving excuses, I will note that the United States was instrumental in winning TWO (2) World Wars, which logistically required the movement of millions of soldiers and materiel across the face of the earth. Both such wars were entered and won in less time than the administration

---

[68] Source: "Health Care Law," www.rasmussenreports.com (November 25, 2013).

has been working to implement Obamacare and to get the requisite website up and running efficiently.[69]

I am firmly convinced that "Obamacare" was nothing more than a ruse and intended stepping stone to a single-payor system.[70] I sincerely believe that even proponents expect that Obamacare will fail. The hope of such persons is that the program will be followed by universal "Medicaid" (an even more massive black hole from which no recovery is likely).

No one has ever demonstrated to me a viable long-term funding model for Obamacare that does not require significant (and growing) taxpayer subsidies. That same limited pool of taxpayers will be required to make Social Security and Medicare solvent and to pay interest on the nearly unfathomable National Debt, not to mention actually paying to run the "discretionary" parts of government (*i.e.* those programs, which most parties agree that government is SUPPOSED to do). One can only go to the well so many times before that well runs dry.

Calling something a "right" (*e.g.* Healthcare) does not make it one. Why not establish a "right" to home ownership? Or, a recurring "right" to a new car every few years? Certainly, everyone could benefit from those things!

A RIGHT is something, which is enjoyed by all persons equally and concurrently without the necessity of contribution from or the diminution in the rights of others. If someone else has to pay to finance your "right" (or he must surrender some

---

[69] World War I - <2 years and World War II - <4 years.

[70] With a quick search on YouTube, anyone is free to hear President Obama say as much in his own words.

other right for your benefit), then the benefit that you receive is a privilege.

PRIVILEGES, as opposed to rights, are not equally distributed, and there is no inherent immorality to the unequal distribution of privileges or wealth (no matter how skewed). Even if there were, government should not be in the morals business. It has never proven itself worthy of the task.

Other than in the enforcement of basic rights, which are truly fundamental and immutable, government should operate on the basis of "quid-pro-quo." The "Social Contract" to be enforced by government is based upon give-and-take, which is brought about by negotiated terms.

If government expects the "wealthy" to pay for all of the "needs" and whims of the dependent majority, then government had better be able to explain to those, who pay the bills, "What's in it for them?"

If the answer is, "Nothing," then government and those who benefit from the largesse of taxpayers should expect to have a fight on their hands and a bumpy road toward implementation.

Robin Hood may have been a populist character in "stealing from the rich to give to the poor," but a thief with supposedly noble ends is no less a thief. Similarly, making government the intermediary by which thievery is effected does not make any such act "moral" or any less reprehensible.

Volume II-B

Befuddled, Beguiled, Bemuddled
Bemused, & Bewildered

261

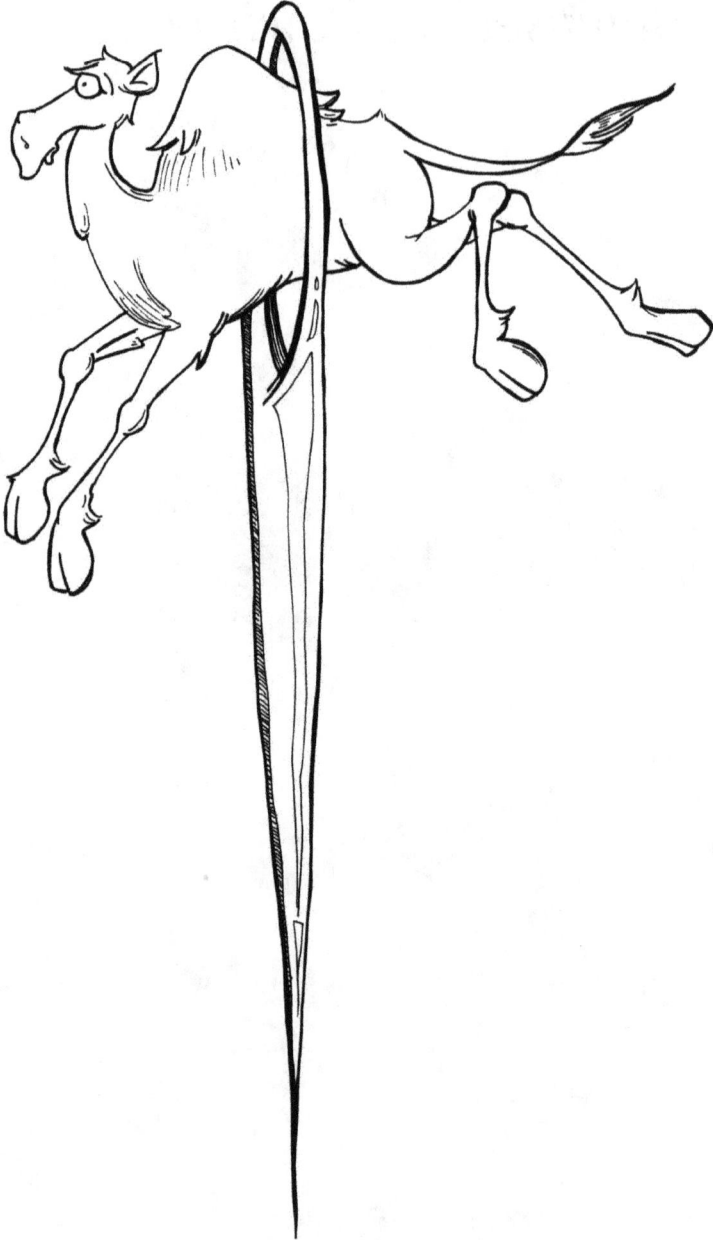

Navigating the Eye of a Needle

Introduction -

A recent internet post provides a graphic representation of the concentration of wealth within the United States. Imagine a two-dimensional martini glass with a wide but shallow bowl so that most of the "volume" is concentrated at the top. This portion represents the combined wealth of the "rich," and the less propertied classes are represented by a long narrow stem, which tapers to a fine point as it approaches the bottom. A graphic representation of income distribution would look very similar.

I must admit that such wealth and income distributions "seem" unconscionably disproportionate. However, the "rich" have always been VERY rich. The richest Americans today (*e.g.* Bill Gates, Warren Buffet, *etc.*) have fortunes, which pale in comparison to the industrialists and robber barons of yesteryear (*e.g.* Ford, Carnegie, Vanderbilt, Rockefeller, *etc.*). However, being rich should not be deemed an inherent character flaw. The Father of our Country, George Washington, was the wealthiest President by far with an estimated worth in excess of half a BILLION dollars (adjusted for inflation). Washington was obviously held in high regard despite his great wealth.

Having personally known individuals and families who would be considered "wealthy" (but not among the super-rich), I cannot say that I am envious of their wealth. With the trappings of wealth, often comes a certain loss of humanity and lack of empathy. This concept is not new or unique. Two thousand years ago, Christ admonished a wealthy man:

> *It is easier for a camel to pass through the eye of a needle than it is for a rich man to enter into the kingdom of heaven.*

However, I do not believe that the accumulation of wealth is itself a guarantee of eternal damnation. I recall the Biblical accounts of Abraham and Job, each of whom accumulated great wealth; although, that wealth was not a shield for either man to avoid the burdens and challenges of life.

It is exceedingly difficult for truly selfless and altruistic persons to become wealthy. Those with wealth tend to be driven to accumulate more wealth. Those who have a calling to serve others generally do not find motivation to accumulate wealth. There is a disconnect between the "haves" and the "have nots," which results in growing tensions. However, I am not convinced that more "evenly distributed" wealth is more efficient (or even more "equitable").

Consider, if wealth were evenly distributed among society, how long would it take for it to be "redistributed" to the current or a similar skewed pattern? Rather than equality, the issue should be one of opportunity.

Access to and Active Participation in Markets -

Historically (and in some cultures even today), opportunity was stifled by cultural norms or legal impediments based upon race, religion, caste, *etc.* As much as nearly any country, the United States today offers opportunity to a broad spectrum of persons, and those opportunities abound in what is collectively, the wealthiest society in the history of mankind.

I would ask, "If one cannot succeed in a country with minimal legal and cultural impediments and with vast accumulated resources, exactly where are opportunities any better?" If one feels that his success is stifled, what changes and expectations would he deem reasonable to alter or rehabilitate this environment?

Many, who are native to the U.S., choose to complain about what they do not have, rather than to give thanks for those things that we have in abundance. Many persons spend lifetimes in the relentless pursuit of the Joneses. Recent immigrants to this country generally have a much different perspective. Many of those immigrants spent years and sacrificed connections to loved ones and to a homeland for the opportunities afforded to them in the U.S. Compared to nearly all citizens, such persons come with the deck stacked against them.

Many immigrants entered the U.S. illegally, with no resources, and not even speaking English; nevertheless, they established themselves and built successful businesses and lives. While I am certainly not a proponent of illegal immigration, we, as Americans, should take note of the innovation, creativity, and initiative of such persons. In doing so, we may be reminded of the still present opportunities to which our ancestors were drawn decades or even centuries ago.

Popular wisdom holds that there is some book, database, or definitive mathematical formula from which to establish economic "fairness" and the "value" of any good or service.

However, goods and services have no inherent value. They only have such value as may be placed upon them by those wishing to acquire a certain good or desiring the benefit derived from a given service.

What is the value of a blacksmith in the age of automobiles or the value of a scribe in an age of near universal literacy?

The definition of Fair Market Value ("FMV") is:

The price at which a given item will be exchanged in a voluntary transaction between independent parties with neither being under any compulsion and both having the benefit of all relevant facts.

Even knowing that definition, *Caveat Emptor*, or "Buyer Beware," should be a constant mantra. There is often a desire on the part of one party or the other (perhaps both) to undertake a transaction where all of the relevant facts are not known to the other party, and some market participants attempt to actively manipulate the market.

For instance, diamonds are prized and valued the world over, but the **demand** for diamonds was artificially fostered by the world's largest supplier of diamonds, De Beers.

The touching romantic tradition of falling upon bended knee to present a bride-to-be with a diamond ring upon her engagement has no historical basis. Instead, it began as a figment of the imagination of some genius of marketing, who positioned that scene over and over again in early motion pictures and who donned the starlets in those movies with diamond studded jewelry. Those jewels then became the envy of moviegoers.

Yes, diamonds are the hardest natural substance on earth, and yes, they sparkle when they are cut and polished. However, they, relatively speaking, are not rare, and even if they were, they can be manufactured for a fraction of the cost which they command in a retail jewelry store. Why then are they so expensive?

Again, we can thank De Beers. Not only did the company spend decades artificially stimulating **demand**, but the company also controls much of the world's **supply** of gem quality diamonds. The company holds a virtual monopoly on commercially available diamonds throughout the world, and not coincidentally, the company also owns the rights to the commercial process for making diamonds.[71] It is this overt manipulation and tight control of the market that assures that the "value" (cost) of diamonds stays high.

So, what is something worth? The answer is, "Whatever someone (else) is willing to pay for it."

You believe Bill Gates has too much money? … Then do not purchase Microsoft products. You believe that Wal-Mart underpays and mistreats its employees? … Then do no patronize the store.

Never has the adage, "Put your money where your mouth is," been so apt. There is not a single product that Microsoft or Wal-Mart sells for which there is not a commercially available and viable alternative. Will shopping be as convenient? Will the product be as inexpensive? Perhaps, not; however, neither question is representative of the most salient point.

---

[71] The process was originally developed by General Electric.

If one wants low prices, those discounts come with the cost of low wages. One should ask himself, "What is better for the economy: A single $150 DVD Player or a household with three (3) $50 DVD players?" Which economy do we encourage by our actions?

As long as we, as a society, choose to shop at the lowest cost provider rather than consider quality and customer service, then we are aiding and abetting in wage disparity. If customers insisted on higher quality and better service (**and** were willing to pay for it), then Wal-Mart would have to respond in kind. Consumers and citizens cannot have their cake and eat it too.

Each of us has choices, and in the hundreds, if not thousands, of individual choices that we make each day, we have the power to alter our economic environment and circumstances. Each time one makes a purchase decision not only does he give support to the supplier of that product or the provider of that service but he also give credence to the company's business model and tacit approval of whatever shareholders choose to do with the proceeds from that transaction. Only when we fully take responsibility for our choices and own the decisions that we make can we effect positive changes in our own lives.

External Market Influences and Protections -

I believe that government has a role in protecting the integrity and fluidity of markets. From the example above, De Beers is not allowed to operate directly within the United States specifically because of its status as a monopoly.

The Sherman Antitrust Act of 1890, Glass-Steagall Banking Act of 1933,[72] and similar legislation in the U.S. were implemented to prevent companies from asserting monopoly powers, manipulating markets, or threatening economic stability. However, I am less comfortable in government taking a more active role in influencing markets. I am not confident in the benign actions of a benevolent government, and I am even less confident that government is capable of effecting an efficient and equitable reallocation of wealth.

Huey Long was a left-wing politician of the early 20th Century. He was a Governor of Louisiana and a challenger to Franklin D. Roosevelt for the Presidency prior to Long's assassination in 1935. Long adamantly advocated for government effected wealth redistribution, and he zealously proposed limits on the amount of wealth that could be accumulated by individuals.

While Long's proposals certainly had populist appeal, how would they work in practice?

How does one incentivize someone who already has $100,000,000.00 or even $10,000,000,000.00?

Should someone stop being productive once he reaches a certain level of wealth, or should society expect such a person to continue to produce and generate new wealth exclusively for the benefit of others?

---

[72] The restrictions of Glass-Steagall were watered down over the years, and the Act was effectively repealed in 1999 with passage of the Gramm–Leach–Bliley Act. The impacts, which the repeal and earlier changes had on the Great Recession, are fiercely debated.

Those who believe as Long did consider "excessive" wealth to an evil in and of itself. To such persons, wealth is a public asset, and the accumulation or hoarding of that wealth is an offense against society as a whole. Long would have no compunction about wrestling assets from wealthy persons and redistributing those assets throughout the less propertied classes. He would argue that it is not only a noble but necessary role of government.

The "Gilded Age"[73] represented a period of growth, wealth, and financial corruption, which followed the Civil War and continued through the end of 19th Century. Into the 20th Century, confidence, arrogance, and short memories gave rise to the "Roaring 20's" following the First World War. Both of these periods of excess and exuberance ended in market collapses and financial depressions.

Many of the "lessons learned" via financial reversals, such The Great Depression, and in response to the oppression of robber barons have been institutionalized in laws, regulations, and government institutions: Federal Reserve Act, FDIC, Civil Rights Act - Title VII, OSHA, EEOC, FLSA, *etc.*

While I would never argue that there is no room for improvement, the improvements that would likely be made are marginal at best. There are not likely to be wholesale systematic changes, because such changes have significant concurrent costs (to someone) with arguably marginal net collective benefits.

---

[73] The phrase, *Gilded Age*, was coined by Mark Twain for his novel of the same title.

The Realities of Class Envy -

In order to promote class envy and animosity, it has been quoted that the ratio of certain U.S. CEO's salaries to line worker wages is just shy of 500-to-1. Sure, you could take an extra $10 Million from an "overpaid" CEO or hoarding billionaire, but distributed to the country's 350,000,000 citizens that is less than 3 cents per person (< $0.03). Even seizing and redistributing $1 BILLION would be less than $3.00 / person. There simply are not enough "rich" people to make an appreciable difference.

But, what about income disparity within the companies themselves?

Five Hundred Twenty-four (524) of the world's 2,000 largest companies are headquartered in the United States (more than 1-in-4 or over 25%). Managerial talent and corporate opportunity are still concentrated in the U.S. So, it is a matter of supply and demand. If you want the best (perceived) talent, then you have to be willing to pay for it.

Of the ten (10) largest U.S. employers, the average U.S. employment is over 300,000. For every $1 Million of income paid to the CEO of such a company one could only increase the average employee wage by $3. This is not a "per hour" increase it is a single payment of Three Dollars ($3.00), which is less than the cost of a workday lunch.

In contrast, to give the same employees a $1 / hr raise would cost over $1 BILLION (with taxes and benefits). It is a matter of leverage, "Where do you get the most bang for the buck?"

There are definitely CEO's who have failed and others, who are not worth the money, but cutting their salaries does not translate into appreciable increases in income to line workers.

People complain that the CEO of Wal-Mart makes more in a single hour than a full-time Wal-Mart associate makes in an entire year. Here again, you have to consider economies of scale. The Wal-Mart CEO makes $35 Million annually (according to cited reports). According to those same reports, Wal-Mart has 2 MILLION employees. If you redistributed the CEO's salary among the employees, each would receive a single payment of $17.50.

HOW MUCH OF AN IMPACT WOULD THAT REALLY HAVE?

I personally know and have met executives in Fortune 500 companies. Most such individuals are basically good persons. They are caring and well meaning people. They have tough jobs and they make decisions regarding opportunities and consequences that the average man-on-the-street can hardly imagine.

When one is tasked with making business decisions, which can result in multi-million-dollar profit swings or which can affect thousands of jobs, those are different kinds of pressure and stress. Most of these individuals take these decisions personally. They take their work home with them every day, even after working 10-12 hours, or more.

Are these executives and managers well compensated for their services? Yes, they certainly are, but those persons with million dollar salaries and bonuses are on the far extreme of the pay scale.

I have had the opportunities to walk in their shoes, and it is not a casual stroll in the park. Are there bad apples in the bunch? Yes, just like there are bad line workers, bad retail sales people, and bad customer service operators. However, those, who are fairly called "Robber Barons," are the exceptions to the rule.

What to Do with All of that Money? -

Some persons may recall *Richie Rich* ("The Poor Little Rich Boy"), from comic books and cartoons. Dubbed the "World's Richest Kid," his family's multiple homes contained bins, silos, safes, and vaults to store vast hoards of cash and gold.

This is the life of the rich that many persons imagine. However, go into the home of almost any wealthy person, and you are unlikely to find a veritable Fort Knox. Similarly, you are not likely to wander into a lair, which is the envy of a dragon hoarding mountains of gold and jewels.

Yes, the rich have houses with luxurious appointments. They have nice cars. They may even have private jets and luxury yachts. However, the bulk of their wealth is often invested in one or more closely held businesses that they founded or run, or it is invested in securities, which represent interests in public companies.

Few "millionaires" could write a check for a million dollars. Even fewer "billionaires" could liquidate a billion dollars at will. Generating and accumulating wealth is not

273

simply a matter of wanting and wishing for it. There is effort involved, and not all persons are cut out for that line of work.

Any investment carries risk, and it is that risk which justifies the return on that investment. The most recent Great Recession clearly demonstrated the realities of risk, when millions lost their "life's savings." If the average man-on-the-street had "more," what would he do with it? Could he invest and retain it, or would it be spent and exhausted in the short term?

Economic growth comes from innovation. Innovation comes with risk. Investing, particularly in start-up companies or growth stocks, is a gamble, and the first rule of gambling is, "Never bet anything that you cannot afford to lose." By definition, the wealthy have a cushion, and they can afford to make investments and take on risks (and occasionally lose that gamble).

Redistributing wealth so that (nearly) everyone has a "nice" house and car, or some money in the bank, does not recognize the realities of life:

- What are carrying the costs of such assets?
- Can the recipient maintain the asset?
- How does government protect persons from themselves, so that they preserve the asset?
- What happens when persons exhaust or lose the asset?
- Do persons get a second bite at the apple (a third, *etc.*)?

Is there a Right Way to do Business/Wealth? -

When considering where to invest, it is important to know that there are competing business models, each with its own risks and potential rewards.

Henry Ford showed foresight and recognized the long-term benefits of pricing his vehicles for the masses rather than settling upon a niche market for the wealthy. His strategy was long-term, and the company, which he founded, is still around a century later, and it is still managed and controlled by the Ford family.

In contrast, many business leaders today are extremely short sighted. The metrics against which public company executives are measured, evaluated, and compensated have a short-term horizon (*i.e.* quarterly financials). There is a tendency, if not obligation, to maximize short-term profitability while mitigating longer term costs. Until and unless the expectations horizon can be expanded to include better accommodation of comprehensive costs (*e.g.* environmental), long-term investments, and a move away from immediate gratification, fundamental changes in the basic model are extremely unlikely.

However, it is not simply an issue of "right" and "wrong." Apple Computers became the most highly capitalized company on earth specifically by "overcharging" for its products. Apple products command a premium over other functionally similar products. Arguably, this advantage in the market cannot be held forever, and there are some indications that Apple's pricing model will likely have to change in the near term. Nevertheless, consumers still choose to purchase higher priced Apple products, even if reluctantly. It is hard to argue that such a model is "wrong," at least as to Apple and its shareholders.

Similarly, the argument that CEO pay should be limited by law to some multiple of the "average" wage of line workers has a certain appeal to one's sense of "fairness." For persons making less than six-figures, a salary of $1 Million per year sounds exorbitant.

Depending on the multiple used and how you calculate average wage, an annual salary of around $10,000,000.00 for executives is often cited as a reasonable "maximum." For the "average" CEO position, the job may be commoditized so that one minimally qualified CEO may be substituted for another minimally qualified CEO. However, relatively few CEO's are paid more than $10,000.000.00 annually,[74] and for those that are, who determines whether or not they are worth it?

I do not fault CEO's for making pay demands, I fault Boards of Directors and (Institutional) Shareholders for not being more forward thinking and more reasonable in their expectations. Nevertheless, a "law" that limits executive pay is not the right answer.

Sometimes, a distinction is drawn between what has been called "old money" and the *nouveau riche* ("newly rich"). The newly rich, by reputation, have a certain air about them demonstrated by ostentation and excess. Whereas, those with established (or God forbid, inherited) wealth may be viewed as having a sense of *noblesse oblige* ("obligation of nobility").

---

[74] Less than two hundred (200) CEO's in 2012 according to *Forbes*.

Even among "self-made" persons, we can see worthy examples of benevolence and philanthropy:

- Carnegie's 2,509 libraries, as well as Carnegie-Mellon University;

- The Gates Foundation; and

- In North Carolina, Duke University and Wake Forest University (both national caliber institutions, which were built with fortunes derived from the much maligned product, tobacco).

Regardless of whether such donations were made out of a sense of obligation, to establish a family legacy, or to assuage some guilty conscience, such gifts are some of the finest fruits borne of excess.

Four Peas in a Pod -

On issues of reasonable compensation and accumulation of wealth, consider two (2) pairs of business partners. All are worthy of legend, but in each case, one of the pair overshadows the other at least in name recognition. The first pair, Bill Gates and Paul Allen were the co-founders of Microsoft. The second pair, Steven Jobs and Steve Wozniak were the co-founders of Apple Computers. The first person in each pair is a household name. However, the "lesser" known of each pair was no less integral to the initial success of his respective company. In fact, depending upon one's belief in the corporate mythologies, their contributions may have been even more important than their more famous counterparts.

Paul Allen secured the DOS program that was the basis for Microsoft's lucrative initial contract with IBM, and Wozniak was personally responsible for developing the first two (2) generations of Apple computers. In interesting twists of fate, both Allen and Wozniak withdrew from active involvement with their respective companies in the mid-80's. (Allen contracted Hodgkin's lymphoma, and Wozniak was injured in the crash of a small plane.)

While both Allen and Wozniak are wealthy as a result of being in on the ground floor of the personal computer ("PC") revolution, the extent of that wealth is almost entirely a byproduct of the drive and determination of their co-founders, Gates and Jobs.

Bill Gates has stated previously that Microsoft is only three (3) years from obsolescence on any given day. Therefore, the company must continually innovate in order to remain viable. Steven Jobs was removed from Apple in the 1980's only to return in the late 90's to salvage the stodgy and stagnant company from near bankruptcy. All of these men could have eked out a comfortable living based on their initial successes, but they would not have been multi-billionaires.

- Should Allen and Wozniak be rewarded with "extra" billions just because they had the initial ideas and were there at the opening bell?
- Should all of these persons have stood pat, rested on the laurels from their initial successes, and risked the fate of the PC revolution to others?
- At what point should such persons no longer be rewarded for past, present, or future successes by attaining additional wealth?

- How much is a Steven Jobs type "worth" to a company like Apple Computers?

- If Steven Jobs were to have said, "Pay me $100,000,000.00, or I quit," who would have faulted Apple for paying whatever amount he commanded?

- If these persons could not be incentivized to continue to innovate, would we have had Microsoft Windows, which is on nearly every PC in the world, or Microsoft Office, the ubiquitous suite of productivity software?

- Would we have missed such technological innovations such as the iPod, iPhone, and iPad?

- Who would have undertaken the philanthropic goals of the Gates Foundation (which is also funded by others among the super rich, including Warren Buffet)?

The Least Favorite Commandment -

One of the least remembered and least favored of the Ten Commandments is the last:

> *You shall not covet your neighbor's house; you shall not covet your neighbor's wife, or his male servant, or his female servant, or his ox, or his donkey, or anything that is your neighbor's.*

After their family transformed the nation's transportation industries and built railroads, did the Vanderbilt heirs "need" to build the nation's largest private residence in the mountains near Asheville, North Carolina?[75] Those mountains, where the Vanderbilts and others summered, as well as the North Carolinas beaches are littered with second homes and vacation homes for

---

[75] In order to appreciate the scale of that undertaking, it should be noted that even today, the operation of the "Biltmore Estate" is one of the largest private companies in the state.

wealthy persons, who by any measure do not "need" those residences.

Resorts like Pinehurst, Grove Park, Hilton Head, and Greenbrier sprang up as retreats for the well-heeled. Should those communities and the persons, who live there, not be grateful and appreciative of those excesses?

When does excess become opulence and opulence become an embarrassment of riches?

There is a Chinese Proverb that translates, "Wealth does not pass three generations." I have heard something similar said, "White collar to blue collar in three generations." There are, of course, exceptions (*e.g.* Ford), but of the families, who have accumulated great wealth (much less those of more moderate wealth), how many such families remain movers and shakers for multiple generations? Are our energies best spent being envious of lives, which represent fleeting flights of fancy?

Also, consider the following:

- Why do we envy that which belongs to others?
- Why should it ever be of concern to us what property another person has, even if it dramatically exceeds that which we believe he or she "needs"?
- To whom does wealth belong?
  - o Does it belong to persons who through hard work and innovation earned it? … OR
  - o Does it belong to the government or to society in general?

- Who gets to determine what best use can be made of the billions of dollars that have been freely given by entities and individuals via market transactions?

- What about government would make it a more efficient and equitable vehicle for redistributing wealth (conceding that it is incapable of initially producing that wealth)?

- How many times can you pluck a quill from the goose that lays a golden egg before she refuses to lay any more?

Conclusion -

Necessity may be the mother of invention, but innovation and growth are spurred by greed and self-interest. Is this "right"? Who is to say? America is the wealthiest country in history. I do not believe that it is an accident that many (if not most) of the major industrial and technological milestones in the last two centuries were set in the United States. Of course, there has been innovation elsewhere, and today, more than ever, competition is fierce throughout the world for that innovation and the resulting rewards.

Nevertheless, the concentration of talent, ideas, and opportunity in the U.S. is unmatched anywhere else in the world. All of us have benefited from these economic, industrial, and technological advancements. One driving force behind that opportunity and innovation is the idea that, in the U.S., one can reap the disproportionate rewards of his own labors and successes. One is not limited to "adequate" remuneration or even "just" compensation based upon some established norm. The sky is the limit.

When wealth is wildly disproportionate, which it always has been, it is easy to think that more equal is more equitable. Rarely do we consider the personal sacrifices that many individuals make to be a "success" in a given endeavor. Even more rarely do we know the motivating factors, which mean the difference between contentment with mere competence versus a drive and commitment to succeed beyond any established measure or standard.

We see the trappings of wealth, but we do not see, or perhaps cannot even understand, the costs associated with achieving that wealth. If we considered those costs, we may not be so quick to envy the lives that the wealthy live.

***

I am for doing good to the poor, but I differ in opinion of the means. I think the best way of doing good to the poor, is not making them easy in poverty, but leading or driving them out of it. In my youth I travelled much, and I observed in different countries, that the more public provisions were made for the poor, the less they provided for themselves, and of course became poorer. And, on the contrary, the less was done for them, the more they did for themselves, and became richer.

- BENJAMIN FRANKLIN
"On the Price of Corn and Management of the Poor"
November 29, 1766.

Benjamin Franklin and Alms to the Poor

Blog Entry – June 29, 2012

The keys to a more contented life are in not defining "happiness" or measuring "success" in reference to a standard of living, which is based upon some societal "norm" or based upon what the "Joneses" have. The United States collectively has the most wealth and the most freedom ever amassed by a society. Yet, we have increasingly high levels of dissatisfaction. The envy, jealousy, and resentment feed upon themselves.

Persons should measure success in life based upon individual achievement relative to the tools, talents, and opportunities afforded to them. If individuals achieved to their own levels of ability and did not squander their skills and opportunities, nearly all arguments regarding the role of government would be moot.

One has to accept that, within a society, certain persons will fail, sometimes at their own hands and sometimes through no fault of their own. Nevertheless, such failures are not necessarily the fault of society, and it is not an obligation of society to make everyone's life smooth and without negative consequence. At some point, we began to expect that poor decisions or bad acts should have no serious consequences.

There will always be poor people. There will always be downtrodden. There will always be persons whose lives are failures by nearly any measure. Those failures should not be an indictment of society, but rather cautionary tales from which to learn and improve. Those following similar paths should expect similar failure and disappointment.

I am taken back to my reply recently to the friend, who pined over the proverbial single mother with three (3) children trying to make ends meet on minimum wage:

> *If you have never made better than minimum wage, and you do not have a stable and established home life, then you probably should not complicate that home life and financial condition by bringing a child into the picture, MUCH LESS THREE (3).*

I feel little sympathy for parents who have children that they cannot afford and are ill prepared to rear. Such parents' lives SHOULD be permanently altered, and they SHOULD be forced to forgo "the finer things in life." One should anticipate and accept the consequences for poor planning, bad decisions, and improper actions. As the adage goes, "God helps those, who help themselves."

While one may have empathy for the children, who are the spawn of such a union, one need not feel a personal obligation to impede his own life in order to correct their misfortunes and to pay for the bad decisions of their parents. Such persons should be in our prayers, and they may be the objects of our charity. Nevertheless, we should not expect that such persons would have their hands plundering through our respective pockets helping themselves to that charity.

As an individual, I recognize an obligation to assist my fellow man. However, "I" should be free to decide what that means, and "I" should be free decide who, if anyone, benefits from my efforts, labors, and resources. I do not care to have my "charity" coerced and my resources forcibly stripped from me by a supposedly benevolent government and to have the fruits of my labors used in a manner entirely inconsistent with what I would do myself.

Governments, in furtherance of some tortured concept of equality and fairness, do not have the luxury of making qualitative decisions about who should benefit from social programs. It is an uncomfortable fact of life that some persons are not worthy of charitable assistance from the government or otherwise. Efforts to or for the supposed benefit such persons often serve only to enable bad behaviors. Ultimately, such efforts buy peace of mind for persons, who need to quell some misdirected sense of obligation, but no real benefit is bestowed to either society in general or the beneficiary in particular.

Suckling on the Teat of Dependence

Blog Entry - August 27, 2013

Compassion for the weak should never be an excuse for suicide of the species. We can be compassionate while continuing to advocate ideals leading toward personal growth and enlightenment. We can be caring while challenging each other to be better and more productive individuals. However, success in any worthwhile endeavor never comes with complacency, and the goal cannot be "equality" since the only possible level of equality is founded in mediocrity.

We must recognize and accept that in life some persons, including family members, friends, and loved ones, will succumb to vice and human frailties thus causing them to fall by the wayside. In excelling as individuals, the hope is to inspire others to purposefully navigate life's difficult journey and to excel similarly.

Those who choose not to grow and excel should not be coddled and benefitted by society, as may be those, who are sincerely limited in ability and hindered by circumstances that are attributable to no fault of their own. This latter group is but a small minority, and the care of the members of this limited group is manageable by the collective.

However, many persons choose to define the group of wanting and needy so as to include all members of society, and defining it in that way will ultimately overwhelm and exhaust the capabilities and resources of the collective (*i.e.* government).

Infantilizing the whole of society does not benefit the individual or the group. It only empowers those, who would lead the pliable masses as sheep to slaughter.

Even if one chooses to view government as acting *in loco parentis*,[76] the goal of any good parent is to aid in establishing the independence and self-sufficiency of the child. No parent or child should want adult offspring to be suckling on the teat of dependence in perpetuity. Is it not time that we all grow up?

I for one would rather be left to my own devices and risk being a victim of social evolution. At least in a fair fight, those, who are among the fittest, should survive and prevail, rather than the government pampering the weak and exalting the timid.

---

[76] Meaning: To act or serve in the place or role of a parent.

Government as Patron of the Disappointed Beggar

Blog Entry – Original Post: August 17, 2012

Introduction -

Several days ago, a panhandler approached me in a parking lot, and he asked me for a couple of dollars. Instinctively, I told him that I did not have any money to spare. From almost any perspective, that statement was a lie. I had a number of bills in my pocket including several $1's, and there would have been no appreciable detriment to me had I given him a few dollars. However, from my personal experience money given to panhandlers or street beggars is rarely well spent.

I have known such persons to take handouts and spend the money directly on alcohol or cigarettes. I have had persons refuse gift cards to local restaurants when offered *in lieu* of cash. I have seen scams repeated over and over with the same pat sob story. I have even known one or two persons, who made a decent living at busy intersections (enough to keep up a vehicle and to maintain comfortable room at the local chain hotel).

Should I have felt guilt for not be being more charitable? Perhaps, but I did not. I made a decision based upon my experience, and having made that conscious and informed decision, it is one that would likely repeat routinely in the future.

Other persons may be more charitably inclined. Such persons may have readily responded to the panhandler's request out of some sense of pity or perceived obligation. Perhaps, their experiences are different than my own, or maybe they just have more faith in human nature than I am able to muster.

Regardless, the actions or experiences of other persons are unlikely to change my own behavior, and I am unlikely to change my behavior as a result of disapproval or rebuke from family, friends, or institutions (be they government or the church).

I have no particular pride or sense of satisfaction in my actions, but those actions result from a decision based upon reason and personal experience. If others, or even most persons, would respond differently, I would not expect some collection of those persons or some institutional authority to forcibly compel my charity. I am certain that no law enforcement officer is going to show up at my door with a citation, which may result in a fine and result in an involuntary contribution to that, or some other, disappointed beggar. Even the idea should seem ludicrous.

"The Greatest of These is Charity" -

Nevertheless, a very similar scenario is proposed by those, who assert that some group or class has too much wealth, as measured by some arbitrary standard, and that the government should compel, through taxes, payment into the public treasury so that moneys can be redistributed to those with a supposed need.

It is appropriate to assert that those with means have a moral obligation to give to those less fortunate. Some would argue that the concept of *noblesse oblige* is lost on the propertied classes. Literally translated it means "nobility obligated," but it may be more easily understood with the adage, "From whom much is given, much is required."

I count myself among the fortunate. At those times when I have slipped or fallen, I have always reached up to find a helping hand. In consideration of the efforts of others, I have always tried to live up to the expectations of those, who were my benefactors, whether their gifts were financial or were in the form of an encouraging word or moral support.

Additionally, I have endeavored to repay the favors of others by repeating their examples and giving freely to persons, who I felt were worthy of the gift. Some persons, who I originally believed worthy, proved that belief to have been misplaced. The accumulated successes and failures represent lessons learned. Reference can be had to the compilation of lessons, when considering whether to make such gifts in the future. Nevertheless, the ultimate decision, with whom to share my property, is my own, regardless of whether that decision is deemed (ir)rational or (im)moral by any supposedly objective standard.

The criteria by which my resources are distributed are mine to determine. I do not argue that those decisions are anything other than subjective, and I contend that process and the result are entirely appropriate. While I care not to compare my charity with that of others, I am comfortable with the nature and quantity of my contributions to other persons and to the public good.

Charity cannot be accomplished by compulsion. It must be freely given. Charity by government compulsion is nothing more than the government assuming the role of the fictional thief, Robin Hood, who stole from the rich to give to the poor.

Theft, even for supposedly noble means, is no less contemptuous.

Institutionalized Charity -

Some would argue that society has an obligation to aid the disadvantaged. This is where I make a distinction between individual morality, by which one has a duty to give aid to his fellow man, and the institution of government, which I would argue is without a moral foundation or function. Government, as I see it, has much more limited function than being utilized as a tool for implementing moral vagaries.

Individuals are free to act collectively in order to a achieve benefits of scale, through voluntary associations with either secular charities or religious institutions. However, I do not believe that it is a fundamental function of government to force charity or to compel altruism on those not so inclined.

Therefore, where persons (or a supermajority of the body politic) wish to use government as a tool through which to funnel their own monies either for their own benefit (*e.g.* Social Security) or that of others (*e.g.* welfare), that is an allowable although not fundamental function of government.

However, where non-propertied parties seek to impose their sense of "morality" on those with the means to fund their charitable aims, such is certainly NOT the proper function of government. "Society," as a class of individuals or as a voluntary collective, may take up such a mantle, but forced altruism is nothing more than theft for a "good" cause (*a la* Robin Hood). In short, I do not believe that society has an obligation to aid the "disadvantaged," if by "society" you mean a government with the power to impress the wealth of one group simply to be disseminated at the discretion of another larger or more influential group.

Government has done good things when no other entity had sufficient power to implement changes. Even those who believe in a government of limited powers would concede that such powers maybe expanded, at times, out of emergency or necessity (*e.g.* natural disaster, war, *etc.*). However, government in recent times has been staggering from crises to crises, and extraordinary actions and powers have become routine. Government powers and programs, originally implemented to address a temporary need, become bureaucratized and institutionalized. What may have been initially a good idea evolves to take on a life of its own.

The thought becomes, "If an inch was good, then a mile must be better." Benefits granted and privileges bestowed turn into birthrights and entitlements. The inalienable right to "pursue happiness" has morphed into a presumed guarantee to BE happy in whatever way an individual chooses to define such happiness and to be free from want, loss, or disappointment in nearly every area of life.

Such expectations of any society are unreasonable, and I believe that government should not be tasked with such a futile burden. I would like to be wrong. I would like to live in a Utopian society, with infinite resources, full of unlimited opportunities, and with complete freedom from want. Nevertheless, I am certain that such a society is merely a figment within the imaginations of idealists, and its existence is limited to works of fiction. In my reality, persons do not contribute to the best of their abilities; individuals' wants are not limited to their needs; and failure and loss are most often attributable to the cumulative actions (or inactions) of the individual rather than some shortcoming or failure in any system or government.

I would like to believe in collaboration and mutual benefit from government, but a collective can seldom unanimously agree how to define and pursue the "common good." In such situations, some persons are deprived of the fruits of their labors, and others enjoy a windfall thanks to government intercession.

Both presidential candidates in the most recent national election were correct in saying that the election was a mandate on the course of America. One path assures a growing government and an increasingly dependent populace. The other path interposes a view of reality that accepts unequal distribution of wealth in favor or greater independence, liberties, and personal responsibility.

Government no longer defines the "poor" as a small discernible subset of the population. Government is expanding to put nearly every citizen on the public dole. The demand on the "rich" is simply too much to bear in the long run. That does not mean that more cannot and should not be expected from the propertied classes; however, it should not be a case of throwing good money after bad. In expanding the role of government, government continues to dig a fiscal hole with a steam shovel, while taxpayers attempt to fill it with a thimble.

It is broken; So, fix it -

Government can properly be used as a tool to allow citizens to help themselves. Government should not be a crutch upon which citizens rely and which prevents persons from taking responsibility for their own lives.

Here is the distinction:

- Personally, I would prefer the opportunity to take the roughly 15% of my income that I pay toward Social Security ("SS") and Medicare, and pay it toward my own retirement, disability, health insurance, and long-term care.

  I am confident that I could make a better use and investment of those funds than I will ever receive under the existing entitlement programs (should those programs, in fact, survive the next 25, or so, years).

- However, I recognize that the average man-on-the-street likely does not have flexibility and commitment to make the same insurance and investment choices.

- For this reason, I accept the fact that I lose the freedom to make, what I would contend are better investment decisions for MY money, and allow the government to administer those funds as part of the old-age retirement programs.

- While I would argue that this is not the best decision for me personally (and further contend that, in a perfect world, all persons would be capable of making such decisions for themselves and such programs would not be necessary), I accept that for the "good of the whole" a decision was made to establish these programs, and I am willing to defer to the consensus decision that the government should establish what are generally understood as "self-funded" entitlement programs.

However, such programs were never understood to be wealth redistribution programs whereby those with greater means take it upon themselves to fund the retirements of those of lesser means. This is evident by the income cap on Social Security (whereas the Medicare cap has been removed). The objective of wealth redistribution completely changes the nature of these programs.

FDR's "New Deal" was (arguably) an effort to address legitimate societal needs growing out of the Great Depression, and it was an experiment on the scope and role of government. Some would contend that those efforts were successful in the battle to address the immediate "needs" but that the war was lost as a result of unrestrained government growth, which now threatens to cannibalize the country's economy.

The gut wrenching black-and-white pictures of undernourished barefoot children in the coal mining sections of Appalachia, which spurred economic social programs, have now morphed into full-color digital video showing a constant flow of persons and entities brawling for the privilege of gorging at the government trough.

The fix comes not from simply changing the perspective of a snapshot of economic policy today. The momentum built from decades of reckless governing has led to habitual budget deficits and an aggregate national debt (soon-to-be) bigger than the entire Gross Domestic Product ("GDP") of the U.S.

economy. Nearly all, who are involved in government, accept this as an immutable part of the *status* quo. However, *if* there is any hope of this nation retaining any level of prominence, government cannot continue to kick this can down the road. What was a ripple continues to grow into a tsunami, which will eventually crash and inundate our country.

We are no longer using economies of scale and administrative efficiencies to assist persons in doing for themselves. Instead, we are engaging in forced altruism. That was never the product that was sold to citizens. Commercials from the entitlement advocate, AARP, are replete with contentions that, "We EARNED our Social Security and Medicare." Well, if one receives benefits at a rate of 3-to-1 (as is the case with current Medicare estimates), that person has not "earned" the majority of those benefits. Retirees, almost without exception, are collecting welfare.

As a people, we have neither shown ourselves willing to limit our demands upon government to be commensurate with our actual "needs," nor have we been honest about the costs of such government programs or adequately funded our government "wish lists." Today, many Americans want reward without sacrifice.

- Is it too much to expect that persons graduate high school and devote themselves to attaining marketable skills?
- Is it too much to expect that persons live within their means rather than demand immediate gratification and insist on having all of the trappings that others around them may have?

- Is it too much to expect that individuals not have children that they are ill prepared to rear and incapable of sustaining?

- Is it too much to ask that persons not blame their positions and circumstances on others (and demand that those others remedy the same) at least until the supposed "victims" can honestly say that they have done all within their own powers to improve themselves and their respective plights in life?

The Tyranny of the Majority -

Such is a function of democracy that the majority can reap from the pockets of the minority, but that does not mean that the propertied classes have any moral obligation to empty their pockets to appease the majority's whims.

In short, the collective can agree to "pool" the assets of the collective for the benefit of the whole. However, where the result is that a dependent majority votes to seize the wealth of a reluctant minority, which receives no material benefit from the transaction, I believe such actions to be beyond the legitimate scope of (our form of) government.

There is an increasingly prevalent fallacy that our country, in fact, is a "Democracy" and that whatever the majority says is "OK," particularly when it comes to redistribution of wealth. The feeling seems to be that it is entirely appropriate for the government to take by social conscription some nebulous (but undoubtedly growing) portion of the wealth of the "haves" and redistribute that conscripted wealth to the self-defined "have nots." As long as such a taking is done by the government in the form of a "tax," there seems to be no further consideration given to the propriety or rightness of the act.

298

More accurately, our federal government is a Republic, which initially had limited enumerated powers. The stated objectives of the drafters of the Constitution were to constrain the powers of government so as to avoid tyranny. The potential source of the tyranny was not only the government itself but also from the majority of citizens collectively exercising the powers of that government. Tyranny by popular vote is no less tyrannical. The forcible taking by a controlling group or class from another for the principal benefit of those in control, even if it is called it a "tax," is institutionalized theft, regardless of whether the controlling class is the ruling elite or the unsated masses.

<u>Enough is Never Enough</u> -

We used to celebrate intellect and personal accomplishment. We used to challenge ourselves to succeed, to overcome obstacles, and to be better. We used to judge ourselves by the best that mankind had to offer. Today, we seem to be in a march toward mediocrity. Instead of working to better mankind, there is a struggle to grasp and hold onto the lowest rung on the evolutionary ladder.

There used to be respect for truth. Intellectual, religious, and social leaders devoted lifetimes in search of knowledge, wisdom, and enlightenment. Today, our supposed leaders shroud truth in self-serving lies, deliberate obfuscations, and conscious efforts to foster ignorance and pray upon naïveté.

Several years ago, the movie, *Idiocracy*, was released to neither critical acclaim nor box office success. Nevertheless, the premise of the comedy is interesting:

Two (2) exceedingly ordinary persons are placed in cryogenic stasis in order to test the process for use by the military. A series of blunders and other circumstances result in the pair remaining in stasis until they are accidentally released five hundred (500) years into the future. They awaken to a world where the less motivated and less intelligent of the human species have bred with abandon, and the species has been dumbed down to the point that the two formerly "average" individuals have the distinction of being the smartest persons on the planet. The stars of the movie stumble into taking over the ineffectual government, and they are able ultimately to save the humanity from itself.

- Will we, as a people, continue to strive and evolve to reach our potential as human beings, or will we be content to a ride a downward spiral toward mediocrity?

- Do we wish to encourage success and accomplishment among individuals?

- Or, do we, in the interest of equality, prefer to reduce all persons the lowest common denominators of society?

Let us hope that *Idiocracy* is just a low budget movie with a humorous plot, rather than a self-fulfilling prophesy about our not-too-distant future.

Some time ago, a New York City police officer was seen buying shoes for a seemingly homeless man living on the streets. Video of the incident went viral on YouTube. Days later, it was announced that the man, Jeffrey Hillman, had government housing available to him; nevertheless, he was once again on the streets and shoeless (apparently of his own choosing on both counts).

Instead of showing appreciation for the stranger's generosity, Hillman said:

I was put on YouTube. I was put on everything without permission. What do I get? ... This went around the world, and I want a piece of the pie.

I have no doubt that some persons are disadvantaged, and if given opportunities, many persons will work THEMSELVES out of a bad situation. However, the responsibility and ultimately the only power to change that situation (regardless of the opportunities afforded to someone, or the lack thereof) rests with the individual himself.

I am all for giving a helping hand, but I have offered that hand often enough to have had it, at various times, ignored, taken advantage of, and swatted away. Such lack of appreciation and personal responsibility does not mean that I will not offer that helping hand in the future; however, there is a realization that some people are beyond help, until and unless they choose to help themselves. My experience is that there are few true victims of unavoidable circumstance, and that opportunities nearly always exist to those willing to seek them out. Failure in life can nearly always be traced to repeated poor decisions by the supposed "victim" and a refusal to apply the personal talents and abilities, which we all possess.

I have no doubt that there are persons, who are aided by the efforts of those who do good works. However, there is a point of diminishing returns, and we as a society have to be able and willing to identify that point. It is irresponsible and unreasonable to throw money, effort, and resources at a lost

301

cause. Persons may disagree as to whether any human being is ever a lost cause. From my personal experience, I would answer reluctantly, "Yes, there are such persons." Perhaps, someone more selfless or more charitably inclined would answer, "No."

I admire the convictions and idealism of others. Part of me hopes that I would be proven wrong, but human history is replete with cautionary tales, which support my positions. Persons are certainly free to pursue their convictions and to reap the intrinsic and extrinsic rewards of their altruism; however, I should not be "guilted" for my supposed inaction or "lack of compassion," when my resources are to be utilized however I choose best.

The ultimate question should be whether the contemplated act is a demonstration of utility or futility. Where the answer is not abundantly clear, the benefit of the doubt should go to the person being asked to contribute his time, effort, and resources.

I recently happened upon a series of local television news reports, which originated from the Boston, Massachusetts area in 2010. The reports contain interviews with President Obama's Aunt, an illegal alien for many years, who receives public assistance. The aunt acknowledges that the President has chosen not to assist her financially, but Obama has no trouble repeatedly picking the pockets of taxpayers to pay for some nebulous common good. According to the President (and those similarly aligned), taxpayers are supposed to give unquestioningly to governments in order to pay for inefficient and bloated government entitlement programs, but the President apparently feels no personal obligation to take some of his millions to support his Aunt.

- Should charity not begin at home?
- What example is Obama giving to Americans?
- Is this an example of, "Do as I say, not as I do"?

I have no issue with Obama not "taking her to raise." I too have family members and friends, who I reluctantly have decided not to assist financially for various reasons. However, I also am not out preaching to the rest of society that THEY should contribute toward the financial well being of those to whom I have chosen not to bestow my charity.

During the TV interviews, Obama's Aunt echoes the sentiments of many persons within and outside of the U.S.: The "government" owes me a particular standard of living, and I am "entitled" to something from a system into which I have never meaningfully contributed. However, every benefit and windfall that government grants to one person has to be wrestled from the increasingly reluctant hands of someone who produced and earned those tax dollars.

For those who would argue that we should be prepared to assist those that fall on "hard times," the bigger problem is that for some people "hard times" represent a way of life. Like government in recent times, many persons catapult themselves from crisis to crisis. While some of these crises may be *force majeure*,[77] the vast majority of the "woes," which befall

---

[77] Meaning: An unexpected and disruptive event that may operate to excuse a party from a contract (*e.g.* Act of God).

individuals are ultimately of their own creation (or could have been entirely avoided by reasonable due diligence).

At some point, you have to say, "You made your bed. Now, go and lie in it." Unfortunately, government is incapable of making those subjective decisions, and many persons, who advocate providing government benefits and services to the "downtrodden," are often excused from personally providing the financing and resources for those government programs.

There can be no altruism without selflessness, and there is no selflessness without personal sacrifice. Of course, anyone would eagerly support everyone (including themselves) having each need and wish fulfilled so long as someone else is bearing the burden and footing the bill.

The Deaths of Self-reliance and Self-sufficiency -

What scares me is the ease and haste in which we, as a people, have lost the desire and pride of self-sufficiency and how it has become second nature to kneel before the almighty government as our lord and savior. With comfort, comes complacency. With perceived safety, comes loss of freedom. We are destroying America in a way that no foreign enemy ever could. Government is not benevolent; it is a purveyor of power and a consumer of riches. With the increase in that power, the corruption of those riches becomes ever more certain.

INDIVIDUALS have morals. Individuals have an obligation to live godly lives. Institutions (including governments and institutionalized religion) have no inherent morality. They are only as moral as their constituent members.

The institution is incapable of instilling or enforcing a prescribed morality in the lives of its members.

In fact, morality by government enforcement social mores is detrimental to the advancement of the species. As the role of government (or religious institutions) expands to define a universal morality for society, the individual members are thereby relieved of personal morality. Instead, they follow by rote the rules established for them without internalizing the "rightness" (or wrongness) of their actions.

Some individuals do succeed in achieving a level of self awareness and spiritual enlightenment; however, there are fundamental human traits that are not likely to be bred or educated out of the species, as a whole (*e.g.* selfishness and self-preservation). Those traits, therefore, will remain inherent to government (and other institutions). The remedies are to advance the development of individuals, to promote a personal morality, and to limit the powers of institutions so that they do not infringe unnecessarily on the rights, freedoms, and liberties of the individual.

Do these things assure equality? They certainly do not. However, I would argue that the results are more equitable than anything that could ever be effected by government fiat.

Conclusion -

Government should NOT have a significant role in the everyday lives of citizens. Government should be a fail-safe to address systematic problems not individual whims. In a more perfect world, interactions with government would be the exception rather than the rule. Government should be a forum of last resort rather than the default for every issue that can possibly befall mankind.

So long as government provides a means whereby the lazy, inept, and reckless among us can demand a self-defined "reasonable" standard of living without taking responsibility for their own lives and without contributing their fair shares to the mix, the pool of consumers will grow exponentially while the pool of producers dries up.

The Mother of Invention, being Necessity, should spawn innovation and self-reliance. Social Darwinism dictates that some (perhaps many) will fall by the wayside. The rest of society would benefit from the cautionary tales that these losses would provide, and society as a whole should not be burdened by the dead weight of those who fail to help themselves.

Otherwise, we all succumb *en masse* to labors that would make Atlas shrug.[78] There needs to be a "new normal" where government is NOT so instrumental in the everyday lives of its citizens. Individuals should succeed, and yes fail, on their own merits, or (mis)fortunes, not with government playing guardian, savior, and scapegoat.

---

[78] Yes, I know that I am mixing my metaphors of mythological gods.

Lessons from Hurricanes Isaac and Sandy:
"Enough is never enough."

Blog Entry – Original Post: September 4, 2012

During 2012's Hurricane Isaac, the levees surrounding New Orleans held to protect the city thanks to the billions of dollars, which were spent by federal, state, and local governments to improve the extensive levee system. This is important for a city, which is essentially built in the bottom of a bowl with sections of the city some twenty (20) feet BELOW sea level.

Whether you call that area of the country the Mississippi Delta, Bayou Country, a flood plain, or swamp, there is one thing for certain ... IT IS WET THERE. More importantly, with a major hurricane event ... THESE AREAS ARE GOING TO FLOOD.

Immediately after the hurricane, those living outside of New Orleans were demanding MORE levees and MORE defenses against Mother Nature. They say, "Yes, it has flooded here before, but never like THIS." Did we learn nothing from Hurricane Katrina?

Here is a thought:

We can demolish the Rocky Mountains ... Truck all the rubble to Louisiana, Mississippi, Alabama, *etc.*, and we can pick up the ground level of the flood-prone states to ... Let's say ... a couple hundred feet above the pesky ocean tides and the flooding Mississippi River. I am sure that will be an effective and efficient use of government and taxes.

No ... it is arrogant to believe that one can tame Mother Nature ...

Here is better thought:

Both acknowledge and plan for the eventuality that your house is going to be flooded ... OR ... MOVE OUT OF THE FLOOD PLAIN.

After late-season Hurricane Sandy hit the Northeast, there were complaints about the speed and efficiency of the recovery efforts. However, reports regarding those efforts hardly showed inaction or inattentiveness.

One report said:

> *As of Sunday, the Red Cross was sheltering some 3,700 people and had delivered more than 4.8 million meals or snacks, and more than 477,000 relief items. ... But, Fran Menchini, 79, who plans to engage a private contractor to clean her flooded home in Breezy Point, said she does not think the Red Cross had anything to offer her, "I saw them up at FEMA (a claim center outside Breezy Point). ... What would they do?* <u>*Were they offering anything? No. I need services, I don't need them to give me coffee.*</u>*"*
> [Emphasis added.]

As a people, we have replaced understanding, personal responsibility, and self-reliance with dependence, complaining, and finger pointing. Persons build shore-hugging houses on a spit of sand, and those homeowners question, "How could it be that my house was washed away with the hurricane induced tides?"

Hurricane Sandy was a once-in-a-generation storm (NOT in a century). It should have been anticipated, yet people complain when the devastation is not completely gone with the light of day. There is a reason that these things are called natural DISASTERS. Otherwise, they would be called, "Weather-related minor inconveniences."

Reports say, "FEMA didn't do this" ... "The RED CROSS didn't do that" ... and ... "The local government didn't do the other!" The more appropriate question should be, "What did YOU do to take care of yourself and to plan for your own well being and that of your family, friends, and neighbors?"

As a result of the recent Fiscal Cliff legislation, the government increased tax revenues by approximately $60 BILLION ($600 Billion over 10 years). In the same month, Congress appropriated more than $50 BILLION in "Hurricane Sandy Relief."

During the debates leading up to this additional spending, Congressman Cory Gardner (R-CO) defended the bipartisan effort by the Colorado Congressional delegation to add to the emergency bill $125 Million for watershed protection and flood mitigation, including about $20 Million for areas in *Colorado* burned by last summer's wildfires.[79]

The sentiment seems to be, "I've suffered a(ny) loss, and the government must pay;" therefore, enough is never enough.

---

[79] NBC News – January 15, 2013.

AMERICAN EDUCATION TODAY:[80]

Down to One "R" and Shrinking

© 2012

As Christmas presents were being opened, the young girl was asked by her father from whom she received a gift. The eleven-year-old sixth grader looked at the cursive script on the tag, and being perplexed, she eventually handed it to her father to read. The problem was NOT in the quality of the penmanship on the gift tag. Instead, it was acknowledged that the child, despite being a good student in one of the "better" local schools, CANNOT READ CURSIVE WRITING.

Surprisingly, her situation is not unique, and another parent confirmed that her child also cannot read or write in cursive. The children are not illiterate. However, our education system has opted to highlight digital communications and to remove emphasis from one of the basic "R's" of education: Reading, wRiting, and aRithamatic.

Ignoring for the moment that we have a new generation of students, who can barely sign their own names and whose handwriting makes them appear illiterate, where are children supposed to learn the hand-eye coordination and fine motor skills that come from learning to write?

Thank goodness for abstract art. Instead of a generation of DaVincis, Michelangelos, and Rembrandts, we will have, at best, budding Picassos, or at worst, a bunch of cave men drawing stick figures.

---

[80] An edited version of this essay appeared as a Letter to the Editor in the *Star-News* (January 1, 2013).

I am certain that the arguments in reply would be along the lines of, "We have to prioritize what we teach," or "Writing isn't important anymore."[81] What is being taught in 2nd and 3rd grades, which is such a monumental undertaking and of the utmost importance that it should be deemed necessary and prudent to squeeze out writing? It certainly is not: Calculus, Molecular Biology, Quantum Physics, or Mandarin.

Grade school is meant to provide a foundation, upon which later learning can be built. Yet, that already precarious foundation continues to erode.

Could it be that our education system is so bogged down teaching to the lowest common denominator that we are losing and stifling the potentials of more apt students? Or, is it that our teachers are tasked and burdened with "teaching to the (end-of-grade) tests" in order to meet some ill-conceived federally established standard of conformity?

It is as if we, as a society, are trying to fill our children's minds with amorphous globs of information without any consideration being given for the quality and benefit of that information. We are attempting to fill the vessel without that vessel being properly molded and formed. When one fails to shore up the foundations of learning, he can hardly expect that those things, which are built upon those flimsy foundations, will be lasting and strong.

In this so-called "information age," persons often mistake access to data and information as being the equivalents of

---

[81] See "The Case against Cursive," *Bloomberg* (September 17, 2013).

personal knowledge and wisdom. Data and information are nothing but garbage and noise, unless persons have the tools to utilize that information and act upon it. Stagnant information is of little benefit unless we use our accumulated knowledge to inspire creativity and free thought.

There is a thought experiment known as the "Big Book." The idea being that a book (database) could be compiled with all information so that, by memorizing the book, one could attain factual omniscience. However, in knowing all "facts," one does not address (much less answer definitively) fundamental questions or ethics and morality. Today, persons equate universal access to information with practical knowledge, or more even more troubling, it is often equated to wisdom. If "a little information is a dangerous thing," then the incessant noise created by an unrestrained and unfiltered flow of information is deafening if not debilitating

To borrow a phrase from computing, "Garbage In equals Garbage Out." A computer is only as good as the underlying software, which provides access to information and allows the user to manipulate vast amounts of data. Today, a near instantaneous Google search can give access to all of the works of Shakespeare. However, that information is of no use if the words on the page fall deafly upon the reader or if the beauty and passion of those words are lost because the reader does not possess the tools, which are necessary for appreciation. Similarly, the vast amounts of information that our children have at their fingertips is useless if they do not have the tools to comprehend and make use of what is being presented.

Today, the tool being lost is cursive writing. Previously, math lost importance as calculators and more recently computers have become ubiquitous in classrooms. Technology makes our lives easier, but it does not necessarily make us better or more able persons. Technology allows us to survive while being less capable and less self-sufficient.

Rather than being used as tools to foster and enable learning, these things often serve as crutches and poor substitutes for true knowledge and learning. Calculators and computers have dulled our abilities to perform basic math functions. Who needs that ability to do math when a calculator is close as hand?

When next you are standing in a retail queue anxiously watching your cashier struggling to make change, remember that such a person is a (by)product of today's system of education.

Who knows? … With the growth of speech-to-text software applications, reading may eventually become obsolete as well. And, this is progress?

Celebrity ... A Love-Hate Relationship

Blog Entry - February 16, 2012

On the morning news, the issue was raised as to whether it was appropriate to lower flags in New Jersey to half staff in memory of the singer, Whitney Houston. The expressed "concern" was that this demonstration of respect may be inappropriate due of Whitney's struggles with substance abuse and addiction (as well as the uncertainty as to what roles these things may have played in her death).

While the question may be legitimate, some persons seemed all too eager to highlight Whitney's human failings and to describe how they tarnished her image as an accomplished recording artist.

Much of the commentary seemed akin to a *Jerry Springer* mentality. Springer's television show allows most viewers to feel good about themselves because those viewers can celebrate the "success" that comes from not being on the lowest rung of the evolutionary ladder. Similarly, people often take perverse pride in tearing down artists, celebrities, and figures of authority. In doing so, the accuser or agitator takes solace in saying, "See ... they're no better than me."

Yes, Michael Phelps smokes pot. Tiger Woods cheated on his wife. Whitney and Bobby embarrassed themselves on reality TV. Lance Armstrong and a host of professional athletes have been punished and even banned from their respective sports for using performance enhancing drugs and procedures.

The list of celebrities who have succumbed to their own fame and success could fill volumes: Marilyn Monroe, Kurt Cobain, Amy Winehouse, Elvis Presley, Jimi Hendrix, Janis Joplin, *etc.*

From the standpoint that such targets of ridicule are human beings complete with the failings and foibles that come from being mortal, they are, in fact, "just like everyone else." However, life should not be measured by the lowest common denominator.

Lives should be measured by successes and achievements that come from hard work and commitment, despite inevitable shortcomings and adversity. No, we should not celebrate failings, but neither should we ignore genuine achievements. We should learn from the former and strive toward the latter.

Where one dedicates his or her life to pursue a skill or passion to the exclusion of nearly every other part of his or her life, it should be expected that some other areas of that person's life would come up short of expectations. In life, success and achievement come only with sacrifices and trade-offs.

We can debate whether such singleness of purpose is a good thing, but so long as society insists on continuously raising the hurdles of success and defining achievement in narrow terms, we should expect that extreme sacrifices will be made and costs incurred by persons, who strive to reach the brass ring.

However, we should contrast artists, who have notable accomplishments and demonstrable talents, to a relatively new cohort of celebrities, who are famous (or often infamous) merely as a result of notoriety. For this latter class of persons, society can shoulder the full blame for placing such persons on the pedestal of celebrity.

While having my morning coffee, the *Today Show* featured an interview with two (2) of the Kardashians, whose apparent claims to fame are being the (step)children of famous persons. Those persons being: The attorney, Robert Kardashian, who defended O.J. Simpson against charges that Simpson murdered his wife and a male companion, and the U.S. athlete, Bruce Jenner, who won the gold medal in the Decathlon at the 1976 Montreal Olympics. At best, the Kardashian children should be considered "celebrity adjacent" or hangers on.

I was trying to draw an analogy to the experience of watching the broadcast. I settled on a comparison to removing my own healthy appendix. Yes, it is a vestigial organ. I can easily live without it, but forcing myself through the pain, agony, and extreme discomfort of removing the appendix without the benefit or a qualified surgeon or anesthesia is as impossible to justify as the vacuous celebrity exemplified by the Kardashians.

Just as a part of me would die from the self-imposed procedure, I wasted a part of my own life by watching the train wreck that is their lives.

It is appropriate that we celebrate the artistry and passion. We may even envy the trappings of success and celebrity. However, we rarely consider what it is really like to BE these persons.

We rarely consider how accurately the mantle of "tortured artist" applies or how much of the individual can be voraciously consumed by the public. No, these persons are not perfect, but we must all take some responsibility for making them who they are. After all, without the spotlight that we shine on them, they would not have grown to be the subjects of our admiration and ridicule.

Bitterness not cured by Butter and Bacon

Blog Entry - July 3, 2013

Paula Deen disclosed in a deposition related to an employment discrimination lawsuit that years earlier she used a racial slur under trying and stressful circumstances. For this admission, she was castigated in the media, lost numerous sponsors, and the release of a cookbook was delayed by her publisher.

I have never considered myself a "fan" of Paula Deen. Like many "celebrities" today she is famous for being famous rather than for any particular talent or unique ability. She is a southern cook, who uses recipes similar to ones, which were ubiquitous in the kitchens of millions of our grandmothers.

Were persons upset because her true persona perhaps does not match her practiced façade or "brand"? Well duh, that revelation was inevitable. She is a human being after all. She is not the love child spawned by an advertising agency and a public relations firm. Close scrutiny will inevitably reveal cracks in anyone's delicate porcelain veneer. When the public is complicit in placing celebrities on an unstable pedestal, it should not come as a surprise when such persons fall from that precarious perch.

I do find it interesting that most of the uproar came not from Deen's fans, but from people, who were likely already dismissive of Deen and her cooking. The cracks in her façade have been pried apart and widened by persons well outside the target demographic of Deen's restaurants and the products that she endorsed. Such persons almost certainly would never purchase her cookbooks or dare to step foot in her butter infused eateries. I am sure that these persons can take great satisfaction and comfort that they and their own celebrity heroes are so much better than Paula Deen.

After weeks of rebuke and castigation of Deen, the lawsuit against Deen was dismissed with prejudice. The court ruled that the Plaintiff lacked standing to bring the lawsuit ostensibly on behalf of other persons, who may have been damaged by the alleged acts. Admittedly, the dismissal of the lawsuit does not mean that some (or even most) of the allegations of unfriendly actions, crass behavior, and harsh words may not be true.

However, contrary to popular belief, there is no law that says everyone (or even anyone) has to be nice to you, and there is no cause of action for having your delicate sensibilities offended. Few very successful people and persons in authority got there because they are nice people and the salt of the earth. The adage, "Nice guys finish last," exists for a reason. I am not saying that everyone should go around being difficult and antisocial, but entrepreneurs do not usually get very far in business by treating employees like many parents do their petulant five-year-olds and continually begging "please" and "pretty please."

If one thinks that his boss is a horse's ass, he should get another job. If one wants to work for a successful business or company, then he should expect that the founder or owner of that business got there by doing things his way. If one thinks that he can do it better, then he should start his own business.

I'm Fat and It's Your Fault

I realize that I am late to the party about the CEO of Abercrombie and Fitch (A&F) discouraging persons of certain bodily proportions from shopping in A&F stores; nevertheless, I MIGHT could understand the uproar if we still depended upon a local General Store for all of our consumer purchases.

If our opportunities were strictly limited to the supply from that single source, then it would be reasonable to expect the proprietor of that establishment to address the needs of consumers (but not necessarily their wants and whims). Thankfully, I do not see any morbidly obese persons running around naked in the streets for want of clothing stores.

Today, we have 100's of boutique and specialties stores (not to mention online suppliers). We have stores for: Big & tall, young & trendy, children, the pregnant, professional clothiers, and yes the unreasonably skinny.

There are stores where I know that neither the style nor the sizing will suit me. I do not complain about the inventory (or lack thereof). I just do not shop there.

While rude and crude may justify rebuke, offense to one's overly sensitive ego does not justify lawsuits and boycotts. It often seems that many persons eagerly seek out things about which to object and complain. Few of us spend enough time showing appreciation for the many options and opportunities that are afforded us each day. It is sport to tear down the popular and strong in favor of the lazy and mediocre. Rather than complaining that others have it so easy, we would all be better served by making the most of what we have.

WHEN IS A TIP NOT A GRATUITY?

Blog Entry - August 1, 2013

NFL Football Player, Drew Brees, was castigated in social media after it was reported that he gave a $3 TIP on a nearly $75 TAKE OUT order. Why would anyone EXPECT a GRATUITY on a takeout order (or at any non-full-service restaurant ... *e.g.* Fast Food, Coffee Shop, Doughnut Shop, Ice Cream Parlor, *etc.*)? And, do not even get me started on the inconsistent traditions and expectations for the host of other service providers: Hair stylists, cab drivers, valets, doormen, *etc.*

Menu items are priced by the restaurant, and the consumer makes a purchase decision based upon whether he deems that price reasonable. As a proprietor, one is free to charge whatever price he thinks appropriate to cover costs and to provide a profit. Thereafter, the customer will decide whether he is willing to pay the established price for the product (and any associated services), but the business owner should not "hide" part of HIS overhead ("OHD") costs (*i.e.* labor) in a presumed TIP.

Persons may point out that the wait staff in restaurants is often paid a reduced Minimum Wage, and persons may use this fact in arguing in favor of freely bestowing or increasing the amount of a gratuity.

For the record, I do not believe that there should be a separate "Server's Minimum Wage" (or Tipped Employee Minimum Wage ... since such a reduced wage can apply to many employees, "who regularly and customarily receive tip income"). Again, the presumption of a tip merely encourages the business owner to manipulate his business model by hiding

323

part of the purchase price and moving some of his labor and OHD costs "off the books." If there is a Minimum Wage, then it should apply across the board.

Nevertheless, a "gratuity" is:

A gift of money, over and above payment due; or something given without claim or demand.

It is a "gift." It is NOT part of the purchase price. I understand if a restaurant would prefer that patrons pay the restaurant's employees "under the table," but it is the OWNER'S responsibility to pay a reasonable wage. Similarly, it is the employee's decision whether to work there for the wage being paid by the employer.

Although we have been conditioned to believe that we "owe" 15% (or as much as 25%) of the price of the meal (and dessert, drinks, *etc.*) as a gratuity, it may be useful for everyone to recall that in many countries, including most European countries, tipping is neither obligatory nor generally expected.

A TIP is something that one EARNS for EXCEPTIONAL personal service. It is not something that someone gets for handing a customer food across a counter, when that is the only means of obtaining the product from the provider.

HOA action may have been Wrong
but didn't affect a Right[82]

Blog Entry – February 25, 2013

An article on the Front Page of in the *Star-News* [02/25/2013] described the actions of residents to reverse a decision of the Rivermist Homeowner's Association ("HOA"). The article reports that the HOA voted to preclude the use of the subdivision's amenities center by political or religious groups.

I will defer to the residents as to the accuracy of their descriptor, "evil," as applied to the actions of the HOA. However, the article contains not less than three (3) statements that the decision of the HOA to limit the uses of its amenities center was somehow a violation of the "rights" of the residents. Admittedly, the writer of the article couched the repeated references as being the statements or opinions of the offended residents, but the writer also did nothing to dissuade the erroneous beliefs of these persons.

While I can appreciate why the residents would oppose the actions of the HOA, those actions were described as un-American and infringements on the First Amendment rights guaranteed by the Constitution. The 1st Amendment states in its entirety:

> *Congress shall make no law respecting an establishment of religion, or prohibiting the free exercise thereof; or abridging the freedom of speech, or of the press; or the right of the people peaceably to assemble, and to petition the Government for a redress of grievances.*

---

[82] An edited version of this essay appeared as a Letter to the Editor in the *Star-News* (March 3, 2013).

The Amendment is a limitation on the powers of the federal government, and by extension through the 14th Amendment, it applies to the states. However, the 1st Amendment has absolutely no application to communications or association between private parties. There is no constitutional guarantee to an audience or forum for one's desired speech, and there is certainly no guarantee that anyone will agree with what is being said.

Similarly, there is no right to have everyone be nice to you or that all persons adhere to your concepts of right and wrong. While I can appreciate the successful efforts to persuade their fellow homeowner's to be sympathetic to their cause and to ultimately prevail upon the HOA to change its position, the article does a disservice to the reader by implying that the actions were anything more than resolving a difference of opinion. Implying that some constitutional right had been violated was nothing short of sensationalism.

"Imagine" by John Lennon

Blog Entry - September 16, 2013

A friend posted a whimsical retelling of John Lennon's classic song, "Imagine." The "sentiments" of the song are things, which each of us should keep in our hearts. We should all keep in mind the possibilities that can brought about by hope and caring. Such lofty sentiments should provide a gauge and point of reference for actions and behaviors. Like all other ideals, however, those which inspired the song should be recognized as practically unattainable by mortal beings.

Mankind has always faced life with limitations of resources, and I do not anticipate that circumstance changing until we develop *Star Trek* style replicators to provide our necessaries and to fulfill our whims. With existing limitations, there will continue to be competitive markets, theft, corruption, and wars, in order to obtain, secure, and distribute limited commodities. Doling out such resources, whether they be wealth, fossil fuels, weapons, *etc.* is a source of power, and power is a vice, which is not easily overcome, regardless of whether the power mongers are corporations or governments.

I can certainly quibble with some concepts within Lennon's song. For example, I believe that religion and countries have places in human society. One may argue that religion is the "opiate of the masses," but some vices are beneficial in preventing "addictions" to more damaging (and damning) vices. Until and unless human beings are born with an innate sense of right and wrong, then there must be some institutional history (some would say mythology) within which to teach those concepts.

However, where such teachings take on a fundamentalist tack or the resulting institutions become destructive, the medicine may be worse than the disease. Lennon's song tends to intimate that the disease continues because a treatment exists. I prefer to take the perspective of "everything in moderation."

Similarly, with the concepts of "tribe" or country, it would be nice to think of human beings as being a single "family." However, unless there is universal acceptance of that concept and mutuality of commitment and joint obligations toward the good of the collective, one must acknowledge that his sphere of influence is much more limited. Therefore, by necessity (due to limited resources) persons are better served by focusing on matters "closer to home." The focus should be more like "as for me and my house" before "town and country" and before "for the good of humanity."

One should listen to the song in the context of its time. It was written in a time of wonder, opportunity, and idealism. I believe that such idealism is good. Otherwise, we get stuck in the "realism" of the *status quo*. I believe that such sentiments force us to ask, "Why can it not be done THIS way?" ... "Why is this NOT possible?"

Reality and practicality may provide very real and immutable answers to those questions; nevertheless, the exercise of asking those questions often provides an opportunity to challenge and change an imperfect reality. It is safe to say that Lennon believed in an achievable if not inherent, "goodness" within humanity.

I believe that mankind is an inherently selfish being and that only in exercising reason and intellect can the individual proceed beyond the more base state of being of the species. However, I also believe that mankind has an obligation to strive toward a higher and better state rather than accepting that the base state is the state of being, which the species is condemned to remain.

Our forefathers were what I would call, "Rational Idealists," and they provided a model that I endeavor to follow. Benjamin Franklin demonstrated this point when he said:

> *In these sentiments, Sir, I agree to this Constitution, with all its faults, — if they are such; because I think a general Government necessary for us, and there is no form of government but what may be a blessing to the people, if well administered; and I believe, farther, that this is likely to be well administered for a course of years, and can only end in despotism, as other forms have done before it, when the people shall become so corrupted as to need despotic government, being incapable of any other.*

Most philosophies and forms of government tend to work well so long as everyone is "equal." By this, I do not mean "equal under the law." Instead, I mean "homogenous," without individuality. If everyone had the same moral base, financial standing, advancement opportunities, work ethic, and commitment to the collective, then "evil" would not exist and any government (or no government) would suffice.

However, so long as there is a single person (or group) with non-conforming intentions and with control of limited resources and/or power, then such a Utopian ideal is impossible.

Additionally, one must realize and accept that the pursuit of such an ideal is not universal among mankind. We are not homogenous. Our wants and needs differ significantly between persons, castes, peoples, and nations. If one applies Maslow's Hierarchy of Needs, then it is easy to accept that a man, who is starving, rarely is concerned about self-actualization, the arts, and the finer points of philosophy.

Any workable philosophy (or government) has to accept and deal with an imperfect humanity, which has disparate wants, needs, and aspirations. Therefore, I believe that an effective government (or philosophy) focuses on the advancement of individuals not the collective.

From my experience, failure comes most often not from encountering an insurmountable wall. Rather, it comes from being unwilling to take the next, or even the first, step, which may be necessary to walk around an obstacle.

Particular individuals excel in reference to their specific talents and opportunities, and such persons provide exemplars for society to follow. However, I do not see the whole of humanity making a significant evolutionary shift *en masse*[83] toward enlightenment, at least not within our lifetimes.

I have no problem with persons dreaming of Utopia (regardless of how one may define that setting for himself and realizing that any ideal locale may have a population of exactly one). Nevertheless, we must all be prepared and properly tooled to live in our singular reality. Reality, whether one believes it to be preordained, haphazard, fortuitous, unfortunate or

---

[83] Meaning: "In a mass" – Movement all together as a group.

inconvenient, has a momentum that is not easily swayed. We may be able to nudge that collective reality on a more opportune and productive path, but it is unlikely that any person or group can make it change course completely.

Imagine

You may say I'm a dreamer but I'm not the only one,
I hope someday you'll join us, and the world will live as One.   John Lennon

Primum non nocere.
First, do no harm.

A Perspective on Abortion from Someone who Should Know

Blog Entry – February 24, 2012

What follows is an excerpt from a lady that, as a newborn, survived a botched abortion. Rarely, could we ever know the story from the perspective of the aborted fetus. One can never say that there can be only one such perspective. Nevertheless, when a human being, who was intended to be disposed of as medical waste, says, "I'm happy to be alive," the rest of us should take notice:

My name is Gianna Jessen. I am 19 years of age. I am originally from California, but now reside in Franklin, Tennessee. I am adopted. I have cerebral palsy. My biological mother was 17 years old and seven and one-half months pregnant when she made the decision to have a saline abortion. I am the person she aborted. I lived instead of died.

Fortunately for me the abortionist was not in the clinic when I arrived alive, instead of dead, at 6:00 a.m. on the morning of April 6, 1977. I was early, my death was not expected to be seen until about 9 a.m., when he would probably be arriving for his office hours. I am sure I would not be here today if the abortionist would have been in the clinic as his job is to take life, not sustain it. Some have said I am a "botched abortion", a result of a job not well done.

There were many witnesses to my entry into this world. My biological mother and other young girls in the clinic, who also awaited the death of their babies, were the first to greet me. I am told this was a hysterical moment. Next was a staff nurse who apparently called emergency medical services and had me transferred to a hospital.

I remained in the hospital for almost three months. There was not much hope for me in the beginning. I weighed only two pounds. Today, babies smaller than I was have survived.

A doctor once said I had a great will to live and that I fought for my life. I eventually was able to leave the hospital and be placed in foster care. I was diagnosed with cerebral palsy as a result of the abortion.

My foster mother was told that it was doubtful that I would ever crawl or walk. I could not sit up independently. Through the prayers and dedication of my foster mother, and later many other people, I eventually learned to sit up, crawl, then stand. I walked with leg braces and a walker shortly before I turned age four. I was legally adopted by my foster mother's daughter, Diana De Paul, a few months after I began to walk. The Department of Social Services would not release me any earlier for adoption.

I have continued in physical therapy for my disability, and after a total of four surgeries, I can now walk without assistance. It is not always easy. Sometimes I fall, but I have learned how to fall gracefully after falling 19 years.

I am happy to be alive. I almost died. Every day I thank God for life. I do not consider myself a by-product of conception, a clump of tissue, or any other of the titles given to a child in the womb. I do not consider any person conceived to be any of those things.

I have met other survivors of abortion. They are all thankful for life. Only a few months ago I met another saline abortion survivor. Her name is Sarah. She is two years old. Sarah also has cerebral palsy, but her diagnosis is not good. She is blind and has severe seizures. The abortionist, besides injecting the mother with saline, also injects the baby victims. Sarah was injected in the head. I saw the place on her head where this was done. When I speak, I speak not only for myself, but for the other survivors, like Sarah, and also for those who cannot yet speak....

Today, a baby is a baby when convenient. It is tissue or otherwise when the time is not right. A baby is a baby when miscarriage takes place at two, three, four months. A baby is called a tissue or clumps of cells when an abortion takes place at two, three, four months. Why is that? I see no difference. What are you seeing? Many close their eyes....

The best thing I can show you to defend life is my life. It has been a great gift. Killing is not the answer to any question or situation. Show me how it is the answer.

There is a quote which is etched into the high ceilings of one of our state's capitol buildings. The quote says, "Whatever is morally wrong, is not politically correct." Abortion is morally wrong. Our country is shedding the blood of the innocent. America is killing its future.

All life is valuable. All life is a gift from our Creator. We must receive and cherish the gifts we are given. We must honor the right to life.

***

In the course of an online discussion concerning the platforms of political parties, I offered the above statement in support of my personal position on the issue of abortion. My argument continued:

It is rather unfortunate that the affected fetus does not have a vote, which can be courted. I think that the abortion issue should be decided certainly not by men, as a limited class, and not by the women, whose rights to privacy and liberty are so zealously protected by [Pro Choice advocates]. Rather, the arbiters of this debate should be the living human beings, who survived botched late-term abortions. Let us take a straw poll among those persons and ask them a simple question, "Would you rather be dead or alive?"

I was originally challenged to offer a single example of a person, who having faced near certain death as a fetus, survived and expressed a preference to live the life afforded to her.

Gianna Jessen's story was available to anyone with a single Google search. That search led to what is to me a very convincing and moving story of life, struggle, and survival. Others would argue however that one example is not enough, and they would demand more proof.

A second Google search readily identifies stories of other persons, who have experienced similar fates, but would ten (10) be enough? ... 100? ... 1,000?

One can also identify statements and videos of nurses, who have assisted in late-term abortions. These nurses describe quite graphically the efforts of the fetus struggling for breath and fighting for life. The idea that such "appendages" can be ripped from their mothers' wombs and be left to die such horrific deaths turns my stomach. Most of us would have more sympathy and compassion for a wild woodland creature struck by a car on the highway than is evident in such procedures.

Hearing and seeing these things produces a visceral reaction in me. If they do not do the same for other persons, then no amount of "proof" is likely to change their reluctant minds. Those who so adamantly advocate "choice" deem the fetus to be the equivalent of a cancer that is not worthy of protection. While nearly all could empathize when the difficult decision to abort stems from a desire to protect the life of the mother, all too often that which is being protected is not the mother's life but her "lifestyle," which would likely be cramped by the addition of a(nother) child.

While I do not doubt that many, if not most, decisions to abort are difficult and come with a recognized toll on the mother. I believe that the primary consideration should be that the patient is (or soon would be) a mother, who in most instances by her own voluntary actions has laid the foundations for the life of her child. With motherhood (and fatherhood), whether by choice or by fate, comes responsibility for that child. I have to believe that aborting a child is rarely, if ever, a proper demonstration of parental responsibility.

Children as Chattel

Blog Entry - May 3, 2013

Children do not emerge from the birth canal happy and productive. Guiding and nurturing them is a decades long commitment. If parents are unwilling or unable to take on that commitment themselves, it is unfair and unreasonable to assume that some other party (*i.e.* family, friends, neighbors, teachers, government, *etc.*) will step forward to act successfully *in loco parentis*.

It is the responsibility of parents to give their child(ren) foundations in hygiene, safety, civility, and learning. It is the parents' joint responsibility to give their children moral, ethical, and religious foundations. When the examples that parents offer are of self-destruction, disinterest, or mediocrity, they can hardly expect their children to excel.

Too often, parents blame their situations on poverty and their own bad family experiences. Those factors should be considered before engaging in self-gratifying activities that are likely to lead to the birth of a child. When such a birth occurs, it should be expected and accepted that the desires, objectives, and yes, the lives of the parents will change forever. The lives of the parents must take on a new singular objective to address and fulfill the needs of the child.

Throughout mankind's history, children at times have been treated as chattel.[84] They were a means to the end of protecting the family unit and lineage. Their numbers were necessary to

---

[84] Chattel: Any article of tangible property other than land, buildings, and other things annexed to land; a slave.

overcome attrition, and their labors were integral to the sustenance of the family (and the accumulation of wealth). Additionally, an effective means to prevent unplanned or unwanted pregnancies did not exist.

Today, the birth of any particular child is not necessary for the propagation of the species. Children's labors in the fields are not integral to a family's survival and wealth. Today, children are often the unintended byproducts of reckless sexual behavior. They are often viewed as accessory items or symbols of status. Too often, they are viewed as burdens or inconveniences rather than the priceless gifts, which they truly are.

I do not make the above statements regarding assessing one's priorities and acceptance of one's responsibilities as matters of cosmic certainty, and I recognize that to every observation there is a differing perspective. Just as to every rule there is an exception.

In 1992, then Vice President, Dan Quayle, made a campaign speech in which he was critical of the fictional TV character, Murphy Brown. The situation comedy of the same name included a storyline in which the fictional TV news personality chose to have a child as a single mother.

Quayle chastised the character (and thus the writers and producers of the show):

Bearing babies irresponsibly is simply wrong. Failing to support children one has fathered is wrong. We must be unequivocal about this. It doesn't help matters when prime-time TV has Murphy Brown, a character who supposedly epitomizes today's intelligent, highly paid professional woman, mocking the importance of fathers by bearing a child alone and calling it just another lifestyle choice.

Quayle's speech and his prior gaffes were parodied on the show, *Murphy Brown*, and throughout popular media. The concept of "Family Values" became both a theme of the presidential campaign and a comedic punch line.

Almost certainly, a character, which was portrayed as a successful and financially stable professional woman was not the appropriate target for the candidate's ire. Such a woman could likely prove herself a fit and capable mother despite the challenges often faced by single parents. However, many persons seem to believe that the existence of any exception negates the application of the rule.

Even in the artificial reality of network sit-coms, the existence of a small child was difficult to manage. Political commentator and cultural critic Mark Steyn observed that the producers did not seem to have a clue what to do with Murphy Brown's son, Avery:

> *In the five years since little Avery's birth ushered in the Clinton era, Murphy Brown has been on CBS every week, Dan Quayle has been back in Indiana (and Arizona). But Avery? As soon as he was born, Murphy made another "lifestyle choice": She stuck him at the back of the closet under the Emmy Awards and the commendations from single-parent outreach groups and mouldering editorials hailing the show for its courage, and the poor kid hasn't been seen since.*[85]

[85] Steyn, Mark, "Murphy Brownout," *The American Spectator* (Arlington, Virginia), pp. 38–39 (January 1998).

Nearly a generation removed from Avery's birth, many would argue that the state of the family unit has continued to deteriorate. Murphy Brown's child would be in his early 20's today. As he and his cohorts look forward to adulthood and children of their own, I wander if they would have similar levels of disdain for "Family Values" as was evident two decades ago?[86]

Occasionally, a long-shot pays off, but more often than not, betting against the odds will result in pronounced loss and disappointment. In making the above observations, it is not my objective to point out particular shortcomings of any individual or to brand anyone for their inadequacies as a parent. It is not my desire to deprive anyone of the joys of life (of which children should be one).

Nevertheless, it would require slightly less of a village to raise children if the parents giving birth to those children took greater care in planning and preparing for their offspring and accepted the personal responsibility and consequences that come with having children. If parents cannot honestly say that a child or their children will be their primary focus and priority, parenting is probably not an appropriate hobby or pastime.

Parents should be free to rear their child(ren) however they deem best within reasonable limits related to health and safety. My objective is not to "impose" my idea of what is right and proper on any such family unit. Nevertheless, I would be remiss

---

[86] See Sawhill, Isabell, "20 years later, it turns out Dan Quayle was right about Murphy Brown and unmarried moms," *Washington Post* (May 25, 2012).

in not pointing out behaviors, the benefits of which I would think to be self-evident, but which are not universally applied.

Man has free will, and he has the liberty to lessen the quality of his own life and that of his progeny should he choose to live in ignorance. My qualm is not so much with the diminution in the quality (if not quantity) of life experienced by the parent and/or children. My biggest issue is blaming any resulting losses on other individuals or the community rather than the parents themselves.

We sometimes hear, "I cannot afford to work for lack of childcare?" Is it fair to expect someone to ask themselves, "Can I afford to have child(ren)?" Yes, I have heard that if one waits to have children until he or she is "ready" (presumably this includes financially stable), then one would never have children. Admittedly, one cannot prepare for every potential shortfall and contingency; nevertheless, some consideration should be given to preparedness.

This is not our great-grandparents' generation. With universal access to birth control, the acts giving rise to having a child are (in all but the most perverse situations) voluntary CHOICES. Those choices should be responsible, and the concurrent actions come with consequences. These consequences may prove to be "bad" (at least untimely) for many persons. Nevertheless, ultimate responsibility is on the parents not the extended family or society at large. Perhaps, more thought and planning should go into having child(ren) rather than treating them as accessory items.

BULLYING: A Battle without Victors

Blog Entry - August 6, 2013

A recent news story included video taken from a camera onboard a public school bus. On the video, three (3) fifteen (15) year-olds are viciously punching and kicking a thirteen (13) year-old boy.

What was his perceived offense against the teenaged ruffians? One of the bullies tried to sell drugs to the victim earlier in the day, and the victim reported that incident to school officials. Most persons would immediately agree that victim did nothing to warrant the wrath of his attackers. However, the "reason" for the offense is hardly relevant. There is no acceptable excuse for such horrendous behavior.

Nevertheless, I am certain that some persons would urge "understanding" for the three (3) thugs and bullies, who cowardly kicked and beat a defenseless boy. Their actions would likely be blamed on social maladjustment arising from a lack of resources or opportunities.

Granted, socially well adjusted and mentally stable individuals rarely commit violent crimes. Nearly everyone, who robs, rapes, kills, and maims, is socially maladjusted and/or emotionally unstable. Nevertheless, crimes should establish a floor, below which society deems such abhorrent behaviors as entirely unacceptable, regardless of the circumstances of one's upbringing and the experience of a hard life.

Each of us comes to crossroads in life, and we have decision points where we choose between right and wrong. Making wrong choices has consequences and rightly so. Those, who would implore empathy and understanding for such persons, argue that the individuals are not inherently "bad" but that their actions are the natural byproducts of a bad environment and the lack of a nurturing home.

What about the people, who grew up in the same or similar "broken homes" or who grew up in the same adverse environs, but who succeeded despite the same supposed lack of resources and opportunities? Do we not diminish the commitment, successes, and achievements of those persons by excusing the bad acts of others similarly situated? How long can one trade on the sins of others as the excuse for his own bad acts?

How long does a person, family, race, sect, country, *etc.* get to use the "woe is me" excuse as a justification for lives poorly lived or as a license to do wrong? A generation, or three ... a century? Are we as a people really willing to say, "It's OK; you didn't know any better," or "You couldn't help yourself"? Do we have no more confidence in the higher human traits of intellect, rationality, and free will than to excuse boorish and base behaviors with the defense, "Life has been so unfair to him"?

Each of us has but one life to live, and each person is the steward of his own life. We are entrusted (and burdened) with making the most of our lives regardless of the lack of fairness and despite the obstacles that the Fates (and others) may place in the way.

My expectations for human beings are much higher than most persons, and as long as we continue to lower the expectations of the species, it is certain that we will never exceed those lowered expectations. How much responsibility

346

should be placed on an individual to improve his own situation and to save himself from the beast within?

Mankind is inherently selfish, and most persons naturally act in their own self-interests. Some men choose not to exercise the reason, intellect, and free will, which distinguish human beings from lower species. Man without intellect and reason is a very crude and cruel beast. Many persons choose to lazily embrace that beast rather than to work diligently to overcome and suppress it.

Civility is not the natural state of man; nevertheless, it is the most efficient and productive state, in which mankind can reasonably coexist. Such a state can be achieved only through enforced adherence and personal enlightenment. We should not tolerate the intolerant. We should not enable those persons, who actions are destructive either toward themselves or the common good. We should never allow those with power to abuse the weaker among us.

Persons have different talents, traits, and goals. Where individual differences are positive, those positive attributes and traits should be openly embraced and eagerly adopted. We should be patient with others and be willing to assist them in their own quests toward enlightenment and self-actualization.

If one chooses not to actively engage in personal growth and fails to demonstrate compassion, then his humanity will atrophy, and his soul likely will suffer death by starvation. Such a death is entirely the responsibility of the person, who allows his life to wither and waste away. Either one consciously chooses enlightenment, or he suffers the consequences of his ignorance.

If we as a species shun enlightenment, then the consequences for our species are dire. It is only in individually embracing and protecting our humanity that we can survive and thrive as a species.

IV. BUSINESS & TAXATION

349

"These Jobs Aren't Coming Back."
© 2012

Introduction -

The quote in the title was the response given to President Obama when he questioned Apple's Co-Founder, Steve Jobs, regarding what it would take for the manufacture of the iPhone (and other Apple products) to be performed in the United States.

Apple employs less than 50,000 persons in the U.S., but those, who work on behalf of Apple elsewhere around the world, number nearly a million. This latter group of persons includes: Assemblers in China, as well component manufactures in Japan, South Korea, and Germany, all of whom complement the relatively small corps of managers and executives in the U.S.

Apple's diversified management, design and manufacturing processes are implemented with consideration given to the costs of labor and manufacturing, as well as the availability of advanced technical expertise and precision manufacturing.

Identifying Problems -

Apple, being the most highly capitalized company in the world, is the poster child of an "American" company, whose corporate presence is primarily outside of the United States. Such global corporations often fail to acknowledge fealty to the United States, despite America often being the place of "birth" for these enterprises and despite the U.S. economy having been a nurturing force for the growth and successes of these companies.

Over the last couple of decades, we have developed a global economy where technology is fungible, transportation costs are negligible, and foreign labor costs are a fraction of that in the U.S.

Domestically, Wal-Mart is often cited as a company, which takes advantage of its low-wage employees and fuels income disparities. First and foremost, I am not a defender Wal-Mart or its business practices; however, the company's business model is a symptom not the sole cause of financial inequality.

I have witnessed "Made in America" manufacturers that sold to Wal-Mart, and those manufacturers cut their margins razor thin just to have the work and to keep their doors open. Wal-Mart would come back year-after-year demanding more price concessions. Ultimately, the manufacturer would lose the contract and close its doors despite the prior efforts and concessions.

The competitor for the business of the U.S. manufacturer was almost inevitably a plant in Southeast Asia with lower costs of labor and often with local government incentives. Some would argue that such competition is not fair, but what we have to recognize is that the game has changed.

Former Labor Secretary, Robert Reich, says:

> *[Big American-based companies] don't care about making Americans more competitive. They say that they have no obligations to solve America's problems.*[87]

---

[87] Reich, Robert, "The Problem Isn't Outsourcing," www.robertreich.org (July 18, 2012).

Reich goes on to say:

> *[These companies] want lower corporate taxes, lower taxes on their executives, fewer regulations, and less public spending. ... [The core problem is] that the prosperity of America's big businesses - which are really global networks that happen to be headquartered here - has become disconnected from the well-being of most Americans. Without a government that's focused on more and better jobs, we're left with global corporations that don't give a damn.*

Reich would likely contend that such corporations are managed as though: (i) There is no real benefit derived from being headquartered the United States; or (ii) The continuity of any such benefits should be the responsibility of others within society.

As to the former proposition, do managers of global companies think that they will have the same certainty of operations and security of their assets and personnel should they be sited in the "growing economies" of China, Brazil, Russia, or the Middle East?

As to the latter proposition, are the countries, in which these "growing economies" exist, less likely to tax the income (or appropriate the assets) of the companies in the long run?

Finally, do "corporate citizens" not have a responsibility to participate (through their actions and by contributions of wealth) toward the common good of the societies, in which they operate?

True Costs of Doing Business -

I do not believe that executives in such companies think that there are "no" benefits to being headquartered in the U.S. or that they have "no" obligations to pay into the systems and mechanisms that yield those benefits. However, I do think that there is a lack of appreciation for the true value of such benefits and a lack of realization of the levels maintenance and responsibility required to assure their continued existence.

Admittedly, the federal government of the United States has taken great strides in recent years to prove itself unworthy of the trust vested in it to provide a fair economic system and stable markets. That government, of late, has proven itself ineffective to instill confidence in the fairness of our political system and the stability in our economic systems among citizens and the world. Assuming that government can right itself and restore its role as a stabilizing (rather than turbulent) influence, the country quickly could be recognized once again as a preferred locale for business.

The historical preference of the U.S. as a home for business is also bolstered by the relative lack of social strife, which is evidenced by an absence of open class warfare, as well as the stability that comes about from adherence to the rule of law. However, there is a price of civility, just as there is a cost of incivility. Citizens will only forego riots in the streets and respect the rule of law when they believe that the economic systems and the rule of law are fair and equitable. When these things are seen as unfair, the people will revolt indirectly by refusing to participate in those systems or directly by way of strikes, protests, and even violence.

The lead that the United States enjoyed in infrastructure and information technologies has been lost somewhat with the advent of the internet, free flowing information, and wireless information systems. No longer is it required that a society incur the cost of being hardwired in order to benefit from the expanding flow of information. No longer is information proprietary. It belongs immediately to the masses.

Bill Gates once said of the venerable Microsoft, "In three years, every product that my company makes will be obsolete." His bet, and that of the United States, is that the economy, on both the micro- and macro-economic level, can stay ahead of the obsolescence curve.

The United States has the benefit of being a place that the world's best and brightest have chosen to congregate for many decades. The country has the benefit of numerous world class educational and research institutions. While this edge has dulled with the more fluid transfer of information and the country's lack of focus on technological innovation and scientific research, there is still a foundation upon which future opportunities and innovations can spring.

It is important that emphasis and resources be placed upon educating our children and training our evolving workforce in order to assure creativity and human resources adequate for tomorrow's endeavors.

If information can be seen as "software," the United States is also at risk of falling behind in "hardware" infrastructure, or guilty of waiting idly while it crumbles. As stated above, the flow of information is no longer tied to hard-wired networks for telephone and digital communications. The U.S. is, at best, riding the tide of wireless communications; it is certainly not at the forefront. Other infrastructure is being ignored or taken for granted: Roads, bridges, utilities, *etc.*

If the U.S. is continually on the defensive, playing catch-up or responding to emergencies, then resources will not be utilized efficiently and longer term costs will soar. Rather than growing and planning for the future, America will be fighting losing battles to maintain the perilous *status quo*.

Government is a primary player and source of expenditures for these infrastructure elements. However, government inefficiencies and distractions have meant that infrastructure hardware is aging and quickly becoming obsolete. Such obsolescence is exacerbated by a sluggish quest for innovation.

Another primary role of government, which has been enjoyed by citizens and corporations alike, is the role that military and law enforcement play in keeping destructive forces at bay. Those forces include not only guerrilla fighters and invading armies, but also persons with criminal intent or subversive political ambitions.

The U.S. military was instrumental in limiting the scourges of two world wars, and containing other destructive forces, which would have been detrimental to the country and destabilizing to the world in general. (This is true despite the fact that the U.S. has acted much too quickly or aggressively with its military might at times).

The world has benefitted from these policing functions for nearly a century. Without the willingness of the U.S. to serve these functions and the ability of the American people to fund such endeavors, the landscape of the world likely would look much different today (both figuratively and literally).

Creative Destruction –

A Public Corporation's primary (some would say sole) obligation is to maximize profits for the shareholders. Such companies do not have the luxury to pad costs in order to appease some notion of collectivism. If a company is not competitive, then it is not likely that it will remain viable in the long term. If a company is not profitable, then it matters not how nice and well-meaning its owners or managers may be. There will not be a business from which to fund their good intentions.

Bain Capital, the company that was co-founded by Mitt Romney, like other takeover specialists, generally took marginal companies and tried to turn them around. It is much like taking junk and making art. Sometimes, the benefit of the end product is in the eye of the beholder. However, if the alternative was to let these companies languish and fail, what is wrong with cutting costs, improving efficiencies, and yes, even outsourcing?

Bain's job was to turn loss into profit, and that certainly does not mean continuing the *status quo*. Rather than apologizing for successes, Mitt Romney, like other capitalists, should undertake an effort to educate the public about economic realities and the necessity of economic evolution.

Manufacturing technology allows companies to do more with less people. Competition, at home and abroad, assures that such companies cannot have legacy employees just because they are nice. Creative destruction is a necessary element of economic evolution. Like natural selection, it is not always pretty. The weak fail, and those that cannot adapt are left behind to perish.

Unto whom Much is Given -

Corporate value to shareholders is tied to profitability, and companies have been rightfully accused of taking steps to maximize short-term profitability to the detriment of long-term viability. There is more to "value" than wringing out every drop of profit, which can be squeezed out in the short-term. There is something to be said for stability, longevity, and continued growth. Such elements of value require investment in things that may not show immediate return. They also require investment in the societies within which the companies operate.

It may be true that corporations have no "obligation to solve America's problems," but they do have an obligation to participate in the solution by being good corporate citizens. As it is said, "If you're not part of the solution, then you're part of the problem." It is unreasonable for an individual or corporation to enjoy the benefits of a stable economic system and civil society without contributing to the continuity of both.

It is a matter of paying now or later. We can pay the price of maintaining civility, or we can incur even higher costs to defend against or repair the damages occasioned by incivility. The more big corporations become "disconnected from the well being of most Americans" the greater will be the revolt from those who become disenchanted:

- Do we in America want Occupy Wall Street style protests to evolve into European-style riots in the streets of our cities?
- Do those in gated communities wish those communities to evolve into fortified compounds reminiscent of affluent Middle East neighborhoods?

The more our society becomes us-versus-them the less likely it will be that any group will be willing to promote the collective good. Productivity and growth comes not from hoarding one's wealth and resources. It comes from utilizing and investing those resources where they are most beneficial. In determining the "benefits" of investment, corporations, and others in business, as well as citizens in general, should remove the blinders of short-term profitability (and immediate gratification), and all parties should be more willing to identify less obvious benefits that may not immediately flow to the bottom line.

Some Solutions -

A friend made the following argument in response to the above comments:

> *Corporations are enslaved by market forces, and those forces ultimately will determine, which corporations succeed or fail. ... Government should not intervene in these market forces because government cannot reliably forecast the best or most appropriate methods for intervention. Government tends to be impatient and in its arrogance fails to demonstrate restraint. Rather than avoiding or correcting all economic ills, many prior interventions by government have created*

or contributed to economic problems. ... In any event, it is inappropriate to coerce corporations to "play nice."

I did not read any recommendation of "coercion" in Robert Reich's original remarks, and I do not believe that "corporations are enslaved by [LEGITIMATE] market forces" any more than I believe that we as human beings are "enslaved" by our natural instincts and animalistic desires.

We, as individuals, have been blessed with free will, reason, and self-determination. Corporations, being institutions comprised of such individuals, are also capable of acting collectively in a rational way for positive self-determination.

Henry Ford provided at least two (2) examples of this principle:

(1) Ford chose to pay his assembly line workers compensation in an amount, which was at the time considered by many to be an exorbitant wage, and he justified this decision by noting that he was building a car for the masses and if the people, which included his workers, could not afford to buy his Model-T then he was narrowing his own potential market. Ford said:

> *It is not the employer who pays the wages. Employers only handle the money. It is the customer who pays the wages.*

(2) In an early 20th Century case, Henry Ford parried with the Dodge Brothers, of Chrysler Motors fame, who were at the time shareholders of Ford Motor Company. While the case has several holdings and applications, the Dodge

Brothers generally argued that Ford had an obligation to maximize short-term shareholder wealth, but Ford argued and received support of the court for the "Business Judgment Rule," which allows much more leeway in determining the **long-term** course of a business.

If the argument is that such corporations allow themselves to be indentured servants to "institutional investors" and "equity markets," that may be a more successful argument. However, such "markets" today are hardly reflections of the long-term viability and actual performance of the subject companies. Instead, public companies are often treated as commodities, much like the colors and numbers on a roulette wheel.

"Investment" on many levels is nothing more than legalized gambling, with a temptation to stack the deck and to manipulate the system. "Investors" are often not working within the system for the benefit of the companies. Instead, they are eagerly trying to pervert the system for their own gain.

The accepted objective is to maximize short-term value, without regard to the long-term effects. How much of the current Great Recession could have been avoided (or lessened) to the benefit of all, including public corporations, had banks, insurance companies, hedge funds, manufacturers, the government, *etc.* taken a broader long-term view of their decisions?

It was obvious to many persons as early as 2004/2005 that the pace of economic growth (in the housing market) could not be sustained. Just as it was obvious in 2000 that the dot-com bubble was about to burst. It was obvious to many persons, who continued to make investment "gambles." Their hope was that they could keep the "hot potatoes" moving quickly enough so as not to be the one left holding the bag.

At their worst, markets and their participants can be like a collection of bullies on a playground jockeying for control and supremacy. If one is among the group of bullies, he must first recognize that only a single party likely will survive to be king-of-the-hill, and the odds are stacked against him. Even if such persons are not naturally inclined to "play dirty," the desire to excel and the will to survive the conflict often motivate such persons to break the rules of civility and fair play.

If one is among the group of bullied students, he may not care much about the infighting among the bullies, because he is going to experience (or suffer) essentially the same treatment and consequences regardless of the victor.

As long as combat is hand-to-hand, the persons most likely to be hurt by the initial infighting are those, who voluntarily choose to participate in it (*i.e.* the bullies fighting for supremacy). Most other persons are aware of the conflict, and they can strive to avoid the abuse and destructive consequences. Collateral damage can be minimized and localized.

However, if the weapons of choice escalate from fists, to knives, then guns, and finally to explosives, then the risk of collateral damage also increases geometrically. If the ultimate result is that the entire school is blown to smithereens (possibly along with all of the students), it cannot be said to be a fight just among the bullies.

362

If we have seen or experienced such extreme negative progressions before, we, as a society, cannot sit back willfully ignorant of the consequences with the naïve hope that history will not repeat itself. In such a situation, those further removed but directly affected by the brawl have not only the right, but the obligation to step in to avert catastrophe.

I have two (2) primary concerns, both of which must be addressed for the "markets" to remain fluid and less dangerous:

First, there have been concerted efforts among some, particularly among those entities deemed "too big to fail," to individualize reward and to institutionalize risk (often through complicit government intervention). In doing so, such market players pervert the risk/reward dichotomy that is absolutely necessary for the free market system to work.

Without individualized risk of loss, there is no disincentive to exposing the party (and others within the economy) to excess risk. The inevitable result is the escalation in economic "weapons" (per my prior analogy) with the ultimate loss being borne not by the actors themselves but by the market and/or consumers.

Following the Great Recession, there SHOULD have been more (or at least some) bankers and managers proverbially jumping from their high rise offices as incidents of Hara-Kiri. Few, if any, of those truly responsible for the actions leading up to the Great Recession have fallen on their swords, and even worse, many such persons have continued to profit from their own misdeeds. There have been few lessons learned and constructively applied.

Second, a free market economy works only if it is, in fact, "free flowing." If the market is not fluid, the rules cannot be applied consistently. If the flow of the market is artificially constrained, diverted, manipulated, or perhaps most damaging, artificially maintained or bolstered, the results will be erratic. There is hubris both in government and among those "in the know." Those in government (*i.e.* Federal Reserve, Commerce Department, *etc.*) believe that the economy can be manipulated for social ends and manipulated to avoid, over an indefinite term, downturns in that economy.

Social engineering through economic incentives and penalties has a sketchy history at best, and as with individualized loss on the microeconomic level, there must also be recessions on the macroeconomic level in order to afford opportunities for market corrections. These are not only inevitable, but shallower and more frequent corrections would be much preferred over artificially delayed corrections that eventually result in a catastrophic decline.

Also, players in certain industries and the equity markets develop skills (some would say "weapons") to make marginalized profits through active manipulations in the markets in which they function. To the extent that such persons can profit from such market manipulations independent of the underlying risks, damage is done to the system as a result of inefficiencies and inconsistent outcomes.

Conclusion -

Large companies and public corporations were not exclusively responsible for recent economic woes; therefore, well intended "corrective actions" cannot focus only on the management and operations of such businesses. Nevertheless, corporate culture and short-sighted objectives did contribute to the economic collapse; therefore, such companies, as well as their shareholders and managers, must commit themselves to being part of the long-term solutions.

If businesses, by and through managers and owners, do not commit themselves to being participants in fixing the current economic problems, America's problems will eventually become their own. Perhaps, then big corporations will "give a damn," if it is not too late.

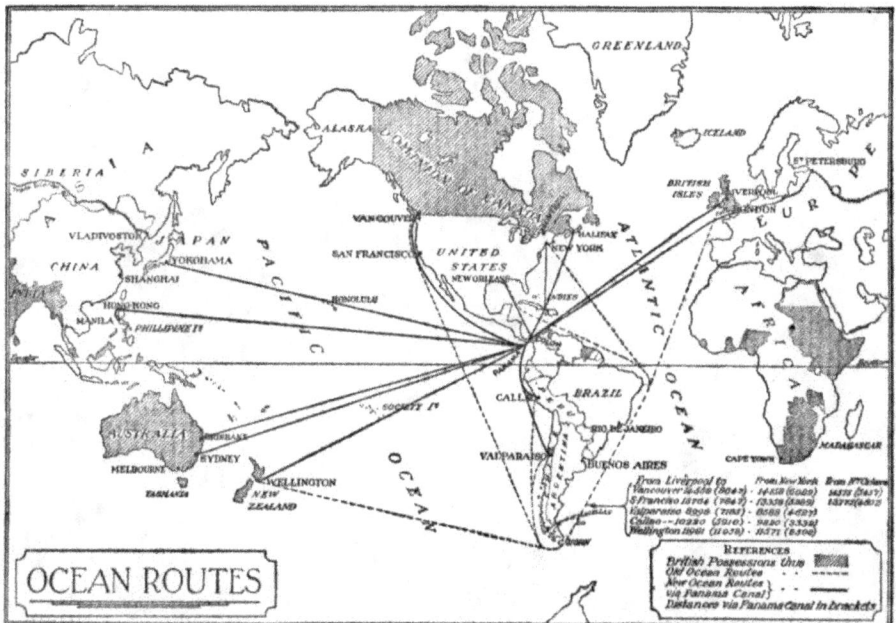

OCEAN ROUTES

Apple versus FaceBook

Blog Entry - May 22, 2012

Introduction -

Apple has the largest market capitalization (value) of any corporation in the world, and it has one of the most ideal business models. It sells "ideas," and the company leverages other people's capital to do it. Apple owns no factories, and its employees worldwide are counted in the tens of thousands. A company cannot get much leaner, and Apple's products command a substantial premium over similar products in the market. Apple also has a corporate history spanning more than thirty (30) years (longer than the lifespan of Mark Zuckerberg of FaceBook fame).

With all of these advantages, Apple's stock currently trades at roughly ten times (10x) Earnings Per Share (EPS). In the recent FaceBook IPO, the value for a company with a twenty-something CEO, no established profit history, and an unproven revenue source, was set at SIXTY-FIVE (65) times the PROJECTED 2013 EPS.

Folks, this is not investing; it is gambling. Investors are betting, as P.T. Barnum is credited with saying, that, "There is a sucker born every minute," and such investors just hope that the line of suckers is unending and readily accessible.

A Primer on the Stock Market -

I have friends and colleagues who are auditors of public corporations and executives at Fortune 500 companies. Their jobs are not so much to "improve the business." Instead, they work to craft and meet expectations among investors, who often have no real knowledge about or interest in the business itself. The "investors" buy and sell what they see as a commodity just like oil, coal, coffee, sugar, or yes, the proverbial "pork bellies."

There is an interesting quirk in commodities trading; there is no inherent "value" in a specific commodity. The only value is in the price at which someone is willing to buy and sell that commodity. Because of this symbiosis, for every dollar "gained" in a commodity trade, someone else "loses" that same dollar.

Everyone should keep that in mind when they are investing in "commodity" stocks (*i.e.* without appreciable underlying worth or demonstrable value). One is betting that he knows something that the guy on the other side of the transaction does not. Are the respective buyers and sellers really that smart? ... REALLY?

There is a story that is told of a financier [sometimes identified in the story as John D. Rockefeller]. The story is set immediately after the collapse of the Stock Market, which lead to the Great Depression. The financier survived the fall relatively unscathed, and he was asked how was it that he knew to get out of the stock market? He replied, "When the cabbies of New York began speculating in the stock market, I knew that it was time to get out."

Investing in the markets may be a game to some, but one should only gamble with assets that he can afford to lose. Life savings and retirement benefits should not be put on a roll of the dice. That rings true whether the investor is an individual or a Pension Fund.

I have often said that there is a difference between being "smart" and "cute." A lot of "investors" these days are trying to be cute playing at the margins. That is not smart. The risks cannot be accurately calculated that precisely, and it is arrogance to think that they can.

The issue that is missed by those "predicting" and attempting to profit from minute market movements is they fail to address a key factor: *Knowledge about the mechanics of a fluid system changes the rules by which the system operates.*

If one is the only person pulling the levers or holding the strings, that is OK, and he can "cash in" on the idiosyncrasies of the system. However, when there are 1,000's or 10's of thousands of people doing the same things (or introducing opposing forces) the predictability of outcomes is inextricably altered.

I was once involved in an industry in which one entity purchased the vast majority of a particularly commodity east of the Mississippi. However, the price of the commodity from suppliers was historically set at a "market" price determined in the Midwest.

Over time, this purchasing entity acquired or merged with several competing entities, and the company integrated production capabilities for the commodity. The dedicated (some would say "captive") production sources sold directly to the manufacturer rather than through the open market. However, the consolidation and integration of the industry fundamentally changed the measuring market.

369

There were fewer buyers in the open market, but the market sellers continued to produce the commodity despite a host of new suppliers (sellers) in the integrated system. The result was a glut or surplus of the commodity on the measuring market. This surplus drove down commodity prices, and this price point carried over to the contract price paid to the "captive" suppliers. This was true despite the fact that these suppliers (sellers) were not actively involved in the measuring market.

The purchasing entity enjoyed a windfall of its own creation. Despite being in an environment with continuing high demand, each purchase was made at a discount because the buyer itself had skewed the market.

The integrated suppliers had fixed production costs, but they were being paid an ever decreasing price. This contractually agreed price formula was unrelated to either the sellers' costs of production or to the ultimate "value" of the finished products sold by the manufacturer (buyer).

The sellers could not fault the "market" because in an effort to assure a guaranteed source for their product they waived participation in the market. In an effort to manipulate risk within the market, they gambled and lost.

The parties ignored the fundamental elements of markets. They had removed the give-and-take of the market transactions. They had interfered with the fluidity of the market. The captive "market" was not representative of a voluntary buy-sell decision. Finally, the selling parties failed to anticipate the effect that a dominant buyer would have on the measuring market. The sellers thought that they were smarter and more proficient than the collective market participants. Ultimately, this did not prove to be true. They suffered the same fate as many of the smaller sellers, who they previously ran out of business.

The dominant buyer consciously and intentionally manipulated the market to its advantage. This is the type of abuse of the market, which should be identified and avoided. In this case, most of the parties were equally complicit, but the situation is demonstrative of why monopoly powers and overt market manipulation should be avoided.

"Index Trading" and "Derivatives" have similar effects of distorting market functionality and fluidity. Such trading treats the underlying stock and securities as commodities. The "value" of the commodity in the hands of the "investor" may have little relationship to the actual income potential, demonstrated profitability, or underlying value of the company or its assets.

Conclusion -

Contrary to popular belief, stocks are seldom traded based upon accounting data, financial planning, or sound economic theory. More often than not, the value is illusory. Markets are made (and lost) based upon an attributed value, which often hinges upon very little other than the someone less informed or less sophisticated being willing to pay a dollar more (or less) than the last sap that bought (or sold) the same stock, commodity, or other instrument.

In essence, the objective of the "trade" in such circumstances is for the seller to convince a buyer that the investment product is worth at least a dollar more than what was

371

paid for it. Where such transactions happen repeatedly, the relationship of the security to the income potential or asset holdings of the underlying company becomes distorted.

Between September 2012 and April 2013, the share price of Apple stock fell from a peak of more than $700 per share to close at $390.53 / sh. on April 19th. It was the first time that the stock closed below $400 since December 2011. In just over six (6) months, nearly $300 billion in market value simply evaporated.

If Apple, one of the most successful and formerly the most highly capitalized company on the planet, can lose nearly one-half (½) of its market "value" in just over six (6) months, what does that say about the supposed "value" of other publically traded companies?

Either Apple was grossly overvalued six (6) months previously, or there is a manufactured and artificial panic forcing the price unreasonably low. Regardless, such "irrational" behavior does not bode well for all of those supposed Wizards of Wall Street.

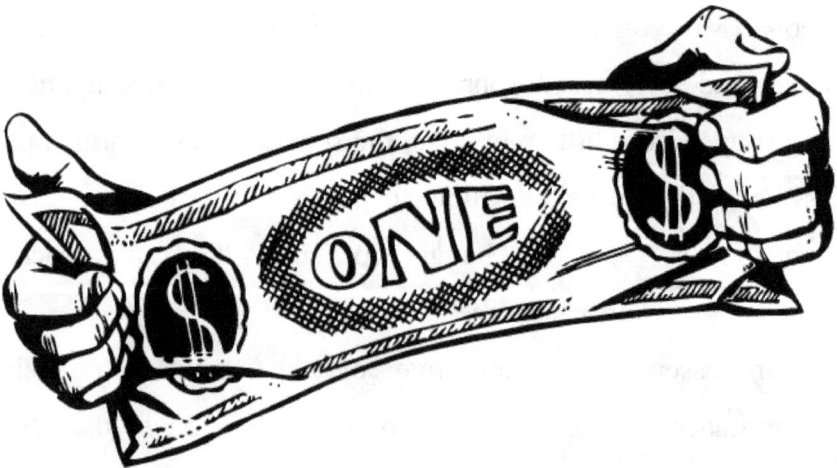

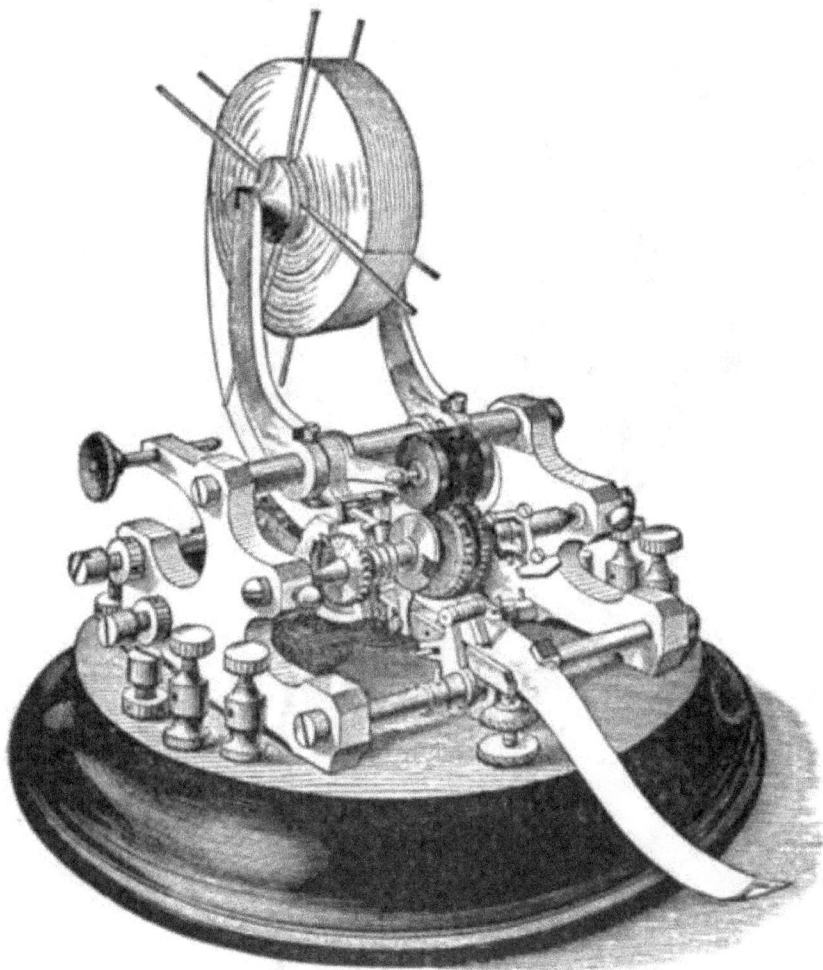

Notes on Ayn Rand and Selfishness

© 2012

From a historical perspective, the lords of the manor needed the labors of the people in order to produce and secure their feudal wealth. There was a further, perhaps "unspoken," exchange between the lord, who provided safety to those in his charge, and the people, who provided something between loyalty and indentured servitude.

A similar dynamic was at play until very recently between barons of industry and their employees. It is this mutual "dependence" that assured some level of "fairness." However, interpersonal dynamics and economic paradigms have changed in recent decades.

Information and transportation systems have been developed, which removed production and distribution impediments. It is no longer necessary to feed the American economy from within. Therefore, production moved (and continues to move) to where facilities are available and where the cost of labor is least.

This loss of manufacturing might is coupled with (or perhaps responsible for) a stagnant U.S. economy. In contrast, certain economies elsewhere around the world are expanding, and each one of these "emerging economies" is striving toward a semblance of the U.S. standard of living. The result is that America is no longer the only game in town as either a producer or consumer nation. Therefore, we are placed in competition for capital, resources, and yes, jobs.

In many ways, public corporations are the new lords of the manner. However, it is no longer necessary for American Companies to "invest" in America either in facilities or jobs.

Apple, the largest company in the world by way of market capitalization, has less than 50,000 employees in America compared to nearly a million employees, agents, and contractors worldwide. If we cannot give companies (American or otherwise) incentives and reasons to invest in America, they will not.

There are two (2) options:

(i)   America can use innovation and initiative and do things better and more efficiently thereby producing a competitive edge, or

(ii)   America can promote open class warfare, which destabilizes not only the economy, but also civility and society, thereby holding the economy and civility for ransom.

In the first case, individuals are rewarded for hard work. In the second, they are paid only as a cost of warding off greater evils, which include inefficiencies, theft, and destruction. Under the first scenario, the bet is that we as Americans can win in the survival of the fittest. In the second scenario, the bet is that America will be just better than the next least favorable alternative.

Inevitably, there will be wins and losses, ups and downs, obstacles and detours, but we can set the general course and the trend. The question is do we want the cream to rise to the top (recognizing that the slag will fall disproportionately to the bottom)? Or, in the futile quest for equality, do we limit nearly everyone to an ever decreasing standard of living, which is below that which many could achieve otherwise?

People should have ample opportunity to provide for their basic needs and those of their family. However, pursuing one's dreams is a privilege and luxury earned from working beyond the minimum required for subsistence.

This is contrary to the thoughts of former Speaker of the House, Nancy Pelosi (D-CA), and those of her ilk. Pelosi was completely out of touch with reality when she asserted that nationalized healthcare was needed so that people could become "artists, musicians, or whatever they want."

Every person's primary goal in life should be to provide for himself (and for his family). If someone wishes to be known as an "artist," they should expect that the word "starving" might also be attached to that description. I can appreciate persons, who wish to contribute to the arts or who choose to follow a calling off of the beaten path, but it is not for any person (or society in general) to be an involuntary benefactor to their whimsy.

The problem, as I see it, arises from imposing a "morality" on political and economic systems. People can be moral, but institutions and systems have no inherent morality. The mechanisms of such systems work best when morality, religion, and concepts of singular rights and wrongs are removed from the equations. Like mathematics, there are rules, which are independent of any morality. Also, there is an "equilibrium" that arises from the give-and-take of life.

Some persons place a high value on "altruism," the philosophical doctrine that right action is that which produces the greatest benefit to others. Other persons are not persuaded by such selflessness. This latter group is most often driven by the dichotomy of risk/reward. They are motivated by the potential rewards that come from taking risks, and the level of risk, which is undertaken by any party, is kept in check by the potential harm and loss that could befall him. Persons of both inclinations necessarily participate in the market of economic and societal privileges.

Many of us recall the story of the "Widow's Mite," which Jesus told at the Temple in Jerusalem. In the story, a poor Widow sacrificially donates two (2) coins of small denominations. Jesus chastises those of greater means, who give more in absolute terms but who proportionally do not demonstrate charity and sacrifice on par with the Widow.[88]

Many persons use this story to encourage (or compel) altruism with the thought being that one should "give until it hurts." Does that mean that each of us must take a vow of poverty and eschew all material possessions? If no one has the capital and means to start businesses and to produce profits, what will be the source of future wealth?

Recognizing the relative wealth of nearly everyone living in the United States, when compared to the rest of the world, what is the level of poverty that we should seek to achieve in demonstrating our selflessness? Do we strive for the federally established U.S. poverty level ($11,500 for an individual or

---

[88] See *Mark* 12:41-44 and *Luke* 21:1-4.

$23,500 for a family of four annually)? Or, do we go above and beyond by striving to achieve "extreme poverty" as defined by the United Nations (subsistence on $1.25-$5.00 per day)?

Who among us should determine the extent of the "pain" that is appropriate for someone else to endure in giving to others, and who determines the appropriate beneficiaries of that compelled altruism? Who determines if the recipient is truly in "need" or whether he is otherwise worthy of the gift?

Should those decisions not be left to discretion of the giver, who would then be guided by his own sense of responsibility and personal morality? Or, should his neighbors, the church, or the government feel entitled to reach into his purse or command a tax or tithe consistent with their liking?

Free enterprise and capitalism do not negate charity, philanthropy, and benevolence. Giving back to one's fellow man can be rewarding intrinsically and extrinsically. Nevertheless, one must accumulate resources beyond the level of mere subsistence in order to be charitable without making one's self the object of another's charity. The overall societal gain and long-term collective benefit should be evaluated before any steps are taken to compel the "charity" of others. Rarely, if ever, is forced altruism or compulsory wealth redistribution an appropriate role of government.

Ayn Rand is often criticized because her Objectivist Philosophy encourages adherents to do only those things which make them happy or which are pleasing to them. However, that does not mean that hedonism, immediate gratification, or short-term financial gain should be the controlling factors for all decisions in life.

In evaluating cumulative benefit and gain, we should have an extended outlook and broad perspective rather than being opportunists and manipulators. However, sacrificing one's self for the benefit of others may be similarly misguided. While such acts will make someone a martyr for a cause, the acts themselves do not guarantee that such a cause is worthy of the sacrifice.

It is up to the parties to determine what value to put on an individual transaction. In negotiating our various privileges in life, we have to surrender something of substance or provide additional value to the other party. The "value" given to any particular resource or act is not dependent upon some inherent or established price (or "right"). Instead, it is a negotiated trade. Some persons will be willing to contribute more or to demand less in order to accomplish the trade and to effect the exchange of privileges. In establishing that relative "selfishness," the value of anything is set by the "market."

The consternation comes when persons are forced to bid for necessaries and other things, to which some persons perceive themselves entitlement by right (*e.g.* food, shelter, healthcare, *etc.*). There is a feeling among some that such things should be freely available to all. It would be nice if that were true, but nearly every commodity is in limited supply no matter how necessary it may be to our existence. Any finite commodity commands a price, which must be paid by someone. The more limited the supply the greater the premium and the more unequal the distribution of the resource becomes.

Where government opts to interfere with natural market activities, the important questions are:

- How long can society or government manipulate and maintain the market artificially?; and

- What may be the eventual costs of doing so?

When markets are not free to move fluidly and to correct themselves regularly, the inevitable result will be a crash or an abrupt correction. Whether this correction is economic or societal, the more natural course is nearly always preferred. The primary problem is that we have removed producers and consumers from a "face-to-face" exchange.

Most persons do not want the inconvenience and discomfort of a *quid-pro-quo*[89] transaction. They do not want to assume the risk of and responsibility for making a bad deal. They do want the comfort and satisfaction of knowing that they got a deal comparable to everyone else, even if that means that the deal imposed upon them is less favorable than may have been available otherwise.

Those, who are confident in an eternally benevolent government, desire that government dictate the collection societal contracts encompassing nearly every area of our lives: Employment, healthcare, mortgage lending, conservation, marriage, and the economy in general.

---

[89] Meaning: "This for that," one thing given in return for another, or a substitute.

The fallacy is that the government in the exercise of some omnipotent wisdom is capable of dictating a single system, which is more equitable and efficient than that which can be fashioned by the billions of collective exchange decisions made by more than 300 Million citizens every day.

In abdicating a personal buy/sell decision, there is no responsibility among the parties for crafting the deal. The parties are not "invested" in the deal or in their mutual success. There is no appreciation of "risk" on the part of either party. As a result, "price" has no real correlation to the product and services being provided.

When the deal (almost inevitably) goes bad, it is invariably SOMEONE ELSE'S fault. Instead of government being the great equalizer in implementing some Utopian ideal, the "equality" imposed by government is more akin to reducing its citizens to pawns or serfs.

Another problem is that mankind is capable of manipulating its environment and the attendant rules of behavior so as to rig the system. Those, who hold the powers of government, manipulate government as a marionette. The political show provides entertainment and distraction to the electorate while the true power plays occur off stage just out of the direct view of the audience. When ignorance, bad behavior, and corruption are rewarded, we all lose. We lose as individuals, and we lose as a species.

As a people, we seem to have stopped striving for a higher purpose and stopped becoming the best persons and human beings that we can be. As individuals, we seem much more content to argue vehemently, that some other person or people occupy the lowest rung on the evolutionary ladder. Instead of striving for the best possible successes of humankind, you can hear it shouted gleefully far and wide, "I'M NOT LAST!"

It is time that we look behind the curtains and understand what is going on within our institutions and in our own lives. It is time that we commit ourselves to living our own lives to the fullest rather than continually suckling at the teat of government. If we cannot wean ourselves from that dependency, we cannot fully mature as a people.

Our political and economic systems always have been and remain today imperfect. However, it should be noted that when parties, including the privileged majority, previously have abused the powers of government overtly (or when the evolution of society necessitated changes to that government), society policed itself.

While societal changes may be slow to evolve, those, who formerly held the reins of government, eventually ceded power, even if reluctantly, in favor of abolishing slavery, granting women's suffrage, implementing the Civil Rights and Voting Right Acts, *etc.* In each of these cases, the evolution was in the granting of additional liberties and personal freedoms. The species and we as a people advanced.

In contrast, many of the eclectic special interest groups, which compete for the control of government today, are not seeking the expansion of individual liberties and personal freedoms. Instead, each group seeks to harness the powers of government to advance their favored objectives or in furtherance of their self interests. When they cannot secure their desired results via voluntary transactions, they seek to compel some action by or restriction upon others within society through government authority.

In gaining control of the powers and purse strings of government, this hodgepodge majority is unlikely to cede power until and unless there is a complete failure of the social and economic system. By necessity, the government expands and grows in an effort to match its power to the multitude of incompatible tasks being thrust upon it.

However, opportunity and wealth are being sacrificed to feed the Leviathan. Similarly, hard won freedoms and liberties are being sacrificed, as we allow ourselves to become indentured servants to government.

Twenty (20) years ago, the cumulative National Debt was less than $4 TRILLION. That was the net amount, which the government had accumulated over a history spanning roughly two hundred (200) years. Today, the cumulative debt is over $16 TRILLION. In ten (10) years, the debt is projected to be between $25 and $35 TRILLION. If history is any indicator, one may want to lean toward the higher end of that range. Atlas will likely shrug if not collapse under the weight of such debt and the resulting interest accruals.

A problem arises when government acts not as a guardian against oppression and corruption but instead intrudes as an active participant in corrupt social and economic systems, which favor perverse self-interests.

Many persons will never grow beyond their selfish and self-indulgent ways. Since entities and institutions (*e.g.* corporations, churches, governments, *etc.*) are nothing more than collections of similarly aligned persons, those institutions take on the foibles, flaws, and failings of the persons, who make up the collective. It is unreasonable to expect that the sum of whole has any more distinct moral compass than its individual constituents.

Politicians generally convince themselves that what they are doing is in the "best interests" of the government (and by extension, for the country as a whole). What they will not express openly is their nearly universal belief that the citizenry is naïve, ignorant, and susceptible to manipulation.

Rather than being seen as a "flaw," this presumed state of being is seen as tool to be exploited in order to make government more "efficient" (*i.e.* easier for those in the governing class). Government plays the role of White Knight riding in to save the dependent masses, who are deemed incapable of managing their own lives.

Rather than implementing efforts to educate and wean the masses from the government teat, the relationship has become symbiotic and co-dependent. A problem arises in that perceived efficiencies and certainty of outcomes require conformity and restriction of liberties.

The individual is no longer tasked or allowed to pursue personal goals and objectives for his own growth and benefit. Instead, the individual's talents and wealth are seen as part of the collective. The governing class effectively controls the dissemination of privileges and wealth by taxation and regulation.

The end result is not everyone rising with the tide but rather reducing the vast majority of persons to a more equal level of misery. Government is no longer the tool of the people. Instead, the institution becomes fixated on maintaining the *status quo* among the power brokers and intent upon assuring its unfettered growth and perpetual survival.

The biggest obstacle to constructive change is the mistaken belief that wealth is infinite. It most certainly is not. Not only is it limited, but it is illusory. Wealth can quickly "disappear" based upon lack of confidence in markets and social institutions.

After more than five (5) years of economic malaise following the Great Recession, the confidence in the markets still wanes, and the collective confidence in government is at an abysmal low. Another fallacy of the Nanny State is the belief that producers will continue to produce for the benefit of the state and the infantilized consumers.

Few persons are going to work while other persons benefit from the fruits of their labors, and those voraciously consuming such fruits will never be sated. Eventually, the supposed "needs" will overwhelm the source, and the well will run dry.

I must take exception to the argument, "It is the government's money to give." Government possesses only nominal wealth of its own. Were the contrary true, it could simply print currency, and taxes would be unnecessary. In collecting taxes, the government should be seen and treated as the steward of the taxpayers' largesse. The crux of the debate turns on the questions:

- Do we have rights to utilize our own assets and resources as we see fit and to enjoy the fruits of our own labors (of which we voluntarily devote a portion to the common good)?; OR
- Does all property belong to the government, which gives license to the people to use some portion based upon an arbitrary notion of "rightness"?

That fundamental debate must be resolved. Either individuals are self-determinant (for better or worse), or we are wards of the state. If the latter is true, the state will seek to establish an egalitarian standard of living for the populace, which will be below that which those with talents, means, and motivation would find acceptable.

Individually, each person must answer the question, "Do I choose to strive toward an uncertain goal of excellence or choose to race headlong toward certain mediocrity?" The first path may lead to obstacles and measured disappointment, but the final destination will always be more rewarding than the other. The second path will be unchallenging, but the benefits attained will be unremarkable.

Who wants to live an unremarkable life? We have but one life to live. We have an obligation to make the most of it. The zealous pursuit of that goal may be deemed "selfish," but the alternative is to squander our greatest wealth.

The Swiss Franc versus the American Cowboy

A news article [10/5/13] told of an upcoming Swiss ballot initiative, which would require the Swiss government to pay to all adult citizens a guaranteed monthly stipend equivalent to $2,800 US (nearly $34,000 annually, presumably net of taxes). The stated objective was to address the income and wealth disparity between economic classes.

This initiative will be considered along with a ballot measure, which would limit the compensation to corporate executives in relation to the lowest paid line workers.[90] Obviously, these initiatives have populist appeal since they were placed on the ballot as the result of citizen petitions; however, the devil is in the details.

Some would say, "If it can be done in Switzerland, why not in the United States?" Even if Switzerland were able to demonstrate incremental success in such programs (as measured by the narrowing of the income/wealth disparity), the country is a unique microcosm.

Switzerland has a population of roughly 8 Million persons and a Gross Domestic Product ("GDP") of less than $1 Trillion. By those measures, Switzerland more closely resembles New York CITY than the United States (with a population exceeding 300 Million and a GDP exceeding $15 Trillion). The per capita GDP of Switzerland is approximately $125,000 versus

---

[90] On November 24, 2013, Swiss voters rejected the proposal limiting the salaries of top executives. About two-thirds of voters said no to the plan, which would have limited the salary gap to a 1:12 ratio. The other referenced ballot initiative has not been voted upon.

approximately $43,000 for the United States (a ratio of nearly 3-to-1).

It would be similar to ask, "Why do all states not pay a citizen dividend like the State of Alaska (which also does not have a personal income tax)?" Such a question ignores the economic realities of comparing a state with a modest population and a funding source derived from extensive natural resources to all other states, which may be much more populous and not have a similar funding source. It is like comparing apples to oranges. I am not saying that positive changes cannot be made in the economy of the United States, but what works on a relatively small (micro) scale does not always transfer to larger (macro) scales.

The news reports offer no description of a proposed funding mechanism for the Swiss stipend, but I would wager that the means to the end would be a tax on the foreign deposits in Swiss banks. This would be a clear demonstration of the fact that governments cannot create wealth, but can only confiscate wealth from others. Governments are very good at skimming and trimming off the top, but eventually they can cut deeply enough to hit an artery! They must assure that they do not kill the goose that lays the Golden Egg.

Persons are slow to realize two (2) things:

(1) In a global economy, wealth is mobile, and some country is willing to bid down the effective tax rate in order to encourage the migration of wealth; and

(2) A man, who has no fear of starvation, has no incentive, to feed himself.

So, let me get this right:

Switzerland is simultaneously seeking to remove both the "carrot" and the "stick," which are used to encourage wealth creation and productivity. Most persons work either because they have to in order to sustain themselves (and their families), or they work to secure the trappings, which can be obtained from compensation and wealth. Should you remove those incentives, productivity will certainly suffer.[91]

The position of the U.S. as a world political and economic leader is HISTORICALLY traced to an ingrained motivation toward self-sufficiency and the rewards of capitalism. One may argue that the U.S. should not maintain its role as a world leader and pursue the objective of to be "better than others." In fact, one Russian legislator argued recently that it was tantamount to "political racism" to assert that the "American Way" was somehow better than any other system. However, if America looses the motivation and incentive to do things, which are "different" and "better," then we, as a society, will join a crowded global race toward mediocrity.

Neither a society nor an individual can excel by resting on its laurels, and not every person (or society) is going to have similar motivations. So, is the "wealth gap" too wide? I cannot say for sure. I cannot define cosmic "fairness." I can say that any effort toward universal "equality" is an exercise in futility without realizing that the only practically attainable equality is a reduction of human behaviors and standards of living down to

---

[91] I am not one, who believes that the average citizen undertakes a lifetime of work solely out of some sense of collectivist obligation or in receipt of some intrinsic reward derived from the work itself.

391

less than desirable levels. Rather than measuring the gap between the haves and the have nots, the objective should be to provide fluidity and fairness within the economic system of a given country.[92]

In this case, "fairness" is not measured by the uniformity of outcomes but rather represents close adherence to the relationships, which should exist among effort, risk, and reward. Those who live responsibly and work hard should be rewarded. The difficult lives of those, who live irresponsibly and slothfully, should serve as cautionary tales to those who would naively follow similarly unproductive paths. However, some lessons are hard learned, and the consequences of some mistakes last a lifetime.

Persons have argued that the recent Great Recession is proof that the market systems are not self-correcting and that they can only work with aggressive government intervention. I disagree with both premises. The most recent "Great Recession" was fundamentally a routine and necessary market correction that was exacerbated by government involvement in and manipulation of the various economic markets.

Would there have been a recession in 2008 (or some earlier or later time)? Absolutely. Is that a bad thing? Absolutely not.

Market corrections (even recessions) are the inevitable, necessary, and natural by-products of a market economy. More frequent shallow corrections and recessions are much preferred to dramatic, deep, and protracted downturns in markets.

---

[92] I limit this to "country" because I do not believe in a worldwide Utopian economy, and I do not believe that an effective sphere of influence extends beyond the borders of a given country.

The depth of the most recent recession and the protracted recovery relate to a precipitous "crash" in the Housing Market. This crash was a direct result of government (political) policies, which dictated banking regulations to encourage home ownership among persons, who historically would not have been deemed credit worthy. Additional federal regulations required that the qualification criteria be applied "fairly" to all persons, who met the less restrictive standards. The applications of these regulations by lenders led to reckless sub-prime lending and excessive speculation (*i.e.* a bubble in the housing market that eventually burst because it was expanded by artificially inflated values).

The problem was further exacerbated when the government deemed certain banks and companies "too big to fail." The only effective restraint (or "self-regulation") of markets stems from the fear of failure. The fear of failure and the potential for commensurate financial losses discourage excessive risk, and the redistribution of assets as a result of such failures is a fundamental function of markets.

In attempting to insulate market participants from that risk, government distorted the markets and fueled "irrational exuberance," to borrow a phrase from the perennial Chairman of the Federal Reserve, Alan Greenspan.

Greenspan's departure in 2006 prior to the fallout from the Great Recession was quite fortuitous. Government's misguided interventions had the same effect as throwing gasoline on a fire. It was the wrong (re)action at the wrong time, and the result was a much more catastrophic series of losses than likely would have occurred had government taken a less intrusive approach.

Government, through its various agencies, cannot dictate a single cohesive economic plan that is better or more efficient than that which results from the billions of cumulative market decisions, which are made daily by informed and conscientious market participants. [93] I do agree that many individuals and companies, who overtly manipulated the markets (some as government co-conspirators), "unfairly benefited" before and after the Great Recession; however, a complicit government is not the proper determiner of fairness.

There are apocryphal stories of stock brokers jumping out of skyscrapers during the Great Depression. What we needed were more bankers and stock brokers making such proverbial leaps in the Great Recession. Many, who were directly responsible for market failures, were not punished for their misdeeds, and any "suffering," which they experienced, was woefully disproportionate to the harm, which they caused. In fact, many such persons, who enjoyed the favor and protection of government, were able to profit handsomely before and after the Great Recession. A government, which was complicit in

---

[93] I recognize the significance and importance of market participants being both "informed" and "conscientious." I also recognize that persons and institutions, including government, actively manipulate and distort market information. It is a proper role of government to prevent (and to avoid participating in) such overt manipulations and to provide consumers with information (*i.e.* education) sufficient to allow them to make informed decisions. The objective should be that the market participants get the benefits of their bargains, regardless of whether those bargains ultimately prove to be "good" or "bad." It is not a proper role of government to assure economic success or to protect market participants from natural corrections and "bad deals."

such behaviors, should not be looked to as a savior of the downtrodden.[94]

Selfishness and self-preservation are inherent human traits; therefore, they are also immutable characteristics of governments. The institution of government, being a creature which takes on the character of those persons who wield it powers, is as much sinner as any corporate baron, partisan voter, or narcissistic politician. That is why, "A government, which does least, governs best."[95] If the formidable powers of government become unfettered, the Leviathan will ultimately destroy those persons, who find themselves dependent upon its charity.

The Nanny State cannot be successful in the long-term. While parents should provide necessaries to their children and should protect those children from significant harm, good parents should not strive to supply their children's every whim and to protect children from any loss or disappointment. Nurturing includes preparation for the child to leave the comfort and security of the parents' home.

The departure of a child from the comforts of his parents' care is much like preparing an eaglet for its first flight. If the child hesitates or falters, a nudge from a nest may be required. This act is necessary and ultimately beneficial despite the fact

---

[94] For additional reading: Allison, John A., *The Financial Crisis and the Free market Cure* (2013). John Allison is the former CEO of Branch Banking & Trust Company (BB&T). After retiring in 2010, Allison assumed the role of President at the Cato Institute.

[95] Some derivation of this quote is sometimes attributed to Thomas Jefferson, among others; however, the quote was actually found in Henry David Thoreau's *Civil Disobedience*. Thoreau was paraphrasing the motto of *The United States Magazine and Democratic Review*: "The best government is that which governs least."

that the child may find himself in an uncomfortable and precarious position before stepping out and taking flight. Despite the risks, independence and self-sufficiency are generally much preferred to a population of adult children suckling *ad nauseum*[96] on the parental teat.

Rather than embracing independence and self-sufficiency, citizens of the Nanny State become increasingly dependent upon government. Such intractable institutional dependence runs counterproductive to the aims of self-sufficiency, individual effort, and personal initiative. Social welfare programs tend to institutionalize complacency. Complacency leads to apathy, and apathy is the antithesis of productivity.

Internationally, Americans are often viewed as embodying the self-reliance, free spirit, and fierce independence of the legendary cowboy. To the extent that Americans view themselves as having those same traits, they will not be well suited to playing the role of government minions.

Perceived safety and government-provided comforts come with costs that include conformity to government mandates (in the interests of supposed "fairness" and efficiency) and losses of personal liberties and individual freedoms.

Liberty and conformity cannot peacefully co-exist. As one is favored, the other must by necessity be restricted and curtailed.

Do you see yourself more as a cowboy or minion?

---

[96] Meaning: To a sickening or excessive degree.

When is a "Surplus" not a Surplus?

Blog Entry – September 6, 2012

Former President Bill Clinton claims a $236 Billion federal budget "surplus" during his term in office. This was the last time that the federal government was "in the black." However, without borrowing from the Social Security Trust Fund and other sources, the actual DEFICIT in his best year would have been $16 Billion. (*i.e.* The combined national debt - public and internal - went up in EVERY year of Clinton's presidency.)

Even ignoring these accounting gimmicks, which magically turned a $16 Billion deficit into an alleged $236 Billion "surplus," it is disingenuous for Clinton to claim primary credit for this supposed feat.

Clinton's administration benefitted TREMENDOUSLY from the stratospheric rise in tech and internet stocks during the late 90's. As the value of the stocks grew and generated Capital Gains (and other income), the taxes derived from those transactions bolstered federal revenues. However, the overinflated "values" of these stocks created a market bubble that burst in 2000 (just as President George W. Bush was coming into office).

This phenomenon was similar to, but not quite as dramatic as, the Housing Bubble that burst in 2007 leading to the most recent Great Recession. Even if one counts the "paper surplus," Clinton did not really DO anything to create it. That is unless he wishes to lay claim to "inventing the internet," much like his Vice President, Al Gore, seemed to do.

The underlying asset values, which led to increased Capital Gains Taxes during the Clinton presidency, were illusory. It was like plugging the federal budget deficit with Monopoly money.

The best thing that Bill Clinton did in his Presidency is that he did nearly nothing. Taking credit for that budget surplus during this period is much like taking credit for the rising tides.

You Didn't Pay for That ... Social Security

Blog Entry – Original Post: November 26, 2012

On Sunday [11/25/2012], the No. 2 Senate Democrat, Sen. Richard Durbin (D-IL), appeared on ABC's "This Week" program and stated:

> *Social Security does not add one penny to our debt - not a penny. It is a separate funded operation.* [Emphasis added.]

Apparently, Durbin has not peeked behind the curtain to realize that there is no viable "Social Security Trust Fund." Nearly all prior receipts have been spent to fund other government activities, and the "Trust Fund" is represented by IOU's from the Federal Government, among more than $16 TRILLION in accumulated national debt.

SOMEHOW that debt, including the IOU's, must be repaid eventually. Either the obligations will be paid by substituting more external debt (*e.g.* to China) for the internal debt, which would be a true exercise in futility, or taxes will have to be raised to pay the future entitlement obligations.[97]

In his op-ed piece from the *New York Times* [11/24/2012], "Our Enemy, the Payroll Tax," Ross Douthat argues in favor of dispensing with the Social Security payroll tax:

> *Payroll taxes are a relic of New Deal Machiavellianism: By taking a bight out of every worker's paycheck and promising postretirement returns, Franklin D. Roosevelt effectively disguised Social Security as a pay-as-you-go system, even though the program actually redistributes from rich to*

---

[97] An equally unpalatable alternative would be to stimulate inflation so that the debt would be paid back with "cheaper" (*i.e.* less valuable) dollars.

poor and young to old. That disguise has helped keep Social Security sacrosanct. But, the costs of this disguise have grown too great to bear.

One of these two supposedly knowledgeable and well-informed individuals is necessarily wrong. Durbin and Douthat are both too intelligent to think that they can both be right.

Durbin wants to maintain the fiction that workers pay into the Social Security ("SS") system over their careers, and upon retirement, each retiree gets "his" money back. From this fiction, those receiving SS (and Medicare) gain a sense of "entitlement." AARP commercials and other advocacy groups often repeat the mantra, "You EARNED your Social Security and Medicare."

The Supreme Court of the United States ("SCOTUS") has ruled consistently that there is no enforceable expectancy in favor of one, on whose behalf, payroll taxes (or Self-employment "SE" Taxes) are paid. No recipient has an "account" from which payments may be drawn, and should payments not be forthcoming, there is no standing for bringing an action against the federal government for breach of promise.

The ability of retirees to collect benefits relies entirely upon the political will of the government to maintain the programs (a will supported by the power of the ballot box) and the ability of other taxpayers (younger employees and wealthier individuals) to pay into the system and to ultimately fund the inevitable deficiencies.

The Problem? ... Old age entitlement programs have been woefully underfunded for generations. Depending on one's perspective, entitlement programs have suffered from a lack of foresight and/or from an insufficiency of political will, both of which would have been required to extract the taxes necessary to have fully maintained the programs. Payments, which will be necessary to fund the programs into the future, must now come from either the future retirees, if it is, in fact, a "separately funded" pay-as-you-go system, or from the more propertied classes, if the programs are merely a guise for a monumental wealth redistribution scheme.

Some persons would argue that the benefits and expectations of these programs, while perhaps reasonable at the outset, have become bloated and unrealistic given current demographics and economic realities. It may also be argued that "fully funded" programs would have long ago crippled the economy.

Former Presidential candidate and Texas Governor, Rick Perry, was castigated following a debate, which occurred during the Republican Primaries. Perry's offense was that he dared to call Social Security a government-sponsored Ponzi Scheme. The horrors of the billion dollar fraud effected by the financier, Bernie Madoff, were still fresh in the minds of those, who heard Perry utter those words. However, the true "horror" is that calling Social Security a Ponzi Scheme may have been a gracious euphemism.[98]

What are the realities? ... Baby Boomers are quickly aging into these entitlement programs, and outlays for old age benefits

---

[98] Salsman, Richard M., "Social Security is Much Worse Than a Ponzi Scheme - and Here's How to End It," *Forbes* (September 27, 2011).

with continue to grow for several years. The relative number of workers paying into the system compared to the number of recipients is declining, as are the gross contributions (even before the ill-conceived "Payroll Tax Holiday").

Eventually, the increasing payments will exceed the decreasing contributions, and the Social Security Administration ("SSA") will have to call in its IOU's from the federal government. At that point, the federal government will issue more third-party debt or raise taxes (presumably on some ill-defined class of "wealthy" taxpayers). However, there is a limit upon how much wealth can be removed from the economic system before the letting takes an adverse toll on the health of the economy. The results of over spending and excessive taxation are much like a mother eating her young.

The growth of entitlements, the mounting national debt, a changing fiscal landscape, and the danger of the United States losing its position as the single dominant player on the world economic stage, all combine to form a perfect storm which threatens fiscal destruction.

The three (3) primary contributors to future government spending will be: Entitlements, Interest on the National Debt, and Defense. In the near future, all other "discretionary spending" (*e.g.* Education, EPA, FTC, FCC, Transportation, *etc.*) could be squeezed out of the budget entirely. It is irrational and unrealistic to expect that there would not be spending cuts within the cannibalizing programs.

There is an accepted and reasonable role that government can and should play in providing fundamental services, including an economic safety net for citizens. Such a safety net should promote innovation by lessening the likelihood of devastation from a single event or inadvertent wrong turn in life. However, if benefits from government are too generous or the qualification criteria are too lenient, such programs are likely to encourage complacency, promote neglect, and shelter excessive risk.

There should be a consensus among the producers of wealth and consumers of benefits on the proper and sustainable role of government. The costs of mutually agreed upon benefits and services from government represent the investment required to maintain a fluid, efficient, and civil society. Everyone benefits from an orderly and efficient system, and everyone should be willing to contribute toward the maintenance of that system. However, no one should have a free ride.

The first step is to identify what are the core functions that we, as a people, want government to provide. Then, we must realistically establish costs and spending estimates to adequately provide for those functions. Finally, we must establish a taxing and revenue system capable of providing the long term funding needs for that level of government spending.

The debate must be frank and honest. The spending and funding plans must be realistic and conservative. It does no one any good to promise the world, if you are unable to deliver on that promise.

Accept this fact, "Your government has lied to you." The government is incapable of providing everything that you want and perhaps even some things to which you believe you are "entitled." One can bemoan that fact and cry, "Woe is me," or he can decide to make a concerted effort toward taking responsibility for and control of his own life and to do what it takes to look out for his best interests and those of his family (or others of importance to him). Is that not the way things are supposed to be anyhow?

"Progressive" philosophies and policies assume that "wealth creators" will not revolt at becoming the pawns and whipping boys of the federal government. The wealth redistribution, which such philosophies favor, results in nothing short of the nationalization of that wealth.

The wealthy need not invest their wealth in the creation of additional wealth. They may very well be content to live off of their accumulated wealth. Additionally, that wealth is mobile. If wealth creators continue to be demonized by the President and the federal government, they need not invest that wealth in such an unfavorable climate. If the last few years have shown anything, it is that government cannot create wealth, and government cannot "fix" the economy.

Active government involvement in the economy is at best a necessary evil and temporary fix. It is time for government to concentrate on its basic functions (*e.g.* Infrastructure, education, national defense, law enforcement, and even a minimal social safety net). Until government can do these things flawlessly (which it has never demonstrated that it can do), it is asinine to expand the role of government to include the micromanagement of the lives of its citizens (*e.g.* healthcare).

A more recent [05/06/2013] McClatchy news service article, "Obama Proposal on Social Security Outrages Backers," highlights the basic problems regarding the entitlement mindset. SS and Medicare are cannibalizing the federal budget, and increasing payments obligations will continue to impair the core functions of government. There is no doubt that old-age entitlement programs in their present incarnations will inevitably be insolvent.

Nearly everyone agrees that significant changes are needed to keep the programs solvent. The referenced article speaks of "Liberal groups angered by Obama's proposed Social Security CUTS." [Emphasis added.] However, no one has proposed "cutting" Social Security benefits; although, actual cuts would likely be prudent. The heated argument is about the proposed DECREASE IN THE RATE OF INCREASE for benefits.

The change brought about by tying future increases to the "chained" CPI in the current year would be a miniscule 2/10's of ONE PERCENT (from a 1.7% annual increase to 1.5%). For the average recipient, it would be a difference of $36 next year ($3 / mo. ... less than 10 cents / day), and the cumulative annual difference would be $360 in TEN YEARS (still less than $1 / day).

If politicians cannot accept a $36 *per capita* change in government entitlement spending annually, there is little hope for addressing the TRILLIONS in budget deficiencies, which are looming!

What Tax Rate is Fair for the "Rich"?

Blog Entry - August 17, 2012

I reposted a YouTube video of Erskine Bowles, former Chief of Staff under Democratic President, Bill Clinton. In the video, Bowles summarized his work on the Simpson-Bowles Deficit-Reduction Commission by saying that gaining control of deficits and debt requires a three-pronged approach:

- Economic Growth;
- Tax Revenues; and
- Spending Cuts.

I have asked repeatedly of those, who are inclined to soak the rich, "What tax rates are 'fair' (given that the rich already pay proportionally as much, or more, in taxes than their collective share of income)?"[99]

According to Bowles, a "tax only" strategy would require:

- Income Tax rates to go up across the board with the Highest Marginal Rate more than doubling to 80%;
- The top Corporate Tax rate, which is already the highest among major economies, to nearly double to 70%; and
- The Capital Gains and Dividends rates to TRIPLE to 50%.

Bowles agreed that such rates would be entirely prohibitive to small business owners, and the resulting tax burden would stifle economic growth.

---

[99] The top 1% of federal tax filers -- those with adjusted gross incomes of at least $343,927 in 2009 -- earned nearly 17% of all Adjusted Gross Income ("AGI") in the country and paid more than a third (37%) of all federal income taxes collected by the government. *See* Sahadi, Jeanne, "How much should the rich pay in taxes?," www.cnn.com (August 30, 2012).

It is time to quit thinking that there is a well out there that will never run dry. Soaking the rich is not a panacea for poor fiscal policies. It is time for reasonable fiscal policies that match effective spending with efficient revenue production. It is time to act like responsible adults, and if there are those among us, who insist on acting like spoiled children, it is time for some tough love.

The necessary changes will result in a rude awakening throughout government and the population. All parties must understand that the social "safety net" cannot be the equivalent of a "hammock." Government social programs can never provide a "comfortable" standard of living. Falling into a safety net is not generally something that you WANT to do.

Falling into such a net, often results in injury of its own. The intent is to avoid a more severe and catastrophic injury. We cannot coast through life taking comfort in the fact that we can rely upon unemployment benefits, "refundable" tax credits, inadequately funded old-age entitlements, and government subsidized food, housing, healthcare, *etc.* Dependency and self-sufficiency are totally incompatible.

I am still waiting for someone to put forth a plan, which pays for existing (and proposed) benefits and entitlements without waiting more than a generation before we stop running budget deficits and stop increasing the astronomical National Debt. The "cuts" being proposed within Congress are not even a drop in the bucket. In the past several years, the federal government borrowed as much as 40 cents of every dollar, which the government spent in a given year.

The underlying premise in favor of the expanded role of government relies upon an uneasy confidence that a benevolent government would only take that which is "fair," and only so much as would be required for the general welfare of the collective.

Gerald Ford said:

A government, which is capable of giving you everything that you want, is also capable of taking everything that you have.

Some would question the "fairness" of fifty percent (50%) of taxpayers contributing less than three percent (3%) toward the common good and general welfare. The other fifty percent (50%), who pay more than 97% (or better yet the 25% that pays nearly 90%) toward those noble aims, reasonably expect a greater say in how *their* money is spent.

I do not believe in a benevolent government. I believe that government, like any institution (or being), has a nearly insatiable drive toward growth and self-preservation. Government will never restrain itself voluntarily. If left unfettered, it will continue to grow and ravage resources until it is crushed under its own weight.

The Federal Government nearly shut down last year over spending cuts that did not even amount to a rounding error in the budget. The necessary cuts are many multiples of the amounts, which are being proposed. Without substantial changes, the

National Debt will be 200%, or more, of GDP by 2037, with just INTEREST on the debt alone being as much as 10% of GDP.[100]

If President Obama were honest and acknowledged that no tax rate on those, who fall within his definition of "rich," would be sufficient to pay for the existing unfunded government obligations, then hope and change would quickly turn into harsh reality.

Republicans know that taxes are ultimately going to rise ... period. There is little chance that taxes will not rise during the next presidential term regardless of who occupies the White House.

The prevailing arguments should be in favor of revenue efficiencies and responsible spending. These changes require substantial revisions of the ENTIRE tax code not just fumbling with the rates. The "rate" does not matter if you do not modify the definition of the "income" (*i.e.* the "base") to which it will be applied. Similarly, each tax deduction and credit should be reviewed and independently justified.

It is fair to say that the infamous "rich" do not pay enough taxes in the U.S. However, neither does everyone else. One cannot have his cake and eat it too, but there is a point at which there are diminishing returns.

Even if a corporation does not pay income taxes itself, taxes are paid on the income of its employees (*e.g.* Income, Social Security, Medicare, *etc.*), taxes are paid on the dividends to its shareholders and interest on its bonds, capital gains taxes

---

[100] A ratio of DEBT/GDP of 80%, or less, is generally favored by economists.

are paid on the increase in value of the stock when sold, and companies pay sales taxes as well as property taxes.

Income Taxes on corporations effectively "doubles" the tax on the income of the corporation. It is taxed at both the entity level and at the shareholder level. If all such income were allowed to be taxed as the maximum rates, without taking advantage of the much maligned "deductions," credits, and exclusions, the tax would exceed seventy-five percent (75%) of every dollar earned. No business could operate effectively in that environment.

France imposed a Seventy-five Percent (75%) tax rate on the super rich in an attempt to plug its fiscal sieve. News stories at the time identified several prominent French citizens seeking to change their citizenship and residence to Russia and other countries in order to avoid the tax.

Wealth is mobile, particularly corporate wealth and the extreme wealth of the super rich, and their wealth will be courted by countries less inclined to pluck the geese that lay golden eggs. However, this issue does not relate to just the Buffets, Gates, and Waltons of the world.

I have friends who are expatriates (*i.e.* Americans living and working abroad). These are not persons with ostentatious or inherited wealth, but they are successful professionals (*e.g.* Doctors, Lawyers, Business Executives, *etc.*). Such persons "compete" financially with colleagues from other countries, who do not have to pay taxes (or pay considerably less taxes) in their home countries.

Although Americans by birth, these expatriates live abroad some times for many years or decades, and some may not have any intention of returning to or permanently residing in the U.S. For this latter group, their only real connections to the U.S. are their passports, and increasingly, many such persons question the benefit of U.S. citizenship in a global society.

While the number of such economic defections is relatively small, that number increasing:

> *The number of citizenship renunciations has surged from 742 in 2001 to more that 1,854 to date in 2013.*"[101]

Personally, I can hardly imagine giving up my U.S. citizenship for any reason, but we must recognize that the higher the price that the government places on citizenship the more likely it will be that some will find that price too high to pay.

Paying one's fair share is an easy concept upon which to agree. However, defining "fair share" is much harder than simply establishing a higher tax rate for the supposed "tax cheats."

The tax rate tables take up less than a handful of pages out of the thousands of pages of Internal Revenue Code (the "Code") and accompanying Regulations. The more difficult procedures relate to defining the "base" of income which is subject to a particular tax rate. This process includes identifying and classifying income as well as identifying deductions, which are allowed against that income.

---

[101] Douglas, William, "Expats Ditching Citizenship over Taxes," *Star-News* (November 28, 2013).

Application of the tax code follows a "law" similar to Newton's Third Law of Motion: *For every action, there is an equal and opposite reaction.* A similar result occurs when one applies pressure to an inflated balloon. "Strengthening" the tax code in one area usually means that some "weakness" will be opened up elsewhere and "exploited" by persons and entities called upon to pay those taxes. Continuing with my analogy, apply too much pressure on all sides, and the balloon will burst.

Persons that resist the call to pay increasingly more taxes are somehow seen as "unpatriotic" or uncaring. However, many, if not most, persons, who promote a more active government, contribute relatively little toward the care and feeding of the growing Leviathan. Many such persons are wards and minions of the state, and such persons are necessarily committed to government's continued expansion in order to assure their own continued sustenance.

Wealthy individuals and corporations did not write the Tax Code. Politicians at some point made informed decisions based upon cost/benefit analyses, which supposedly justified the definitions and concepts, which are presently in the Code. One may disagree with those decisions, and the resulting laws are certainly subject to change. However, when an increasing majority of U.S. citizens contribute nearly nothing to the general welfare, assigning blame to higher income taxpayers and corporations for "not paying their fair share" is without merit.

Our new Constitution is now established,
and has an appearance
that promises permanency; but
in this world nothing can be said to be certain,
except death and taxes.

- BENJAMIN FRANKLIN
in a letter to Jean-Baptiste Leroy
1789.

WHAT'S WRONG WITH
A FEDERAL BUDGET DEFICIT?

Blog Entry – February 27, 2013

Prior to the "Great Recession," the largest Deficit under President George W. Bush was less than $500 Billion (which was too high). In EIGHT (8) years (and with two concurrent wars), Bush accumulated less than $3 TRILLION in debt (which again was too much).

With the initial "stimulus" following the recession, the 2009 deficit was $1.4 TRILLION, which was more than 40 cents of every dollar spent by the federal government. (As a percentage of the Gross Domestic Product ("GDP"), it was the largest deficit since WWII.) That was President Obama's first year in office.

Starting from that astronomical number, thank goodness that the annual deficit it did not GROW any more. Nevertheless, the cumulative deficits during Obama's first FOUR (4) years in office have been more than $4.5 TRILLION (> $1 TRILLION / yr.). Currently, the accumulated debt of the United States is approaching $17 TRILLION (more than the entire annual GDP of the U.S.).

The most "aggressive" proposed "cuts" in spending do not result in a balanced budget for a generation (*i.e.* 2035). Within the next decade, the accumulated deficit will likely exceed $25 TRILLION, and by 2035, the debt is projected to be 250% of GPD (2.5 x GDP). Many economists warn that debt, which is more than 80% of GDP, is likely more than can be sustained by an economy over a longer term.

Currently, the federal government benefits from historically low interest rates, but if rates return to historical averages (say a modest 6%), just the INTEREST on those projected debt loads would overwhelm reasonably available revenue sources for the federal government. THAT is why spending cuts are needed.

Obama himself proposed cutting the deficits "in half" by 2013 after passage of HIS nearly $800 BILLION stimulus bill (the 2nd one). However, annual spending of more than $3 TRILLION has become the "norm." That level of spending is nearly $1 TRILLION (1/3) more than can be sustained by current tax revenues. Historically, tax revenues and federal spending have been roughly 20% of GDP, which according to many economists is the level supportable by a given economy without interfering with economic growth.

When you have only 50% of taxpayers making significant contributions to the "general welfare," there is a limit on the amount that can be siphoned off by the federal government. Contrary to popular belief, there is not an unlimited pool of hoarded "wealth" that can be used to fund unrestrained government spending, and the government cannot print enough money to spend its way out of deficits and debts.

Obama and the Democrats speak of "reducing deficits" not "debt." They have given up on reducing the debt burden carried by the United States. Instead, they wholeheartedly expect that debt burden to continue to grow commensurate with the hoped for growth of the economy without any dollar reduction whatsoever. Politicians no longer ask is it appropriate (or authorized) that government should implement some program or provide some benefit. Instead, they respond to constituent wish lists and to the demands of special interest groups. Politicians are continually pushing the envelope in an attempt to empower government to do even more.

Having made the decision to have an ever expanding federal government, politicians then look to fund that overcommitted government. When tax revenues fall short, because taxpayers resist the forced contributions to government, that government, undeterred, goes out and borrows money to fund the shortfall.

What happens when there is a true "emergency?" What happens when there is a global depression, not recession? What happens when we have a contested war with a formidable foe, rather than fighting a ragtag group of mercenaries from a third world country or banana republic? What happens when, not if, a large chunk of southern California slips into the Pacific Ocean from a major earthquake?

If we have maximized government spending and there are no reserves, what then? Do we go to China with hat in hand and ask for more money?

Consider that China very well could be that "formidable foe" given its propensity to thwart the United States and given China's involvement in repeated cyber attacks against U.S. companies and government agencies.

Does no one see a problem here?

It's Easy Spending Someone Else's Money

Blog Entry – April 16, 2013

The tax system for the State of North Carolina is in need of significant overhaul and modernization. That system has not had a major overhaul in over seventy (70) years. The current system was implemented originally to address the ills of the Great Depression at a time when North Carolina had an agricultural and manufacturing based economy. The economy of the time was tied to tobacco, furniture, and textiles. A lot has changed in the intervening decades, but God forbid, that we touch anyone's sacred cow in order to modernize the tax system. Until politicians are willing to sacrifice a few such cows, we will continually be fed a bunch of bull.

A newspaper article clearly demonstrates why tax reform and modernization is such an elusive beast.[102] I was *shocked* to learn that the state was considering whether to ask those that use a particular resource to actually pay for that resource.

The proposed scheme would have required boat registrants to pay a portion of the costs for inlet dredging. I must admit that my feigned sympathies regarding the maligned "TENFOLD INCREASE" waned quickly and completely. I realized that the proposed change would increase registration fees from a miniscule FIFTEEN DOLLARS ($15.00) annually across the board up to a modest and tiered $150.00 / yr. (the amount applicable to boats 40' or longer).

Lest you think that only a privileged class of boaters would have such adverse reactions to fee increases, one might recall

---

[102] *Star News* - "Bill Revised to Scale Back Boat-fee Hikes" (April 16, 2013).

that legislators in districts served by state ferries were aghast at the proposal that ferry fees actually cover the cost of operating the ferries! HAVE YOU EVER HEARD OF ANYTHING SO APPALLING AND ABSURD?

Then there are those shore-hugging beachfront property owners, who expect the federal, state, and local governments, to fork over tens of millions of dollars to repeatedly "renourish beaches" in order to protect their investments.

Here is a thought:

Do not build a million-dollar house on a spit of sand that you know is likely to wash away in the next tidal surge spawned by an inevitable hurricane!

Regardless, the cost of maintaining property should be an accepted (and planned for) cost of ownership and utilization. Citizens, who demand government services, should be willing to contribute appreciably to the provision of such services.

As an example, why is it deemed unreasonable to implement a gas tax that is sufficient to handle routine and necessary maintenance of the state's road and bridges and to assure their continued development?

We have been sold on the idea that government will provide ever increasing benefits and that the sacrifices required in funding those benefits will be borne by someone else. Too often, taxpayers collectively are required to heavily subsidize benefits that extend to a limited few. Those persons and entities that directly benefit from government projects and programs often are too far removed from the cost element of the cost/benefit analysis to appreciate the necessary sacrifices of taxpayers.

Such an analysis, including complete costs and realistic funding mechanisms, should be required to justify the existence of any benefit or government program. Without being able to appreciate the true cost and required sacrifices, it is impossible to make an informed decision whether to implement or continue a program. If citizens wish to continue or to expand the benefits, which government provides, it is time that all of us know the actual costs, and it is time that citizens feel the requisite pain of providing those benefits. Only then, should decisions be made collectively regarding the implementation or continuation of any specific benefit, project, or program.

The "tax" debate is ultimately a debate on the proper role of government, and the process of defining that role is influenced by the highly subjective concepts of philosophy, ethics, and morality. Unlike many of my colleagues, I am not certain that a discussion regarding the scientific and technical theories of finance, economics, and accounting are entirely determinative of the hotly contested issues.

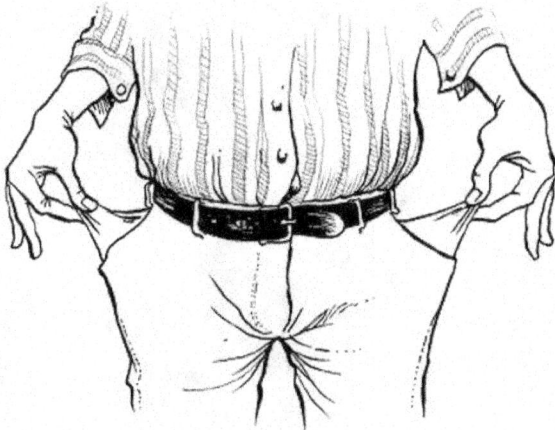

I'M FROM THE GOVERNMENT, I'M HERE TO HELP

Something between the Nanny State and Big Brother

Blog Entry – June 6, 2012

Those with means used to recognize that with privilege comes an obligation to contribute to the benefit of society in general and to give to the less fortunate (but not to deprive others of the opportunity and satisfaction of providing for themselves). Learned persons sought to enlighten the less experienced and to provide intellectual tools, which are necessary to assure that all persons are capable of making more informed decisions (without imposing a particular world view upon them).

The concept is summed upon the adage:

Give a man a fish, and you feed him for a day, but
Teach a man to fish and he can feed himself for a lifetime.

Today, one extreme of the political spectrum seems to want to infantilize the citizenry in order to assure permanent dependence upon the state. The feeling being that the masses are incapable of helping themselves. The other extreme seems to prey upon and exploit ignorance and fear among members of the populace. The idea being that, in darkness and uncertainty, persons can be led as sheep to slaughter.

Either position provides a base from which to assert power and control for the benefit of those wielding that power. The guiding objective for all persons in government (and society) should be to promote knowledge and ability among citizens and for those citizens to combine those tools with opportunity and self-reliance so that each person has a fair shot at success and fairly can assume responsibility for his own shortcomings.

Generally, I do not give politicians credit for being smart enough to intentionally bring forth the evils, to which they often give life. I believe that it is more like unleashing the evils contained in Pandora's Box, which once unleashed upon the earth, cannot be undone.

Politicians are told by bureaucratic wonks that there is a secret that only they know, and if the government and society at large should only put their trust in this secret knowledge, then all will be better off. However, the supposed secret is not so much the spawn of knowledge and wisdom as it is a coveted source of power and control. Power, once accumulated and focused, gives rise to an ever expanding fiefdom. The Leviathan grows constantly feeding upon its environment.

I am all for charity, but I believe that charity begins at home. It is easy to argue that someone deemed "rich" should pay more toward the general welfare. However, what are others willing to do for their fellow man (and for themselves)? Did the biblical tithe (which is 10% by the way) not apply both to the rich man and the widow?

The one immutable fact is that there is not enough wealth in the United States to fund that to which many persons believe they are "entitled" from government. Another point that should be made is that you cannot "cut" taxes for persons that do not PAY taxes (the misnomer, "Earned Income Credit," among others, notwithstanding).

First and foremost, taxes must and will rise in the coming years. Yes, this will disproportionately affect the "rich," but EVERYONE must be prepared to pay more and receive less.

Retirees did not "earn" their Social Security and Medicare when they collect 2-3 times (or more) in benefits than they paid in. That is welfare pure and simple. It may be the "right" thing to institute a Nanny State, but everyone needs to be honest about and understand what is going on.

Those receiving such benefits need to acknowledge and accept that they are beholding to the "wealthy," who, in effect, are writing checks for welfare to the masses, and we need to accept that a government, which takes on the mantle of "parent," assumes the power to treat its citizens like children.

Forced altruism is not charity. It is conscription, and institutionalized theft in the form of a "tax" is no less damnable. Regardless of one's leanings in favor of individual rights or egalitarianism, it is most important that we understand and accept that wealth is finite and mobile. Burden the "rich" too much and they hoard their wealth or relocate their money, ideas, and innovation to a more favorable locale.

I do not disagree that "unfairness" and "inequality" exist in the world, and I would likely echo many of the personal sentiments against avarice and greed as may be argued by the most liberal among us. However, I believe that it is unreasonable, and perhaps even counterproductive, to seek the elimination of all "unfairness" in life and to attempt to insulate individuals from the adverse effects of their bad decisions. Regardless, I do not believe that is a proper role of government to implement some egalitarian notion of economic equity and fairness. Additionally, no matter how noble such a goal may be, I believe that the mechanism of government is completely ineffectual to achieving that goal.

I reposted a story online about the Chinese Premier, a man famous for his humble upbringing, who parlayed his position and power for the benefit of himself and his family to the tune of nearly $3 Billion. Government is no more a benevolent master than the wealthy capitalist. For both, there are concurrent addictions to power and wealth. The only differences:

For one, Wealth begets Power, and

for the other, Power begets the Wealth.

Government complains about and is envious of the profitability (*i.e.* economic efficiency) in the private sector. Rather than promoting these economic efficiencies, government chooses to intervene and manipulate markets so that the resulting transactions favor various special interests.

Also, legislative bodies sometimes pass legislation in response to some real or imagined crisis. The objectives of the act itself may be well intended; however, such acts are often enabling legislation whereby the ultimate promulgation of regulations and enforcement of such regulations will be undertaken by one or more government agencies. The applications of burdensome regulations often lead to interference and micromanagement by government bureaucrats unless such administrative powers are constantly reviewed and challenged.

In the wake of the WorldCom and Enron accounting scandals, the federal government imposed Sarbanes-Oxley[103] ("SOX"). Supposedly, the legislation was passed to tighten internal controls and to increase some concept of "transparency" in public companies. However, the practical effect is to burden the private sector with levels of bureaucracy and inefficiencies similar to those suffered by government. If large companies are plodding and cumbersome, rather than spry and adapting, government is better suited to controlling the activities and outcomes of the private sector.

SOX has done little to nothing to improve the efficiencies of the market or the reliability of information reporting. Companies are required to spend more time documenting and "justifying" actions, and that time could be better utilized making informed decisions and increasing productivity. Managers are distracted by their fears of sanctions and penalties, which may be imposed for inadvertent acts, and they are distracted from more productive and profitable endeavors. Therefore, such regulations should be reexamined and curtailed, if not abolished entirely.

Liberals believe that government can be harnessed as a tool so that the downtrodden and needy can be made (more) equal to the wealthy. I believe that those who act as puppeteers and who control the functions of government have no desires to free the dependent citizens from their bondage. With dependence comes compliance ... with compliance comes support ... with support

---

[103] Also known as the "Public Company Accounting Reform and Investor Protection Act" (in the Senate) and the "Corporate and Auditing Accountability and Responsibility Act" (in the House of Representatives) – 2002.

comes power. The only way that a man can improve his station in life is through his own concerted efforts. The government will not "build that."

When you have a single source provider or single payor source (*i.e.* government), the lack of competition and alternatives foster inefficiencies, waste, and corruption. Do not expect this immutable fact to be changed by an increasingly powerful government. Benevolence comes from prudence and humility, and an unfettered sovereign government and its minions have neither.

Government wants to dictate regulations by fiat for nearly every industry and every aspect of life (*e.g.* Obamacare), and we are told: "Trust us. We know what we're doing, and we certainly don't have any ulterior motives."

Some might call me a paranoid cynic. Perhaps, I am fairly called a cynic, but it is not paranoia if it is true. Governments are NOT benevolent, and the only good government is a restrained one with limited powers. Unleashing the Leviathan is an invitation to disaster!

Supply and Demand versus Right and Wrong

© 2012

Introduction -

We, as a society, need to pick up a Thesaurus and use adjectives that remove "morality" (and subjective concepts of "right" and "wrong") from discussions of property rights and economics.

Someone's wealth or earnings may be described as "disproportionate" or "unfathomable" or "disconcerting" by some persons, but not all individuals will feel similarly. A rule or privilege, which may seem perfectly acceptable for the "average" person, may seem "immoral" to some when that same rule or privilege benefits someone making $100 Million per year.

We all expect to retain the fruits of our labors, and those "labors" include capital investments. The same "favorable" Capital Gains rates apply to all persons. Are tax laws somehow "immoral" because someone benefits from code provisions exactly in the manner in which they were intended by Congress?

It is appropriate to discuss taxing strategies based upon fiscal need and cost/benefit analyses, but accumulating (and even hoarding) wealth is not intrinsically immoral. The "morality" is in the use of such riches, and I would argue that government has hardly proven itself a worthy and "moral" steward of the wealth, which it confiscates from its citizens.

429

A Nation of Laws -

A world of finite resources has always existed, and the basic laws of supply and demand remain in play. I have argued for years, and continue to believe, that many persons, who work for "minimum wage," do so because they have failed to apply themselves in order to acquire skills, which would make such employees more valuable and marketable to (other) employers.

If one drops out of high school, can he reasonably expect to draw a salary of $100,000 annually? If one's dominant skill is the ability to punch a time clock, what is that true value of his services to an employer?

I do not disagree that there is room for improvements:

- The Minimum Wage has been stagnant for too long, and it should be tied to inflation so that it does not devalue over time, and

- There is no real justification for Capital Gains rates to be one-half (½) of maximum ordinary income tax rates.

Nevertheless, the controlling laws were consciously made by elected representatives, who were supposedly weighing the interests of their respective constituents in passing legislation. The remedy, if one is needed, is to elect legislators that are more inclined to the view that a particular voter espouses, or who weigh the competing interests differently.

There is little benefit to demonizing a duly elected representative or his constituents as being inherently immoral. Each person is entitled to vote his or her convictions and to act in his or her own self-interests. Government, however, should not be the arbiter of morality.

The Grass isn't always Greener -

The "math" required to bring the entire population of the earth to even a fraction of the standard of living of the United States in the near term is utterly insurmountable. So, I will not even identify that as an objective.

However, there is some credibility in a "collective" outlook and philosophy. There are certainly efficiencies and economies of scale, which are at play when persons work together. Mutually beneficial activities should be fostered and encouraged. However, "collectivism," whereby social and economic controls are vested in a central authority, inspires much less confidence. Collectivism may work well on paper, but it functions terribly in practice (as demonstrated by history).

No amount of regulation (or religion) will ever rid society of inherent self-interest toward which most persons strive. Because of this, all persons and all institutions are corruptible. I believe that it is easier to instill morality and proper behavior at the individual level, and I believe that it is impossible to institutionalize morality and ideal behaviors.

The more powerful the collective (or individual) the more susceptible to corruption: "Power corrupts, and absolute power corrupts absolutely."

Individuals will "conform" to dictated behaviors only when it can be demonstrated that such behaviors are in their own best interests or when noncompliance has such dire consequences that conformity can be compelled.

Where government fails to convince persons that the desired behavior or dictated prohibition is in best interests of the individual and thereafter attempts to manipulate citizens by the imposition of penalties or sanctions, society must consider the costs of enforcement in comparison to the supposed benefits. Where laws are based upon less than universally accepted positions, the costs of enforcement (as measured by expenditures for law enforcement and penalties imposed upon violators) may be extreme. We have the history of Prohibition to prove this point.

Definition of Value -

The "value" of one's services and wealth is determined by that for which it can be exchanged. Nothing has economic value except to the extent that some other party in the open market is ready, willing, and able to exchange some object or service having a corresponding value.

What is the value of a scribe in a society with near full literacy? What is the value of a blacksmith in a motorized society?

In more recent times, computers made entire classes of jobs obsolete. If one dedicates his or her life to these obsolete skills, it would be unreasonable to expect that he or she would be well compensated for services that have little demand.

In more contemporary terms, I once worked with a lady who graduated from a teacher's college with a degree in Latin just as that "dead" language lost favor as a required college prep course. Rather than pining away and mourning the "waste" or "loss" of her education, she used her intellect and personal talents in developing more marketable skills. She adapted by learning new skills in public accounting.

Some union workers, particularly in the auto industry, grew to expect more and more compensation and benefits while the companies, for which they "toiled," failed to adapt to technology or foreign competition. Even the most skilled blacksmith must be willing to adapt his compensation expectations or develop new skills. However, institutionalizing a particular skill set and increasing compensation (by union contract) makes such skills inefficient and such compensation unsustainable over time.

Before changes were forced by the Great Recession and the resulting downturn in the economy, as much as $3-5,000 from the unit sales of "American" branded and domestically manufactured automobiles went to pay benefits to RETIRED auto workers.

Like unions, governments are more adept at institutionalizing and protecting the *status quo* rather than assuring true progress and innovation. Whether it is the Military-Industrial Complex or teacher/government employee unions, change is not easy to advance.

Market forces may seem harsh at times (inevitably there are "winners" and "losers"), but I believe that an open and fluid market makes a better allocation of privileges and resources than a government bureaucracy whose inevitable role will be to protect an ever growing collection of fiefdoms.

A Marketplace of Ideas -

I think that most persons could ultimately agree on the societal goals and ideals, but many persons would likely disagree as to the most effective and efficient route(s). Political debate is quickly brought to an impasse when one (or both) side(s) asserts that its positions are based upon an immutable revelation from the Divine or from omniscience, which is available only to a privileged few.

As much as I may abhor an ostentatious lifestyle of one who hoards inherited wealth, I do not believe that being rich is a sin, and I do not believe that government should be an instrument of charity through which the majority can redistribute the wealth of others. It is easy to be charitable with other people's money.

The fallacy of most political arguments today is the belief that there is a single immediately implementable right answer that will apply to all persons and situations in perpetuity.

We must accept incremental improvements and incremental failures (from which we can learn and adjust). We must also accept that what may be reasonable today may not be the best solution in the future. When a man is afraid to commit any failure, the result is inaction and timidity. We should not fear or detest changing paths, but it would be beneficial to recognize that most persons will be inclined to take their first steps toward any destination on the path, which is best known and most familiar to them.

I readily acknowledge the existence of what, in the best of times, might be described as "indifference" among market forces when it comes to satisfying one's basic needs. I also will acknowledge that, at its worst, such indifference can develop into malevolence (often fed by greed). Liberal minded persons would interpose the government between the market participants in order to ameliorate the potentially harsh outcomes of market forces.

However, I no more believe in an entirely benevolent state than I do in the existence of a benevolent dictator (and for the same reasons). Just as I believe that it is against human nature for one to be altruistic, I also believe that it is the nature of institutions (including governments) to be concerned more with the perpetuation and self-preservation of the institution rather than serving constituents. I believe that it is only when individuals consciously forego egoism and bureaucrats stop protecting their fiefdoms that exceptions are made to those general rules.

I prefer market forces for four (4) reasons:

(i)   There is a fundamental admonition, *Caveat Emptor* or "Buyer Beware," rather than a naïve belief someone else (*i.e.* government) is looking out for the "consumer's" best interests;

(ii)   The consumer is in the best position of negotiating for his necessaries, so that he can evaluate his personal needs (and wants) and can establish priorities for the same;

(iii)   The interplay between "consumers" and "producers" establishes a value for scarce commodities, and the "face-to-face" value exchange determines the availability and distribution of the commodity; and

(iv)   Through direct participation in the *quid-pro-quo* transaction, all parties have a better understanding of and appreciation for the costs of production and the ultimate value of the goods and services, as opposed to an irrational belief that such things just "are."

This process is not inherently "fair" if one defines fairness in terms of equal distribution of resources or the absence of unmet needs. However, I contend that the process, even if unequal, is equitable, or at least there is no evidence of a more equitable solution, which has proven effective in the long term. This process is uncomfortable because we do not like the idea that basic necessities are (and will be) rationed.

Society has an ever expanding definition of "necessaries," yet there continues to be a finite pool of resources (*i.e.* wealth), from which the government can draw to fill the growing demands of citizens. This is the realization, which most people find difficult to grasp and understand, and even those who understand it, find it difficult to accept.

Conclusion -

We have ample history from which to draw:

- Marxism and Communism work in theory, "From each according to his ability, and to each according to his need;" BUT

- The practicalities are that wealth and resources shrink in an environment where the effort (risk) is individual but the benefit (reward) goes to the collective.

With illusions of "safety" come dependence, and such dependence decreases initiative and increases the demand for more institutional resources and services. To paraphrase Margaret Thatcher, the end result in the Nanny State is that, "You always run out of other people's money." Additionally,

436

with certainty of outcomes, comes the prerequisite of conformity, and that conformity is incompatible with personal liberties. Irrespective of the dollar cost, the loss of personal rights and individual liberties are too high a price to pay for illusions of safety and perceived comforts.

I am not relegating government to the role of bystander. There are times when abuses in the markets result in inherent unfairness and when active manipulations of the markets affect the fluidity. It is the role of government to curb such abuses and to assure fluidity in the market (*e.g.* Anti-trust Laws). It may be argued that what some would describe as micromanagement and excessive regulation are just the government doing its job. However, the objective should not be to choose winners and losers.

The objective should be fluidity in the market not a guarantee of a desired result. After all, "losing" in the market is the primary mechanism to keep risk and bad behavior in check. Similarly, market corrections are natural (and necessary) elements of the markets. While they should be anticipated, the market should not be artificially maintained to avoid them. If government removes the potential for loss, such actions encourage excessive risk and other abuses.

So long as parties get the benefit of their bargains, the market has done its work, even if one party makes a bad bargain (or chooses not to participate in the market at all). Individual losses and collective failures should serve as lessons learned so that the efficiency and fluidity of the markets are continually improved.

437

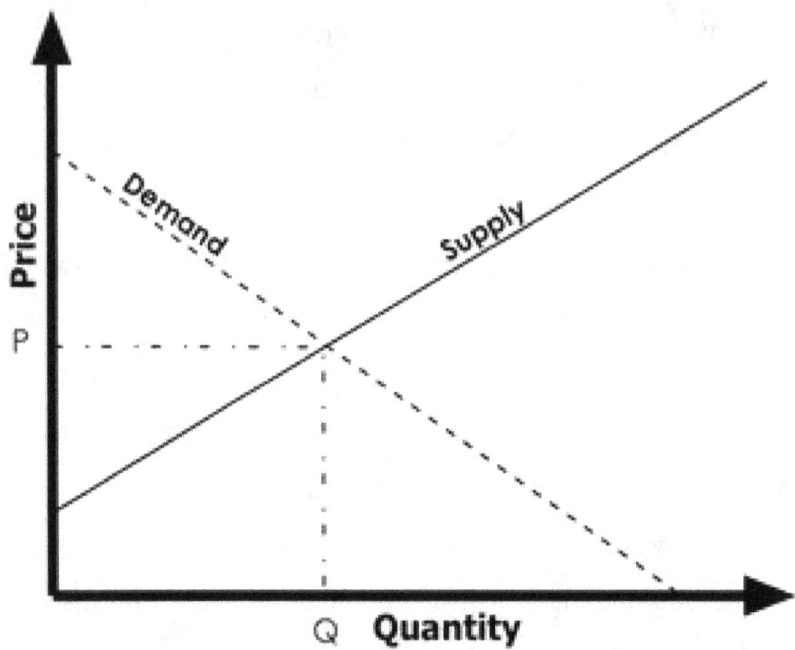

V.   RELIGION & PHILOSOPHY

Love is Gender-Neutral:

Love Thy Neighbor as Thyself - Mark 12:31

In the 2012 general election, the State of Washington legalized same-sex marriage by popular vote. I recently saw a series of sixty (60) photographs, which were snapped on the first day on which such marriages were legal. The photographs portrayed several same-sex couples (and others in attendance) as those Seattle-area couples exchanged marriage vows. The pictures created a beautiful and moving collage of the lives of those couples and illustrated how the collective love of those many couples was celebrated on that day.

We may debate the semantics of the word "marriage," but anyone looking at this series of pictures can hardly debate the existence of "love" and "commitment" in the lives of these couples. Are those not the attributes that marriage is supposed to signify and celebrate in any relationship?

Having asked that question, which was intended to be rhetorical, I was confronted by a reply, which was in essence:

> *I am offended by the decision of those persons to marry, in that marriage is a religiously defined institution, and homosexuality is morally reprehensible under the teachings of my religion.*

The responding opponent of same-sex marriage went on to justify his position by analogizing same-sex romantic love to an incestuous relationship between himself and his mother. He stated that he found both situations equally repulsive.

Apparently, the individual, with whom I was engaged in debate, was familiar with a rhetorical device utilized by

Supreme Court Justice Antonin Scalia, in which Scalia questioned whether constitutional guarantees in favor of homosexuals might destroy the "moral" justifications for laws against bestiality or even murder.[104]

I responded to the opponent of same-sex marriage that the key factors in any successful romantic relationship are reciprocal love and mutual sexual attraction, along with concomitant capacity, care, and commitment. If all of those things truly exist, then government should have neither involvement in nor fear of the relationship.

One can experience familial love, brotherly love, agape love, and romantic love; nevertheless, comparing one to the other is like comparing apples to oranges.

Some would argue that children and others with delicate moral sensibilities should not be "forced" to witness or even acknowledge the existence of homosexuality in any form. This is not just an aversion to witnessing lewd and lascivious sex acts, which would certainly be understandable, but the objection includes merely seeing such persons just "be" themselves and also having to interact with them within society.

Anyone is free to shelter himself or his children behind the walls of any moral or social façade that he cares to create. However, the reality of life is that Lesbians, Gays, Bi-sexuals, and Transgendered ("LGBT") persons exist. Deeming such persons inherently immoral will do nothing to stop them from living openly and conspicuously within society.

---

[104] See *Lawrence v. Texas,* 539 U.S. 558 (2003) - Dissent.

Any individual is at liberty to associate with like thinking persons, and persons are free to adopt and espouse the dogma of any group (religious or otherwise) that supports similar positions and beliefs. We can debate the issue of whether homosexuals are the creations of their Maker or the products of their environments. However, the ultimate answer is irrelevant. Resolution of the argument of nature versus nurture is neither going to remove an entire class of people from society nor will it fully integrate them within a reluctant populace.

Nevertheless, it is entirely unacceptable and ineffective to use the authority and compulsory powers of government to segregate any class of persons on the basis of less than universally accepted religious dogma and to discriminate against such persons by limiting the rights afforded to those individuals by that government.

I would be entirely supportive of government getting completely out of the marriage business and stopping its attempts to socially engineer families. The institution of government is ill suited to either task. Once marriage becomes a strictly personal choice (without government interference), persons then would be free to commit to, cohabitate with, and yes, marry anyone of their mutual choosing. If any person or church wishes not to recognize such marriages, then they are free to disavow the same. If the spouses' friends and family choose not to recognize the union, the loss is theirs to suffer. Nevertheless, the government should not have an interest in the decision regarding whom someone loves, with whom they choose to share their life, and whom they call family.

Individuals ultimately choose their own moral foundations. Religions establish and promote dogma, which define moral ideals and which can be used to compare and contrast one's actual behavior to those institutionalized ideals. Government does not establish morals. Government establishes laws. Laws do not dictate ideal behavior. Instead, laws identify minimum levels of behaviors, below which any actions are entirely unacceptable by society.

Using a specific moral position or religious teaching as the foundation for establishing secular law, is contrary to the rights of free expression and association, both of which are guaranteed by the Constitution. LGBT persons are inextricable constituents of society. They should not be labeled as second-class citizens for the sake of promoting some artificial social construct.

Then comes the cry, "But, you are redefining the word, 'Marriage'!" I can call the union of same-sex persons, "Marriage." Another person may call it a, "Civil Union." Someone else may call it something different. "Marriage" as a word is not sacrosanct.

As Shakespeare wrote, "[A] rose, by any other name, would smell as sweet." The sanctity of the institution of marriage depends not upon what it is called, but rather by what import and commitment is placed upon that relationship by the spouses involved.

"Marriage" means different things to different peoples of the world. Historically, marriages have been based upon business or contractual relationships among individuals or families, and the resulting unions were often a means to

444

consolidate power or unify kingdoms. Only more recently, has the notion of romantic love become integral the concept of marriage.

Certain religious authorities have embraced marriage among homosexuals. Any number of churches and religious institutions can have an entire slew of definitions for marriage. The definition of marriage differs within the *Holy Bible* itself.[105]

Some persons have argued that even using the word "gay" (originally meaning joyful, happy, merry, *etc.*) in reference to homosexuals is an "abuse of the [English] language." The objection is raised despite the fact that "gay" has a sexual connotation since the 17th century, and the word has been used in reference to homosexuals for nearly a century. *In lieu* of "gay," those persons, who wish same-sex relationships to be viewed exclusively in a negative light, prefer that homosexuals should be universally referred to as "sodomites."

Since we are exploring the definitions of words, let us look at the word "sodomy." Most recently, sodomy has become synonymous with homosexual sex, but in historical contexts, the term also encompasses oral sex between persons of opposite sex, including husbands and wives. In fact, the felonious offense of "Crimes against Nature" (*i.e.* Sodomy) is still on the books in North Carolina; although, the enforcement thereof cannot be characterized as "strict."[106]

---

[105] Opponents of same-sex marriage are not very credible when they argue that, at some point in history, the definition of marriage (and other acts which are deemed "right" and "wrong") quit evolving and that it is just a happenstance that the interpretation espoused by them and their church is the only real and right one.
[106] N.C.G.S. § 14-177.

Nevertheless, case law as late as 1980, confirmed the validity of a government prohibition against oral sex between consenting heterosexual adults. Of course, such a broad definition would be uncomfortably restrictive of heterosexuals, and it would have a potentially chilling effect upon sexual relations throughout society. As a matter of convenience, it is easier for society to "change" that pesky definition just to mean homosexual sex acts.

An admonition against the evolution and "redefining" of words is a bit of a sticky wicket. Without "abuse of the language," the word "Sodomite" would be limited to meaning: "An inhabitant of the locale of Sodom." Since "Sodom" was reportedly destroyed by an act of God, it is safe to say that no homosexual alive today was or is an inhabitant of that locale. Calling a homosexual a "sodomite" (with a lowercase "s") is itself a perversion of the original word. It is only with custom and use, developed over time and across cultures that "sodomy" and "sodomite" took on their current connotations.

Those who equate "Sodom" with deviant sexuality should familiarize themselves more closely with the story of Sodom and Gomorrah. The only "sex" to which reference is made in *Genesis* 19 is the threatened rape of Lot's house guests.

However, sexual behavior was not the focus of the condemnation of the inhabitants of Sodom, as evidenced by Lot offering up his two (2) virginal daughters, rather than his guests, to be ravaged by the mob outside his home.

Interestingly, the sin which was being most exemplified and condemned was the sin of being inhospitable to guests and visitors, as evidenced by the violence of the mob and the proposed degradation and humiliation of male-on-male rape. In this context, the sex act through violent assault was a symptom not the sin itself.

Lest one thinks my reading of *Genesis* 19 is off base, the *Bible* says in *Ezekiel* 16:49 (*KJV*):

> *Behold, this was the iniquity of thy sister Sodom, pride, fullness of bread, and abundance of idleness was in her and in her daughters, neither did she strengthen the hand of the poor and needy.*

Nowhere in the Bible is there found a condemnation of a loving committed same-sex relationship between consenting adults (if for no other reason than the concept of such a relationship is a relatively new construct within society).

Therefore, the bigger condemnation in calling someone a "sodomite" would be in describing one who is inhospitable and unwelcoming of strangers into his home or presence. Given that perspective, persons should consider this broader meaning of the story and contemplate whether they are themselves "sodomites" in excluding homosexuals from their houses of worship and from the Christian (or other) faith.

Notwithstanding the "un-Christian" hate speech spouted by many persons, who profess to speak on behalf of the faith, Jesus himself said:

447

A new commandment I give unto you, "That ye love one another; as I have loved you, that ye also love one another." By this shall all men know that ye are my disciples, if ye have love one to another.[107]

The ministry of Christ is consistent with promoting a personal faith, and that faith is based upon an individual's relationship with God, rather than adherence to any fundamentalist dogma of an institutional Church. This evolution of the faith recognizes that "state of mind" and "intent" are important in determining the culpability (*i.e.* sinfulness) of an act. The early Christian faith recognized the need for a guiding principle (*i.e.* "Golden Rule") that would supplant formalistic rules of the faith.

In the parable from which comes the admonition, "It is easier for a camel to pass through the eye of a needle than a rich man to get into heaven," Jesus spoke to the Rich Young Ruler, who had dutifully followed all of the Commandments of Moses.[108] Instead of praising the Ruler for his devout adherence to dogma, Jesus called upon him to undertake acts of selflessness for the benefit of others. The lack of love and compassion in the words and actions of many piously religious persons makes it hard to identify such persons as "disciples" of Jesus.

Regardless of how persons and religious institutions may define marriage, the government has no legitimate interest in defining the word or the resulting union. The entire reason that there is a First Amendment to the Constitution of the United

---

[107] *Gospel of John* 13:34-35 *KJV*.
[108] See the *Gospels* of *Matthew, Mark,* and *Luke.*

States is so that reasoned minds can disagree on matters of philosophy, morality, and religion. Within any free association of believers, persons can adopt any belief, morals, and dogma, which are supportive of the ideals of the association; however, when one attempts to enforce that dogma on non-believers using the compulsory powers of government, those persons and that government have overstepped their legitimate authority.

No one is demanding that any individual personally embrace the marriage of any same-sex couple. No one is required to step foot into their home. No church is obliged to sanctify their marriage, and no church has to open its doors to celebrate their union. Persons are perfectly free to shun them individually or collectively; however, such persons are not entitled to the sanctioning and enforcement of that belief by government action.

Some persons have taken my arguments in support of same-sex marriage as an assault on Christianity. My assault is upon bigotry and prejudice. However, I do not cite Christianity as being the source of bigotry and prejudice. On the contrary, I believe that Christianity teaches inclusion and love for one's fellow man. The opponents of women's suffrage, desegregation, religious tolerance, *etc.* cited portions of the *Bible* by chapter and verse in vehement support of their prejudices and bigotry.

One can attempt to explain how "true" religious teachings were perverted by such persons, but that does little to repair the damage done to the institution of religion by those who professed the faith. Despite now being (nearly) universally panned, those who are now said to have perverted the faith

449

communicated their espoused beliefs with no less certainty or sincerity as others, who today would use Christianity as a sword to cut homosexuals out of society. Persons, who would use religion in that way, will ultimately be seen as being on the wrong side of history. On this issue, history itself will be the final arbiter.

While I believe that there are persons, who honestly believe that their particular prejudice is mandated by their religion, I do not believe that Christianity teaches or requires such prejudices. Bigotry stems entirely from individuals not the religion. If one honestly believes that his position against a committed same-sex relationship (*i.e.* "gay marriage") is on a sturdier religious footing, than slavery, misogyny, racism, religious intolerance, *etc.*, then I will allow that hair to be split by religious scholars more adept than me.

Nevertheless, I will offer that the religious authorities, who formerly used the *Bible* to support such bigotries, were not among the fringe elements of the Christian church. These bigotries and prejudices were preached directly from pulpits of nearly every Christian denomination in locales throughout the country. So, if there is a distinction to be made between those prior "misguided" teachings and the current institutional teachings against homosexuality, I will err on the side that current teachings will also been seen as "misguided" with time.

Nevertheless, my issue is not so much with any particular church or denomination. Any group (religious or otherwise) is entitled to establish its own mores and to set standards for membership. However, I am not requesting membership into

450

any church with moral and religious positions different than my own. Were that the case, I would wholeheartedly agree that I could (and arguably should) be denied admission into the fold. My objection arises when someone else's religious beliefs dictate laws, which limit the rights of persons not similarly aligned and which do not advance any legitimate interest of the state.

I have been accused of suborning hate by pointing out prior misdeeds undertaken either with the blessing of or in the name of "the Church." Truth is often ugly, and unfortunately, being confronted with the ugliness of that truth is often the only way that some deniers of truth will acknowledge it. Prejudice and bigotry should not be excused as being mandates from God. It would be disingenuous not to point out a history of the institutional church, which is replete with examples of scripture and dogma being manipulated in furtherance of ignoble aims. I am confident that inclusion and love will win out over exclusion and irrational fear.

My discourse also has been described as an indictment of "all Christians," of whom I am one. As a Christian, I am no less confident in my faith than other Christians, whose opinions and positions on theology differ from my own. I cannot speak as to the mind or motivation of any specific individual, and I give the benefit of the doubt that any espoused belief is held sincerely. In drawing distinctions between current positions against same-sex marriage and prior discredited positions supporting racism, misogyny, *etc.*, persons making those distinctions argue that

451

prior positions were not consistent with the teachings of "their" church.

They would argue that there is but one true church, coincidentally their own, and presumably that church adheres to a clearly defined and biblically sound set of tenets and mores, including prohibitions against homosexuality. Such protectors of the faith attempt to paint as heretics and blasphemers all other (little "c") "christians," who view their faith differently.[109]

It may be that a single church or denomination speaks for the faith and that its interpretation of the *Bible* represents the singular cosmic truth. However, history does not give credence that any religion, denomination, or mortal individual can speak definitively on issues of faith. While I disagree with persons that would hold that Christianity dictates opposition to government sanctioned same-sex marriage, it is certainly one's right to zealously hold to that opinion, as being consistent with the tenets of their religion.

Similarly, it is my right (if not obligation) to point out what I believe are inconsistencies and hypocrisies of those, who profess to speak on behalf of God. Nevertheless, my primary objective is not to change any particular person's mind. Rather, my objective is to prevent anyone from using the proscriptive powers of government to impose a particular view of morality on the population as a whole.

Senator Rob Portman (R-OH) recently took a personal stance in favor a same-sex marriage. The senator is part of the

---

[109] Presumably, such persons would be similarly dismissive of adherents of non-Christian faiths.

Republican Party establishment. He was a key adviser to Mitt Romney during his Presidential campaign, as well as his debate-prep partner, and he was seriously vetted for Vice-President on the GOP ticket. In acknowledging his new policy position, Sen. Portman cited a change of mind upon learning that his son is gay. Some persons have stated that such a change in position would be more influential, if triggered by some motivation other than his son being gay.

I respect a man, who changes his mind in the light of experience and reason. I have a harder time respecting someone, who stands on personal principle, even if that principle flies in the face of all reason. Copernicus and Galileo were deemed heretics by the Catholic Church for opposing a geo-centric view of the universe. Today, it is (generally) accepted that the earth is not flat, and that the planet revolves around the sun within a heliocentric solar system, which is a minor element of the larger Milky Way galaxy traveling among roughly 100 billion other galaxies in the universe. Obviously, knowledge, like our concept of the universe itself, is expanding.

Most persons, who "know" homosexuals only from caricature and stereotype, understandably have a poor impression of LGBT persons. Similarly, if all heterosexual persons were presumed to live their entire lives mirroring the *Girls Gone Wild* series of movies, euphemistic "gentlemen's clubs," and bachelor parties, the proverbial Sodom and Gomorrah would pale in comparison.

As individuals come to know LGBT person as sons and daughters or friends and neighbors rather than through the dichotomy of "us versus them," societal attitudes will inevitably change for the better. Sen. Portman's "evolution" is entirely indicative of the changes taking place throughout the greater society. Just was we should love our sons and daughters unconditionally, so should we love our neighbors, even the gay ones.

Can you have Free Exercise of Religion
without Freedom of Speech?

Blog Entry – September 12, 2012

The morning of 9/11/2001 is etched in our collective consciousness. Those etchings serve as memorials to innocents lost and fitting tribute to those heroic Americans who sacrificed their lives on that fateful day. May that collection of memories, painful though they may be, survive the erosions of time and complacency.

Embassy attacks on 09/11/2012[110] were spawned by a trailer from a soon-to-be-released movie. The trailer shows the prophet, Mohammed, and some aspects of the Muslim faith in a negative light. President Obama took presidential candidate Mitt Romney to task for criticizing an official Press Release from the U.S. Embassy in Egypt. Political Correctness aside, it is entirely inappropriate for the U.S. government to call the Freedom of Speech "misguided" and "abusive." And, exactly what was so damnable?

The internet trailer was said to offend Muslims and "hurt [their] feelings." So, do we now police the internet for anything that may be offensive to someone, or accept this as a justification for open violence? Freedoms of speech and of religion require the acceptance of opinions, which may be offensive to yourself or others. What happened to, "I may not

---

[110] This essay was originally written in response to initial news reports. Subsequent reports and evidence distinguished the alleged motivations for the attack in Benghazi, Libya from the motivation for attacks and protests in other parts of the Middle East.

agree with what you say, but I will defend unto the death your right to say it?"[111]

A subsequent headline reads, "Why Films and Cartoons of Muhammad Spark violence." Does one really feel the need to ask, "Why?" These things happen for the same reasons that gave rise to the Spanish Inquisition ... the persecution Copernicus ... the Salem Witch Trials ... the Ku Klux Klan. Persons exploit ignorance and pervert religious dogma in order to secure power and personal gain. Nevertheless, violence in the furtherance of dogma cannot be tolerated.

The YouTube video which gave rise to the violence in Egypt is entitled, *The Innocence of Muslims*. It is cheap and poorly made. It demonstrates a dearth of talent and nearly no production values. No one with an ounce of decorum and common sense could take the piece seriously.

Is it a farce about a topic which should not be the subject of ridicule? Perhaps it is; nevertheless, Freedom of Speech protects not only the lofty and urbane but also the crude and crass. That, which cannot be questioned and ridiculed, cannot be fully examined nor understood. Go ahead ... view the video for yourself, and see if its existence justifies the killing of four (4) innocent people.

A picture, which was presented in news reports, shows the body of murdered U.S. Ambassador Christopher Stevens after it was pulled from the burned out embassy in Benghazi, Libya. If

---

[111] Although these words are regularly attributed to Voltaire, they were first used by Evelyn Beatrice Hall, who wrote under the pseudonym of Stephen G. Tallentyre, in *The Friends of Voltaire* (1906). She wrote this as a summation of Voltaire's beliefs on freedom of thought and expression.

peoples choose to act like savages, then we, as more civilized countries, should not tolerate them within the international community. If countries cannot police their own citizens, then we should leave them to their own devices. It is time to cut our losses rather than enabling their bad behaviors with largesse from our country's limited treasury. Religious fundamentalism should not be accepted as an excuse for violence.

The subject film had no direct association with, nor endorsement by, the U.S. Government. If failure to censor speech is sufficient justification for attacking a foreign embassy and causing the death of an Ambassador, then we had better arm up. Such actions do not demonstrate tolerance or a desire to coexist within the world community. Such violence only feeds the fears and distrust of those, who see the Muslim community as a threat to American ideals (including Freedom of Speech and Religion).

President Obama says, "Egypt is not an ally OR an enemy?" Yet, we provide the country BILLIONS in aid. In any relationship, the worst reciprocal emotion is not hate, but (depraved) indifference. Enemies with drawn guns do not scare me nearly as much as the ones who come with feigned smiles and hidden daggers.

In the words of the much maligned former President Bush shortly after 9-11:

> Over time it's going to be important for nations to know they will be held accountable for inactivity. ... You're either with us or against us in the fight against terror.

The United States should NEVER apologize for any constitutionally guaranteed right exercised by the country or any of its citizens. The First Amendment guaranteed right to Free Speech is sacrosanct, and no agency of the government should ever describe its exercise as "misguided" or "abusive." More importantly, the U.S. should not seek to appease bullies, thugs, and tyrants, who act in the name of a religion that has been perverted to suit their selfish ambitions. In doing so, America is made to appear indecisive, unsure, and weak rather than assuming the mantle of leadership.

COEXIST

Fundamentalist elements of the Christian religion are accused of ignoring scientific evidence, impeding the rights of minorities, and seeking to impose religious will on civil governments. The path dictated by some religious authorities is "straight and narrow." It does not allow for deviation, diversion, or even an alternate path to a similarly situated destination. For adherents, the path is certain, clear, and singularly right. For those not of the faith, the path may seem unnecessarily restrictive, irrational, or even misguided.

"Fundamentalism" in any religion is an impediment to rational discourse because it insists upon infallibility of Holy Scripture, not only in matters of faith and morals but also as a literal historical record, and it holds that such teachings are essential to the faith. However, this singular perspective is most often based upon some presumed authoritative interpretation of scripture by one or more individuals, who necessarily suffer from the frailties of the human condition, and whose motives, sources, and veracity often can be called into question.

In an effort to highlight history so as to avoid repeating it, the Christian Church (in the persons of Saint Cyril I, Patriarch of Alexandria, and his followers) was responsible for the horrific death in 413 A.D. of the Greek female astronomer, mathematician, and philosopher, Hypatia, who was the developer of the Astrolabe.

In form and function, the Astrolabe resembles the Sextant (a more recently developed nautical instrument for navigation), and it is an instrument capable of predicting the locations of planetary bodies and stars from a fixed position on earth. By reference to such celestial bodies, the Astrolabe can provide accurate information about the current time at any locale, day or night, and it can be used for surveying and triangulation. While replaced today by more modern technologies, the instrument was extremely advanced for its day, and its development was indicative of Alexandria's role as an incubator of knowledge and intellect.

For her knowledge and teaching, Hypatia suffered execution by the Church as a witch and heretic. The death of Hypatia followed the destruction of the Library of Alexandria some centuries earlier.[112]

The library was originally established by Alexander the Great with the objective to house all of the knowledge of the Ancient World (secular and religious). Alexander understood that with knowledge comes power.

The loss and destruction of the information troves contained within the library, including one-of-a-kind papyrus scrolls, are alleged to have set back the development of mankind by centuries and to have been a factor in the onset of the Dark Ages.[113]

Knowledge and its resulting power are often envied and feared by leaders within the institutional Church, whose power

---

[112] The actual date (or period) of the destruction of the Great Library at Alexandria is uncertain. Stories of the destruction are set as early as the 1st century A.D. [Julius Cesar] and continue into the 7th century [Caliph Omar]. Regardless, Alexandra was a center for the accumulation of knowledge and scholarly study for centuries.

[113] A historical period between the 6th and 13th Centuries marked by the decline of the Roman Empire and the cultural and economic deterioration in Europe.

is derived by manipulating information and controlling its flow. Intellectual advancement is not the enemy of religion; however, arrogance and hubris are.

History, ancient and recent, is replete with examples of ambitious men, who used religion as the means to ends, which include power, oppression, and corruption. The biggest threat to the Church (however that singular institution is defined) is not an external brute force. Instead, such a threat comes from an internal cancer, which can destroy the body and corrupt the nature of the institution from within.

An institution established for dissemination of moral teachings and to afford salvation to mankind is not naturally a proper guardian or patron of scientific development, diversity of thought, and political philosophy.

The greatest tools that our forefathers gave us in protecting personal freedoms and individual rights from the tyranny of mob rule was the paramount right of free speech and a guarantee that religion shall be maintained as a personal right to all peoples but shall not be an overriding authority with the power to impede the development of knowledge and to subvert truth.

Those inspired gifts from our forefathers are likely exceeded in quality and import only by the gift of conscious reason granted to us by our Maker. Among earth's creatures, human beings are unique in that we are ordained with both sentience and intellect, and these traits provide us with self-awareness, independent thought, and free will. These collective powers are immense, and with such immense powers come the responsibility that they be used for good.

We are stewards of the intellect given to us. As stewards, we have an obligation to expand the wealth of knowledge, and each person is individually responsible for the use or waste of the talents afforded him. Willful ignorance is not a defense to misuse or waste of intellect and reason, and one should never voluntarily surrender one's intellect to the control and direction of another. Each of us is blessed and cursed concurrently by the fruits of the tree of the "Knowledge of Good and Evil."

Information and knowledge in the abstract have no inherent moral qualities. The ways, in which we, as individuals, choose to utilize our acquired knowledge, determine whether that knowledge takes on the character of good or evil. Only from the applications of knowledge can wisdom be divined. Wisdom and enlightenment should be the goals of all humankind, as should be the emancipation of slavery of thought, which unfetters the shackles of ignorance, bigotry, and prejudice.

Man once surrendering his reason, has no remaining guard against absurdities the most monstrous, and like a ship without rudder, is the sport of every wind. With such persons, gullibility, which they call faith, takes the helm from the hand of reason, and the mind becomes a wreck.

— THOMAS JEFFERSON

GOD'S LAW: Judge, Jury, and Executioner

© 2012

Introduction -

Charlie Fuqua, a Republican candidate for the Arkansas House of Representatives, called for expelling Muslims from the United States in his book, *God's Law*. He also wrote in support of instituting the death penalty for "rebellious children." In Fuqua's 2012 book, the candidate wrote:

> *The maintenance of civil order in society rests on the foundation of family discipline. Therefore, a child who disrespects his parents must be permanently removed from society in a way that gives an example to all other children of the importance of respect for parents. The death penalty for rebellious children is not something to be taken lightly. The guidelines for administering the death penalty to rebellious children are given in* Deuteronomy 21:18-21.

For the benefit of the curious, what follows is the passage, which is cited by Mr. Fuqua in his book, supposedly supporting the killing such rebellious children:

> *[18] If a man have a stubborn and rebellious son, which will not obey the voice of his father, or the voice of his mother, and that, when they have chastened him, will not hearken unto them: [19] Then shall his father and his mother lay hold on him, and bring him out unto the elders of his city, and unto the gate of his place; [20] And they shall say unto the elders of his city, This our son is stubborn and rebellious, he will not obey our voice; he is a glutton, and a drunkard. [21] And all the men of his city shall stone him with stones, that he die: so shalt thou put evil away from among you; and all Israel shall hear, and fear.*

463

However here are just a few other Biblical passages, of which Mr. Fuqua should make note before condemning "rebellious" children to death:

- But Jesus said, "Suffer little children, and forbid them not, to come unto me: for of such is the kingdom of heaven." - *MATTHEW 19:14*.

- He that is without sin among you, let him first cast a stone at her. - *JOHN 8:7*.

- And as ye would that men should do to you, do ye also to them likewise. - *LUKE 6:21* - The "Golden Rule."

- Then said Jesus, "Father, forgive them; for they know not what they do." - *LUKE 23:34*.

Please allow me to also note a few Biblical examples where children were NOT killed by their parents, or the village elders, despite actions, which would be deemed "rebellious" or even horrendous:

- Cain kills Abel - *GENESIS 4*;

- Joseph's brothers sell him into slavery - *GENESIS 37*;

- Lot's daughters get him drunk; have sex with him; and conceive children by their father. - *GENESIS 19*; and

- Prodigal Son - *LUKE 15:11-32*.

In fact, I am aware of no example given in the Bible where parents sought, much less secured, the death of a rebellious child, as proposed by Mr. Fuqua.

Right versus Reason -

Fuqua, and others of a similar ilk, choose to adopt dogma over reason. In submitting to a prescribed interpretation of scripture, they seek to remove from themselves any responsibility for a personal determination of right and wrong. However, reason is all that mankind has to overcome fear and ignorance.

I have seen the question asked, "How could someone this misguided occupy a pulpit [or position of authority]?" However, occupiers of similar pulpits directed: The Inquisition, Salem Witch Trials, and centuries of Holy Wars resulting in the deaths of millions. Those pulpits have often been occupied by dangerous personalities such as Jim Jones and David Koresh, as well as the humorous and covetous, Jim and Tammy Faye Baker, and the more base, Jimmy Swaggart and Ted Haggard.

Favorite sermons have extolled the virtues of misogyny, slavery, segregation, and racial or ethnic supremacy. In response to the question above, such persons do serve a purpose. They are foils against which persons of true love, honor, and righteousness can be readily identified. Only in shining light upon the darkness of lies and ignorance can truth and grace be discerned and appreciated.

Institutional Religions are often focused on the defense of the *status quo* and the dissemination of power and authority. The practices of many such religions have nearly nothing to do with personal spirituality. True religion must be internalized not institutionalized.

Do as I say not as "I Do" -

I am certain that Mr. Fuqua would count himself among the self-appointed protectors of "traditional" marriage. "Marriage," as an institution, is evident in [nearly] all peoples as the religious, social, contractual, and anthropological union of a man and a woman. However, the "definition of marriage" differs not only among such peoples, but it also has differed within specific groups over time. For many persons, "marriage" has no religious component, and none is required for a legal or civil marriage. For others, there is no "ceremony" or license at all (as with common law marriages).

Are persons in these latter groups any less "married" when compared to persons who undertake "traditional" religious/ceremonial marriages?

Marriage is said to be "until death do us part." Religious teachings and authorities historically condemned separation and divorce. Nevertheless, fifty percent (50%) of U.S. marriages end in divorce. What then is the "moral" state of 2nd and successive "marriages"?

I will refrain from highlighting all of the oft repeated types and standards of "marriage," which are identified in the *Bible* itself. Suffice it to say that many identified unions seem unusual (*e.g.* brother and widow), if not repulsive (*e.g.* rapist and victim), by current standards. By necessity, "traditional" marriage proponents dismiss these unions as being "outdated" and inconsistent with some superseding dispensation or revelation. Regardless, marriage, as an institution today, has evolved. It has changed to address changes in society and to acknowledge our continued understandings of human behavior.

Does that mean that all changes within the institution of marriage have been for the better? That is for theologians and philosophers to debate, but certainly not politicians. If any religious body (or other social group) wishes to implement mores and restrict marriage to a specific definition, then so be it. Where membership to any group is voluntary, then one chooses to be bound by the rules of the controlling authority. However, such restrictions should not apply to what has become a civil and legal institution rather than a religious union.

For Better or Worse -

Christianity's source (*i.e.* the words of Christ) outlines a very personal and individually spiritual religion. Christ taught in the temple as a young boy. Later, Christ rebuked the temple money changers in his only recorded demonstration of anger. The Golden Rule contemplates that "right" and "wrong" are determined within the heart of the actor. Christ himself chastised blind adherence to religious laws.

The standard liturgy for the wedding ceremony states, "That which God has joined together, let no man put asunder." If two people come together and wish to formalize their relationship by joining publicly in a loving committed relationship, I am not worthy of questioning whether their relationship is ordained by God, and neither is anyone else.

"Marriage" is a contractual relationship, which carries certain legal rights, privileges, and obligations. Those aspects of marriage are not related to religious dogma, and the concept of equal protection of laws will eventually be interpreted and applied so as to assure that the legal definition of marriage will be extended to include any two consenting adults having legal capacity, including same-sex couples. As long as government is in the business of marriage, it cannot legitimately deprive a segment of the population of the benefits of marriage.

Conclusion -

Overt evil will not be the downfall of humanity, because it will always be identified and defeated. Humanity will fail when reason, God's distinguishing gift to the species, is ignored in favor of the charisma and certainty offered by false prophets. Such prophets presume to speak for God when no man holds that power or right. Reason is not incompatible with the legitimate teachings of religion, but such teachings are entirely incompatible with hubris and bigotry.

A recent Pew study found that the United States is becoming more "secular," and more persons than ever are shying away from organized religion. Interestingly, the decrease in religious participation is not so much a rush toward evil or to the "Dark Side." Instead, it is an indictment against the hypocrisies prevalent in many institutionalized religions. Many among the "religious" fail to live their individual lives, as examples which persons would choose to emulate. If we do not individualize and take to heart the positive principles of religion, no membership in any "church" is going to redeem our bad acts.

The power and authority of the "Church" require a fixed dogma, a certain collection of laws for the purpose of controlling the flock and to distinguish between the faithful and the heathen. The Church often demonizes those, who do not follow its dogma so as to maintain its power and control over the impressionable flock. Church leaders fearfully realize that such power and control are illusory, and with the destruction of ignorance and bigotry, their collective hold onto such power slips away.

The true power of the teachings of Christ is derived from inclusion and love. The false teachings of many current religions concentrate upon are exclusion and damnation.

To which "church" would you rather belong?

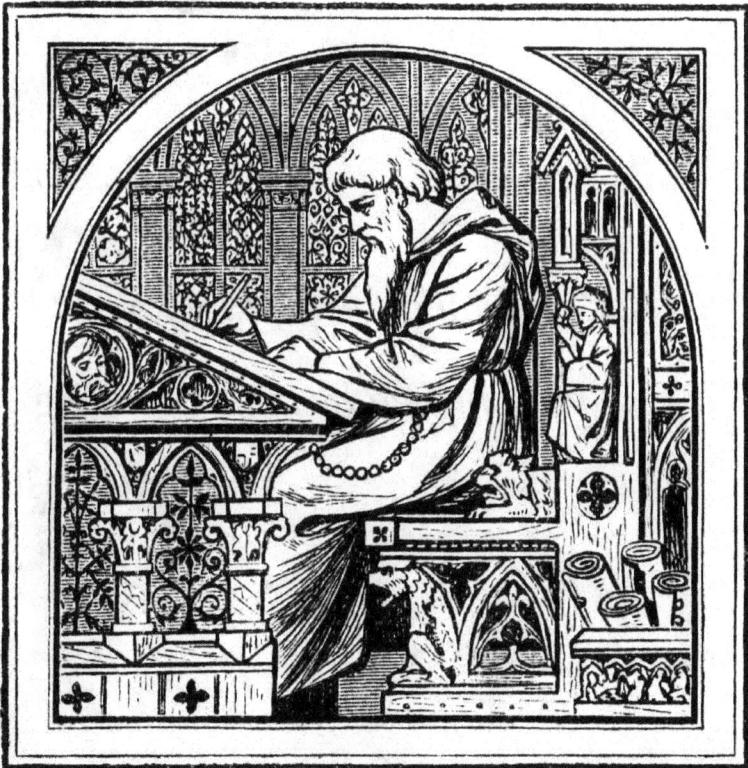

Peace ... *cannot be kept by force.*

It can only be achieved by understanding.

- Albert Einstein

Judeo-Christian Ethic: A Late Adopter of "Equality"

Blog Entry – March 4, 2012

[Former] Presidential candidate, Rick Santorum, said:

I love it because the left says, "equality, equality." Where does that concept come from? Does it come from Islam? Does it come from other cultures around the world? ... No, it comes it comes from our culture and tradition, from the Judeo-Christian ethic.

Does Santorum read the same *Bible* that (many of) the rest of us read? ... "Equality" from the Judeo-Christian ethic?

Let's see ... much of the *Old Testament*, including the oft quoted *Leviticus*, is spent dictating that the Jews segregate and separate themselves from all other peoples. It is not until the *Gospels* of the *New Testament* that Christ teaches a more inclusive philosophy that includes charity, grace, and compassion for harlots and the downtrodden, and Jesus does this not by highlighting the righteousness of the religious but in the story of the Good Samaritan from the *Gospel of Luke* beginning at Ch. 10:30:

A man was going down from Jerusalem to Jericho, when he was attacked by robbers. They stripped him of his clothes, beat him and went away, leaving him half dead. [31] A priest happened to be going down the same road, and when he saw the man, he passed by on the other side. [32] So too, a Levite, when he came to the place and saw him, passed by on the other side. [33] But a Samaritan, as he traveled, came where the man was; and when he saw him, he took pity on him. [34] He went to him and bandaged his wounds, pouring on oil and wine. Then he put the man on his own donkey, brought him to an inn and took care of him. [35] The next day he took out two denarii and gave them to the innkeeper. 'Look after him,' he said, 'and when I return, I will reimburse you for any extra expense you may have.' [36] *Which of these three do you think was a neighbor to the man who fell into the hands of robbers?*

Even after this admonition by Christ, equality is hardly a tradition that has been universally adopted by the Christian church:

- There were the Crusades against Muslims immediately after the first millennium;

- There was the Inquisition of "heretics" beginning in the 12th and 13th centuries;

- There were further persecutions of the Church that led to Protestantism in the 16th Century; and

- There continue to be numerous factions, denominations, and congregations among the collective of "Christians," and each group considers its creed superior to all others.

Such is the nature of religion. It is hard to escape the notion that there are the self-declared righteous, and all others persons are infidels. Santorum's idea of "equality" is acceptance of and inclusivity with those that agree with him and an uneasy toleration or pity, at best, for those who disagree.

This is hardly the type of equality, which was fostered by our Founding Fathers and which is required under the laws of the United States. Thomas Jefferson wrote of his concerns regarding the influence of clergy and the Church on the teachings of Christ (and thus on society in general).

In a letter to John Adams dated October 13, 1813, Jefferson wrote about his compilation, "The Philosophy of Jesus of Nazareth:"

In extracting the pure principles which he taught, we should have to strip off the artificial vestments in which they have been muffled by priests, who have travestied them into various forms, as instruments of riches and power to themselves. We must dismiss the Platonists and Plotinists, the Stagyrites and Gamalielites, the Eclectics, the Gnostics and Scholastics, their essences and emanations, their logos and demiurges, aeons and daemons, male and female, with a long train of ... or, shall I say at once, of nonsense. We must reduce our volume to the simple evangelists, select, even from them, the very words only of Jesus, paring off the amphibologisms[114] into which they have been led, by forgetting often, or not understanding, what had fallen from him, by giving their own misconceptions as his dicta, and expressing unintelligibly for others what they had not understood themselves. There will be found remaining the most sublime and benevolent code of morals which has ever been offered to man. I have performed this operation for my own use, by cutting verse by verse out of the printed book, and arranging the matter which is evidently his, and which is as easily distinguishable as diamonds in a dunghill. The result is an octavo of forty-six pages, of pure and unsophisticated doctrines.

---

[114] Jefferson's use of "amphibologisms" refers to the residues found in all religious texts that result from the habit of the faithful to interpret a phrase in a way that suits them best, and then insist others accept their interpretation as the truth. *See "The Jefferson Bible."*

"Equality" and diversity of thought are hardly trademarks of religions generally, and they cannot be said to be cornerstones of the Judeo-Christian religions. Jesus spoke of an individualized relationship with God, and He taught against religion merely as a set of rules to be kept by the faithful. Nevertheless, tolerance for diversity of thought among philosophies and religious teachings is a much more recent concept, and it is one which continues to suffer resistance from zealots and fundamentalists of all faiths.[115]

=quality

---

[115] See *A Letter Concerning Toleration,* John Locke (1689).

Family Dissension -

Abraham is an important figure in the Judeo-Christian faiths. Hebrews (Jews) trace their lineage to Isaac, who was the second son of Abraham, and the only son by his wife, Sarah. Abraham is also a principle figure in the Islamic faith, and a fork in the family lineage of Abraham is significant in the development of the various faiths.[116]

Abraham had an older son, Ishmael, who was born to Sarah's handmaiden, Hagar. While Ishmael, plays nearly no role in the development in the Judeo-Christian faiths, he is instrumental within the Islamic faith. In fact, traditions of Islam hold that Ishmael was an ancestor of Muhammad and the progenitor of all Arabs.

The issues arising from the "legitimacy" of the birth of Ishmael carry over into the teachings of Judaism and Islam. The split in the lineage of Abraham also explains, at least in part, why many Muslims feel that they have been treated as "bastard step-children" in religious and political circles for more than 1,500 years.

The Christian "Jihads" -

Christianity is an offshoot of Judaism. Christianity spread throughout the Roman Empire into what would become Europe thereby replacing the pagan religions of the time. As Christendom grew throughout the continent, the powers of the Catholic Church and Christian monarchs also grew. The

---

[116] See *Genesis* Ch. 16.

Crusades were spawned from a desire to assert those collective powers and to establish the dominance of the Christian religion throughout the known world.

For more than two centuries, Western powers sought to retake parts of the Holy Land (now Israel) in order to assure access to the holy shrines and places, which are located therein. A secondary but closely-related objective was to rid the western world of the influences of Islam. This series of religious wars helped to define the Middle Ages (also referred to as the "Dark Ages").

The Christian kingdoms successfully limited the influences of Islam, and they succeeded in removing Muslims from parts of the European continent. Toward these ends, the control and influence of the Moors ended on the Iberian Peninsula, and the Moors were driven from what are the modern-day countries of Portugal and Spain. However, the Christian kings failed in maintaining significant influence in the Middle East, and the wars failed in establishing Christianity as the dominant religion in that region.

A Second Birthright Lost -

These factors are significant in understanding the effects of Islam on current geopolitical affairs. However, the rift between Islam and the Judeo-Christian faiths is not the only schism, which is important to a complete understanding of the current political landscape of the Middle East. A second issue of religious "lineage" arose within the Islamic faith after the death of the Prophet Muhammad in 632 A.D.

After Muhammad's death, a series of religious leaders ("Caliphs") were elected consistent with the teachings of the Quran, and those Caliphs continued to lead the majority of Muslims. Those, who supported and followed this line of succession, have become known as the Sunni branch of Islam, and adherents are known as "Sunnis."

A smaller group of Muslims believed that Muhammad personally ordained his cousin and son-in-law, Ali, to be his successor. Ali was eventually named fourth Caliph (and first Shia Imam) in 656 A.D. following the assassination of his predecessor. Ali's reign saw the onset of the First Fitna (Islamic civil war, of which there have been five). The First Fitna ended with Ali's own assassination in 661 A.D.

This Islamic minority is the source of the Shia branch of Islam, and adherents are known as Shiites. The major distinction between the two religious lineages is in the perceived legitimacy of the leaders, who head the respective branches. Shiites believe that the successive leaders ("Imams") are divinely appointed. As such, Imams are believed to be infallible and bestowed with special insight into religion and spiritual teachings.

Sunnis account for the vast majority of Muslims throughout the world. Although precise counts are impossible, more than three-fourths of all Muslims are Sunnis, and some estimates are as high as ninety percent (90%). The Shiites represent a much smaller minority, likely between 10% and 20% of all Muslims, but Shiites are the majorities in certain key countries.[117]

Muslims have fought collectively for religious "legitimacy" and geopolitical significance for more than a millennium. Shiites, as a minority within a minority, have struggled even longer to assert themselves as the rightful "keepers of the faith." It is this fight for recognition and legitimacy that colors, if not defines, the ongoing conflicts and struggles throughout the Middle East.

Thumbnail History (after the Dark Ages) -

Beginning in the 14th century, the Ottoman Empire asserted dominion over much of the Middle East, as well as portions of Eastern Europe and Africa. This dominance within the region continued for more than five (5) centuries. The leaders of the empire were self-declared Caliphs, spiritual leaders of Islam, and the resulting government, or Caliphate, maintained control over the military, administrative agencies, and the clergy (of all religions, including Christians and Jews). By the 19th century, the Ottoman Empire was in decline as a political power, and the empire ultimately collapsed and was fractured during the political reshuffling, which followed World War I.

Thereafter, Western powers (*e.g.* Great Britain and France) established colonies in the Middle East (and other Muslim/Arab countries), and those European powers asserted substantial control and political influence in the region well into the 20th Century. As the colonial influence of such countries diminished in the latter half of the century, a cultural and political vacuum

---

[117] Iran (90-95%), Azerbaijan (85%), Iraq (60-65%), and Bahrain (65%).

resulted in successive power struggles, civil wars, and military coups in the region.

In the midst of this turmoil, the United Nations ("U.N.") established the State of Israel in 1948 at least partially in response to the systematic persecution (and attempted extermination) of Jews during World War II. The world's only Jewish majority state was established in Palestine, which had been under British control following the collapse of the Ottoman Empire. In establishing the State of Israel, world powers effectively disenfranchised the indigenous Palestinians, who continue to live in the region.

These events set a stage fraught with continuing conflicts among the Arab States and spurred fresh conflicts with the newly-created Jewish State of Israel. The resulting "morality play" culminates is a very acrimonious family reunion, which has been centuries in the making.

Conclusion -

Over time, a myriad of events occur, which can trigger open conflicts among the various states and factions in the Middle East, and the implements of war continue to change and develop always resulting in greater destruction and loss of life. In trying to avoid violence and warfare, it is important to acknowledge and to understand the underlying dynamics, which go back decades, centuries, and millennia.

A resolution to these destructive dynamics is not likely to be brought about in the short term. Nevertheless, only in acknowledging the complexities of the conflicts and the depths of the perceived slights can any productive steps be taken to lessen the likelihood and scope of violence and war in the region.

To Hell with Freedom and Democracy

© 2012

"TO HELL WITH FREEDOM AND DEMOCRACY, WHEN IT THREATENS THE PEOPLE'S RELIGION AND FAITH."

This translated statement was quoted in news reports after it was shouted by a man on streets within the Middle East. [09/15/12] In condemning "Freedom" and "Democracy," the speaker was not only implicitly condemning America, but he also identified the existence of two completely incompatible social perspectives.

In the modern world, a theocracy is a viable social construct only within a homogeneous society or one, in which dissent is actively stifled and minority points of view are oppressed. Within the more diverse American culture, it is important that we acknowledge and zealously protect our fundamental rights, including freedoms related to of speech, association, and religion.

Anyone choosing to oppose such freedoms does not wish to integrate into the broader society. The only alternatives, which are compatible with such an exclusionary perspective, are either to destroy any open society or to convert all other persons to the prescribed way of thinking. Neither alternative is reasonable.

I do not believe that the sentiment, which is evidenced by the above quote, is ubiquitous among all Arabs, but it is pervasive among significant segments of the populations. This is not simply a disagreement about shades of gray. This perspective is entirely incompatible with the ideals of the

481

America, which our forefathers fought to establish and died to maintain. In an effort to appease and pacify bullies, thugs, and tyrants, we cannot tarnish the ideals of: Freedom of Speech, Freedom of Association, Free Exercise of Religion, *etc.*

These ideals are not uniquely American, but the United States is in a unique position of leadership. Any compromise by America on these ideals almost certainly assures that others will bend to similar pressures. Our foreign policy objective should not be to "make" all other countries in our image, but we should strive to demonstrate the benefits of our fundamental freedoms in such a way that others around the world will choose to emulate those ideals. We, as a people and a country, have failed to project that positive example in recent times.

The idea of a "Melting Pot" is to create an amalgamation of the better aspects of different individuals and cultures in order to develop and grow as a people and a nation. We often fail to appreciate that the smelting and refining processes are ones, which require extreme heat and destruction in order to extract the purified trait. People(s) are reluctant to recognize better traits in others or to acknowledge their own shortcomings.

By necessity, persons should be "equal" under the law, and one may even argue that persons should have equal "opportunity" to thrive and succeed. However, the reality is that situations and circumstances are almost never entirely equal, and understandably, we are reluctant to fault one, who is a victim of circumstance. Even so, many persons do not take equal advantage of the opportunities afforded them. It is proper that one's actions (or willful inaction) are the subjects of either praise when warranted or rebuke when justified.

Those, who choose to act out with violence, do not deserve to be seen as "equals." Such actions should be unequivocally and universally condemned. Such persons are worthy of rebuke, and the supposed religious dogma, which serves as justification for such actions, should be identified as a perversion. Dogma and philosophies that advocate or promote violence and excuse the killing of innocent persons should be excluded from the mix of positive attributes and traits toward which human beings should strive.

Seeking to include such perspectives for the sake of "diversity" is detrimental to our growth as a nation and as a species. Condemnation of such violent actions should be definitive and not tepid. The tacit acceptance of such behavior, as being the natural product of any responsible religion, is not appropriate.

Religious compulsion should not be allowed as a defense to bad behavior or horrific acts. Even in situations where one's religion may be presumed by birth (*e.g.* Judaism, Amish, *etc.*), adherence to any religion is ultimately a voluntary choice. Any free association of individuals may espouse any belief and impose whatever conditions and expectations that the group may choose for itself and its members. However, where government and a particular religion are inextricably intertwined, the favored religion enjoys the mandate of law and police powers. There is no voluntary association, and the government can dictate adherence to the (religious) law.

In a theocracy, religious dogma, as interpreted and applied by some supreme (and presumably inerrant) religious authority, serves as the basis for all law, and there can be no allowance for differing opinions or points of view.

Where adherents adopt a religion, which is consistent with their personal beliefs, such persons exchange certainty of continued association and approval of the religious authority *in lieu* of free will and independence of thought. The broader society, however, should not normalize abhorrent behavior outside the confines of the group for the sake of and under the guise of equality or diversity.

Where government enforces religious dogma on persons not so inclined, the results are suppression of liberty and oppression of religious dissidents. One cannot have liberty without diversity of thought, and within the confines of a theocracy, one cannot exercise free will.

A theocracy is essentially a compulsory religion. Such a concept is not only incompatible with freedom and democracy, but it is inconsistent with most persons' understanding of religion. Morality presumably requires voluntary adherence and free will. Again, one can respect the right of any voluntarily assembled group or association to establish their rules and mores, but it is not necessary that such traits be incorporated by broader society, or even allowed outside of such group.

As Americans and Christians, we often conveniently forget or omit the less savory aspects of our own social and religious histories:

- The Salem Witch Trials, Spanish Inquisition, the persecution of "heretics" like Copernicus, white supremacy, *etc.*;
- Christians participated in battles to remove Moors [Muslims] from the Iberian Peninsula, comprising what is today Spain and Portugal; and
- Christians fought in the Crusades in an effort to "free" Jerusalem from Muslim rule.

Such conflicts, battles and wars were efforts to establish religious supremacy. One would hope that history has shown the futility of such hostilities and that, as civilized men, we can apply these lessons in today's world.

Western Civilization survived the Dark Ages, during which intellectual and social developments were stagnant for centuries following the decline of the Roman Empire. It was with the rise of Renaissance throughout Europe that the foundations of modern political and social thought were laid. We forget the efforts, struggles, and lessons learned by those, who lived those histories.

We act as though our present situation and freedoms "just are." We take them for granted, and we fail to appreciate the sacrifices that were necessary to establish these things as well as the continued sacrifices and contributions that are necessary from each of us in order to maintain our way of life today.

Islam is divided into sects considerably more diverse than our Christian denominations. The more mainstream sects are closely identified with the tenets of Christianity. Fringe sects exist, in which individuals have intentionally perverted the holy teachings in order to promote their own interests and personal gain. However, this phenomenon is not unique to Islam. Christianity has historically produced numerous cults and false prophets, which choose to use the religion as a weapon of exclusion rather than a light to salvation (*e.g.* Westboro Baptist Church, Jim Jones, David Koresh, *etc.*).

I have friends, who practice the Muslim faith. I do not fear them, and they do not despise me or seek my demise for my religious beliefs. Christians, Muslims, and Jews all revere and worship the God of Abraham. Our religious texts bear different names,[118] but the basic teachings remain the same. We share a God of love, grace, and compassion. We share many of the same prophets.

Today, Christians accept Jews despite the fact that Judaism teaches that Jesus was not the Messiah. However, Jesus is common to both Christians and Muslims. We should seek common ground and accentuate our similarities, and learn from our differences. However, those who choose not to embrace inclusion and mutual respect should be isolated not tolerated among more civilized peoples.

We as Americans must be committed to our ideals of inclusion and individual liberties. We as Christians should be committed to the ideals of the Golden Rule. In living that ideal, we are likely to realize that many persons, who we do not know well, are more alike than different. However, inclusion and acceptance of persons and peoples should not be excuses for sacrificing ideals, normalizing heinous actions, or enabling ignorance and lies.

---

[118] *i.e. Holy Bible [Apocrypha], Koran [Quran],* and *Torah [Tanach].*

If truth and mutual respect are the objectives toward which we strive, we should be willing to acknowledge and address our own shortcomings and should not be reluctant to insist that others do the same. Only in doing so can with grow toward further enlightenment.

Bringing it Home -

Some months ago, media sources reported that fourteen-year-old Malala Yousufzai was shot in the head by members of the Taliban as she was returning home from school in Pakistan. A teenage girl was marked for assassination because she dared propose that children, who sought knowledge and wisdom, should be afforded the opportunity to learn, even if they are female. She was marked to die because she simply wanted to read and go to school.

In response to such horrendous acts, many of us want to so "something." However, we cannot impose civility upon the uncivilized, nor can we impart wisdom to those, who are blissful in their ignorance. It is unlikely, that any of us can directly impact the life of Malala.

Nevertheless, we have in the U.S. millions of schoolchildren, who seemingly would accept the deaths of intelligence and reason rather than to apply themselves and take advantage of the near boundless opportunities afforded to them. We can have a dramatic effect on the lives of these children.

These stark differences in perspective can give up new insight into old problems. We could stand to learn from the challenges and struggles of others, who long for basic services and necessities that we take for granted.

Similarly, we, as a people should set a better example to the rest of the world about what it means to be civilized, respectful, cooperative, and compassionate. In all these things, we have a lot to learn.

¹ ...[B]e ready to do whatever is good, ² to slander no one, to be peaceable and considerate, and always to be gentle toward everyone. ...
⁹ [A]void foolish controversies and genealogies and arguments and quarrels about the law, because these are unprofitable and useless.
¹⁰ Warn a divisive person once, and then warn them a second time. After that, have nothing to do with them.
¹¹ You may be sure that such people are warped and sinful; they are self-condemned.

Titus – Chapter 3 (NIV)

Semantics: *The Building Blocks of Our Reality*

© 2012

Introduction -

Debates are as much a matter of crafting the issue as it is couching an argument. Polls can be skewed depending on the phraseology of the question being posed, and statistics can be applied to support a number of disparate positions. Placing someone in the proper perspective or providing the framework of thought and understanding is imperative to communicating philosophies and ideas.

Never is it more dangerous to compare apples to oranges than in the debates about religion and morality. While there may be cosmic truths just as there are laws of physics, the application of those truths and laws rely greatly upon perspective and relativity.

Open to Wonder -

Few moments of intellectual clarity stand out in one's life. These are eureka moments when consciousness is expanded.

One of these moments came to me as a young boy. I was admiring the stars and discussing the night sky with slightly older aunts. In that moment, I came to realize that those stars were more than specs of light in the night sky. I realized that each one of those twinkling specs represented a star similar to our sun.

I imagined then the "thousands" of stars that must be in the universe and the equal number of planets that may be circling those stars. While the concept of life on those planets did not follow immediately, it was the first time that the "smallness" of myself and earth first became known to me. [119]

On Defining God -

A second such incident came in college. I was taking a philosophy class, and the young professor regularly scheduled a free-flowing study session at his home. Rarely, were the discussions limited to recent assignments. More often than not we began pondering among ourselves the mysteries of morality, religion, and the dichotomy of good versus evil. During one of those sessions, we began discussing the existence of God and debating what relationship man could have with the Divine.

The first step toward a fruitful discussion was to define, "God." Rather than debating the form, which God may take, and contemplating whether God existed in "man's image" or vice versa, we did not define God as a collection of physical characteristics. God did not take on the form of a Michelangelo fresco. In removing the human form of God, we also removed the associated human frailties.

We avoided any specific religious construct. We resisted the urge to define the Deity by certain attributed acts or powers. In avoiding debates regarding God's scope of powers and any potential limitations, we skirted conflicts regarding creation myths or explanations for miraculous events.

---

[119] More accurately, there are roughly 10,000 stars visible in the night sky. In our own Milky Way Galaxy, there are estimated to be 300 Billion stars. Within the Universe, there are estimated to be as many as 200 Billion Galaxies, and the total number of stars is estimated to be One Septillion. That is 10^{24} stars or "1" followed by 24 zeroes!

We settled on a definition, upon which everyone could agree. We reached agreement despite differences of experience, religious convictions, and perspective.

We agreed that the Supreme Being is: *That above which there is none other.*

Using that definition:

- God has no gender, race, or even humanoid form; therefore, the prejudices associated therewith disappear;

- There is no requirement to debate God's powers but simply to acknowledge that those powers are unequaled; and

- There is no personification of God merely an acceptance that something is the pinnacle of the universe of sentient beings (believing that consciousness would be required of a Supreme Being).

The God that exists under this definition may take many forms depending on the perspective and beliefs of the individual, but the differences were like viewing someone from different perspectives rather than questioning their entire existence. The descriptions differed, but the picture was recognizable regardless of the person, who was speaking.

When one conceptualizes God as a collection of positive ideals toward which we might all strive, that cumulative concept of a Deity does not seem so farfetched, and the existence of such a being is readily imaginable.

Appreciating Creation -

Similarly, the importance of the Biblical Creation story becomes lost in debates about the length of a "day" or how dinosaurs and man could have lived simultaneously in contravention of existing fossil records. To me, the most fascinating things about the Biblical Creation was the order in which it occurred and the fact that the story is not told that everything came into existence simultaneously.

I was always curious as to why an omnipotent God did not simply will everything into existence instantly. Later, I was fascinated that the course of creation followed (somewhat) consistently with scientific theories of the Big Bang and Darwinian Evolution.

At this point, if the potential reader is not at least open to the possibility that the "Six (6) Days" of Creation represented periods of time other than an absolutely fixed span of time consisting of exactly twenty-four (24) hours (1,440 minutes – 86,400 seconds), then said reader likely quit reading a couple pages ago. I will note that the sun and the moon, which were to "be for signs, and for seasons, and for days, and years," were not created until the fourth (4th) day of creation. Is the act (or process) of creation any less miraculous whether it spans a period of exactly 8,640 minutes or a scientifically estimated 13.8 Billion years?

Another fascination for me is that on Day One creation effectively began with God saying, "Let there be light."[120] I noted above that those celestial bodies primarily responsible for

---

[120] *Genesis* 1:3.

giving (or reflecting) the light that we perceive today (*i.e.* sun, moon, and stars) were not created until Day Four.[121] So, for three (3) days there was "light" without an identified source of that light.

Scientists tell us that space and matter (and even time), as we know it, came into existence as result of a "Big Bang," the original cause or source of which is scientifically unproven. Regardless, that "miraculous" event could have very well been the onset of Creation.

Interestingly, "light" is a form of energy. Immediately after the Big Bang energies (in various forms) were all that existed. Energy existed before matter came to be.

Days Two through Four concern the creation of: Air and Water [Day Two], Separation of Land from Water (and Plants) [Day Three], and Celestial Bodies (e.g. Sun, Moon, and Stars) [Day Four].

I will resist any attempt to seamlessly synthesize the Biblical Creation Story with scientific theory. (Such an effort has been undertaken by others, who are involved in promoting Intelligent Design theories of Creation).

Instead, I will merely note that, if one allows for the possibility that the "elements" of creation came into being over some period of time, the scientific process is generally consistent with the outline in the Bible:

---

[121] *Genesis* 1:14-19.

493

1. Energy from the Big Bang beget basic matter (*i.e.* Hydrogen);

2. The force of gravity caused Hydrogen to form the heart of stars;

3. Intense pressures caused Hydrogen to begin the process of nuclear fusion so as to create helium, thereby begetting stars;

4. Those early stars experienced death and rebirth;

5. Through successive series of destruction and rebirth all other complex elements, which are naturally occurring on the earth (and in the universe) came into being;

6. As the massive clouds of cosmic dust sorted themselves, the planets in our solar system came into being;

7. Water, the compound most important to life as we know it, was delivered onto the face of earth;

8. The crust of the earth expanded and contracted to form the continents;

9. On those continents and in the oceans, there developed flora representing the earliest stages of life; and

10. From these building blocks, higher life forms developed:

   a. Day 5 – Fishes and Birds;[122] and

   b. Day 6 – Other Animals, including man.

---

[122] Interestingly, scientists hypothesize that modern birds are the distant evolutionary descendants of dinosaurs. Higher order animals, again including man, followed creatures from the oceans and feathered "dinosaurs." Allowing for the length of the given "day," the similarities between this ordering and scientifically supported evolution is uncanny.

For those for whom a literal interpretation of the Creation Story, which is contained in *Genesis*, is an article of faith, the information, which is contained in this essay, is likely seen as blasphemous and heretical.

I am not trying to "prove" or "disprove" any particular theory or belief related to Creation with cosmic certainty. Instead, I ask, "Why does it matter?" Is the existence of the Universe, much less our place in it as sentient beings, any less "miraculous" regardless of how we came to be?

In Search of Heaven -[123]

Maurice Sendak, a self-professed atheist and noted author of the children's book, *Where the Wild things Are*, died in 2012. As Sendak came to terms with his own mortality, his words, as expressed in an interview, gave additional credence to the old adage, "There are no atheists in foxholes."

As each of us faces death, we want to believe that there is something bigger than ourselves. We hope that there is life after death whereby we can continue to participate as part of a greater consciousness after our passings or that we at least leave some legacy whereby our lives can have meaning and have an impact on future generations.

Each of us is comprised of a complicated collection of energies, which have inexplicably achieved sentience and consciousness. Is it so hard to imagine an afterlife or collective consciousness among all things (a conversion to a state of being where our consciousness spends eternity among others similarly

---

[123] Originally posted as a Blog Entry (January 10, 2013).

situated)? Could this state of collective consciousness be considered heaven or nirvana?

Is God a fiction? Is religion a delusion? Some persons would adamantly answer both questions in the affirmative, but without hope and a belief in something greater than ourselves, our individual lives and temporal existences on the cosmic stage have very little meaning.

Conclusion -

One of the most interesting and intriguing analogies that I ever heard related to the existence of God and the interrelatedness of all things. The analogy went thus:

> *Imagine that our solar system* [or universe] *is merely an atom on the thumbnail of God.*

If we allow for the existence of the "Big Bang" and concede that all, which we perceive as having substance and comprising the matter of the universe, was once pure energy condensed in an area smaller than the size of an atom, is it really so strange to imagine an interconnected universe with a intelligent and sentient Supreme Being more capable than mortal man?

Live a good life. ... If there are gods and they are just, then they will not care how devout you have been, but will welcome you based on the virtues you have lived by.

If there are gods, but unjust, then you should not want to worship them.

If there are no gods, then you will be gone, but will have lived a noble life that will live on in the memories of your loved ones.

— Marcus Aurelius, *Meditations*

The Nature of the Beast

Blog Entry - July 27, 2013

A recent internet meme contained the quotation:

If you expect the world to be fair with you because you are fair, you are fooling yourself.

That is like expecting the lion not to eat you because you did not eat him.

Life is not fair. Humankind is often not humane. Expecting to disprove either of these immutable facts will lead to a lifetime of disappointment. All that anyone can do is to live his own life as a worthy example for others and to hope that such an example will be followed.

Morality, or the lack thereof, is strictly an individual trait. Each individual has the wherewithal within himself to battle and conquer a selfish and corrupt nature. Success in this battle requires one to admit weakness and fault, as well as requires that one accept responsibility for his own fate. Some persons are too vain to acknowledge weakness or too fearful to strive toward enlightenment and self-discovery. Therefore, many persons succumb needlessly to human frailties and weaknesses of the flesh.

Faith that any institution or government will impose morality and enforce proper behavior is misplaced. Similarly, blame for one's moral failings and personal shortcomings should be directed only at one's self. Morality and good deeds can neither be imposed by fiat nor enforced by the sword of government or by the threat of eternal damnation from the church. It is up to each person to battle his own demons and to be a worthy steward of the life and talents bestowed upon him.

Each day should begin with a conscious and deliberate pause, during which each of us takes a moment to look deeply into our respective souls while asking:

What can I do today to prove myself a worthy steward of the life that I have been privileged to live?

Introduction -

In an internet meme, a photograph of Ayn Rand, philosopher and author of the novel, *Atlas Shrugged,* is juxtaposed beside a portrait of Jesus Christ. Beneath the picture of Rand, there is a quote from her:

> *[Faith] is a sign of a psychological weakness. ... I regard it as evil to place your emotions, your desire, above the evidence of what your mind knows. That's what you're doing with the idea of God.*

Under the portrait of Christ, is scripture from *Mark* 10:25:

> *It is easier for a camel to go through the eye of a needle, than for a rich man to enter into the kingdom of God.*

The pictures contained the bottom caption, "Republican Party ... You're doing it wrong," with the obvious implication being, if you are rich, then you cannot be moral. By extension, if you are Republican and/or you oppose liberal political philosophies and government entitlement programs, then you are un-Christian.

In this essay, I address specifically the message or argument presented by the aforementioned meme. Liberals / Progressives, through the Democratic Party, propose to use the conscription powers of government in an effort to establish a prescribed standard of living through entitlements funded by coerced altruism (*i.e.* taxation). Nevertheless, I would offer similarly adamant objections to the "Religious Right" / Social Conservatives pursuing a social (read "moral") agenda through the Republican Party. Such platform elements unnecessarily limit individual liberties and personal freedoms without sufficiently advancing any legitimate state interest.

Is God a Democrat or a Republican? -

Which political party is the true standard bearer for Christianity:

- Democrats, who advocate on behalf of constituent groups for the alleviation of want and need, with such perceived deficiencies being defined in a manner that is quite fluid and expanding, and who advocate in favor of Same-sex Marriage and adopt a Pro-Choice platform?

- Or, does that honor fall to Republicans, who advocate on behalf of propertied interests, and who promote the rights of the unborn and zealously protect the sanctity of "traditional" marriage?

- Can the members of any party or the proponents of any political philosophy, on the whole, be identified as saints versus sinners?

Morality seems to be very much in the eye of the beholder. Are all rich people going to hell? If so, what is the threshold, at which one is "rich" and therefore subject to damnation?

It should be noted that nearly every American is "rich" in relation to the United Nations' established standard for "extreme poverty." Approximately 1.2 Billion persons (nearly 1-in-5 of all inhabitants of earth) subsist on no more than $1.25 per day (less than $500.00 / yr.). In comparison to these persons, how "rich" are you? In light of this fact, do Healthcare, Social Security, and Medicare seem like "rights" or "privileges"?

Liberals seek to use government as a tool to mold society in an image that they feel is appropriate. In the names of "fairness" and "equality," they seek to establish a minimum standard of living for all. Given the disparities among individuals' talents, traits, efforts, commitments, and needs, is it realistic to expect that all persons will be on equal financial footing? If not, then what is the appropriate minimum "standard"? And, by "all" do liberals mean everyone on earth, only Americans, or just those in our own subdivisions?

What sacrifices should we, as individuals and collectively as a society, be willing to make in pursuit of this Utopia? Economic efficiencies require conformity. Conformity smothers individuality. Without individuality, there can be no freedom. So, are losses of personal freedoms and individual liberties among the costs that we should be willing to pay for perceived incremental improvements financial security?

In response to the analogy of a camel passing through the eye of a needle, the disciples asked Jesus how it was that anyone could be saved, Christ responded in *Mark* 10:27:

> *But Jesus beheld them, and said unto them, "With men this is impossible; but with God all things are possible."*

Jesus taught his disciples that the important factor was not the wealth of the individual (or even his specific charitable acts) but the individual's personal relationship with God. Far be it from individuals, much less government, to challenge any man's relationship with his God by critiquing the morality of another person's acts or by measuring the sufficiency of another person's charity.

Matthew 7:1-5 provides:

> *Judge not, that ye be not judged. [2] For with what judgment ye judge, ye shall be judged: and with what measure ye mete, it shall be measured to you again. [3] And why beholdest thou the mote that is in thy brother's eye, but considerest not the beam that is in thine own eye? [4] Or how wilt thou say to thy brother, Let me pull out the mote out of thine eye; and, behold, a beam is in thine own eye? [5] Thou hypocrite, first cast out the beam out of thine own eye; and then shalt thou see clearly to cast out the mote out of thy brother's eye.*

Understanding the "Social Contract" -

Every citizen has the mutual obligation and responsibility to not actively and materially interfere with the concurrent and concomitant rights of other citizens. However, it is not proper, or even feasible, for government to impose laws mandating "Good Samaritan" acts or which codify the "Golden Rule." Such ideal human behaviors can be supported and mandated by religious teachings and morals, but the rule of law is entirely ineffective in guaranteeing and enforcing such behaviors.

Contrary to current thinking, individual citizens have no affirmative obligation to advance the efficiencies and supposed effectiveness of government. Citizens are obliged not to do "wrong" acts such as would interfere with the established rights of others. Those same citizens do not have affirmative obligations to advance goals or objectives, which may be established by a self-serving government when the acts prescribed by that government (or its power brokers) have been

502

deemed "right" but such acts would be contrary to the best interests of the contributing individual(s).

As much as it may seem beneficial and prudent to some parties to legislate morality (or government efficiencies), the extent of human beings' social and civic obligations is to avoid actively harming their fellow man. Individuals cede powers and authority to government in order for that institution to serve as the intermediary or arbiter between citizens so as to assure the security of property, fluidity of transactions among parties, and to afford safety to the citizenry from oppressive and destructive forces (both domestic and foreign).

Without a showing of proximate harm to another person or entity, government should not seek to correct individual behaviors and should not mandate which path among many is appropriate for any individual or group. With freedom, come the benefits of self-determination and the burdens of personal responsibility. Success or failure should stem from the acts or omissions of the individual. Government is not an insurer of a life without want, loss, or failure.

There is no civic obligation to sacrifice one's own property and well-being primarily for the support, comfort, and aid of another. Are such sacrifices worthy of admiration and duplication? Perhaps, they are, but such sacrifices should not be the subjects of government mandates to be enforced under threat of government prosecution and persecution.

Nearly no one would argue that government is authorized and empowered to enforce a tithe prescribed by a religious faith

503

or ecclesiastical body. An uproar would be heard regarding the required "Separation of Church and State."

Similarly, few would argue that the government should be empowered to require gifts to specified individuals or charitable contributions to a predetermined organization, group, or class of "needy" persons under threats of garnishment, levy, or incarceration. Those persons, from whom such transfers, contributions, and payments would be compelled, likely would object citing guarantees in favor of owning personal property and restrictions upon the taking of such property by government.

Each of these situations would have identical effect:

The imposition by government fiat of a standard of morality or sense of "right" and "wrong," as defined or established by a controlling group or bloc of voters.

While most of us think of religion in terms of "theism" (*i.e.* a belief in the existence of a God or gods), the definition of "religion" is itself not so limiting:

A specific fundamental set of beliefs and practices generally agreed upon by a number of persons or sects.

In this expanded context, Communism and Humanism,[124] are no less "religions" than are Buddhism and Catholicism. Therefore, what distinction is there between a religiously compelled "tithe" and government coerced altruism? Is social "rightness," as determined by a democratic majority, any more compelling than religious dogma?

---

[124] Meaning: Any system or mode of thought or action in which human interests, values, and dignity predominate.

504

A valid distinction must rest upon something other than the existence of a deity and associated mythologies. This is especially true since political rulers often have been deified, and governments (or political philosophies) tend to create their own mythologies and legends, which may differ materially from fact and reality.

If government were to require the propertied classes to pay a religiously instituted tithe or if it were to require taxpayers to make direct contributions to fellow citizens in satisfaction of civic obligations, such requirements would almost certainly be struck down as being well beyond the purview and authority of government (particularly the federal government).

Today, the bottom fifty percent (50%) of taxpaying citizens contributes less than five percent (5%) of the required funding for the operations of the federal government and for the general welfare of the population. Therefore, the propertied classes, who represent a minority of the electorate, are forced to shoulder an ever increasing burden to fund the operations of government and to fund the growing entitlement programs of the Nanny State.

Imposing government as an intermediary between the propertied classes (*producers*) and those receiving government benefits (*consumers*) for the purpose of conscripting personal property (*taxes*) and redistributing wealth somehow makes the resulting payments of entitlements through taxation palatable (and for some a moral imperative).

The Maligned and Misinterpreted Rand -

Much has been made about the supposed hypocrisy of Ayn Rand collecting Social Security in her advanced age. It was Ayn Rand herself, who addressed this issue during her lifetime. To paraphrase her argument:

> If the government is committed to paying a benefit through conscription of my personal property, it would be entirely unreasonable and irrational for me, as a citizen from whom those assets were conscripted, to refuse to accept the benefits, which the government pays to everyone else.

In a similar vein, I will collect without compunction whatever Social Security and Medicare that the government will pay to me when I am eligible. However, I would opt out of both programs if given the opportunity. I am confident that I could provide a better benefit to myself if I could choose how it is that my monies were spent. But alas, that choice is not mine to make. So, I will wait eagerly to see if Social Security and Medicare remain solvent until my retirement.

Ayn Rand was a humanist. She relied upon rational thought and human reason as the foundations for her philosophies. Therefore, her disdain for a theistic religion, as evidenced from the introductory quote, should come as a surprise to no one. However, her philosophies have been distorted and misconstrued by both supposed adherents and opponents. Focus has been placed on the "transactions," which she saw as inevitably occurring between persons, and most commentators have defined the consideration exchanged in such transactions solely in terms of money or monetary value.

Hence, her philosophies are often considered cold, greedy, and selfish.

Nevertheless, Rand's philosophies anticipate and allow for interrelated personal transactions using "currencies" or mediums of exchange independent of money. Voluntary exchanges can be for joy and pleasure, as well as for personal services, companionship, and emotional comforts. Her philosophies do not eliminate the concepts of charity, philanthropy, and benevolence, but in those philosophies, she did oppose compelled altruism as being disingenuous and irrational. While her philosophies were, and continue to be unconventional, they should hardly be seen as "evil."

Admittedly, Rand's philosophies attempt to divest emotion, theology, and institutionalized morals from decisions about "right" and "wrong." However, the absence of a traditional religious faith in and of itself should not disqualify her philosophies as irrelevant or baseless. Even the much revered Thomas Jefferson, developed a personal theist theory of religion, which would hardly be consistent with any "traditional" or "fundamentalist" views of religion today.

In fact, Jefferson said in considering the respective roles of religion and government:

It does me no injury for my neighbor to say there are 20 gods, or no god. It neither picks my pocket nor breaks my leg.

Among the proper functions of government are to protect and enforce property rights and to impose a level of safety and security for the citizenry. However, it is not a proper role of government to define, establish, and impose a moral code or religious standards for that citizenry. Such actions would result in a theocracy.

Transacting in Morals -

Moralistic arguments are all-or-nothing propositions. They do not allow for divergence of opinions. The resulting mindset is, "If you are not with us, then you are against us." The liberal mantra can be summarized, "If you are not as 'generous' with your property as the self-defined 'moral majority' wants you to be, then you are a bad and evil person."

None but the most ardent anarchists would ever argue that government should have no role in society. In fact, government is entirely necessary in protecting individual rights and personal liberties. The debated positions regarding the proper roles of government do not necessarily represent differences of moral ideals or societal objectives, but those differing positions almost certainly represent opposing personal beliefs as to whether government is a proper and viable means to achieve the desired ends.

Nevertheless, there is a massive chasm between a truly needy or disabled individual, who requires care and sustenance via society, and the advancement of the cradle-to-grave Nanny State, in which the government acts *in loco parentis* for all citizens. I would argue that the nature, type, and extent of the roles of government are not subject moral determinations. The proper and accepted role is a matter of negotiation, give-and-take, and *quid-pro-quo*.

508

Illusions of safety and increased certainties of outcome are mutually exclusive to the concepts of self-determination and individual liberties. How much liberty and freedom are we, as individuals and as a society, willing to give up in the pursuit of economic efficiencies, financial security, and perceived safety? Those parties wishing to expand the roles of government must be honest about the costs of the supposed "benefits," and such parties must acknowledge that the associated costs include, not only monetary costs, but also significant losses and curtailments of personal rights, liberties, and freedoms.

Those wishing to tax the producer and to deprive him of the right to determine the most productive use of his property must be creative but sincere in explaining the benefits to that taxpayer, if any.

It is fair to ask, "What is the 'producer' getting in return for that next dollar of taxation?" The answer to that question cannot be, "Nothing."

Upon receipt, the government has a duty to act efficiently and effectively in using conscripted property in furtherance of the common good (as opposed to payments to special interest groups or merely for the self-preservation of the state). Unfortunately, government has not proven itself a worthy steward of the taxes that it takes, and when government expands its own role into areas, to which it is entirely ill-suited, government ineffectiveness and inefficiencies will likely be even more pronounced.

Institutions: The Sum of Their Parts -

I consider morality and its associated acts on the micro-level (individuals) rather than at the macro-level (institutions). If thousands of years of religious (institutional) mandates and teachings, with the coercive power of eternal damnation, have not been effective to instill a sense of morality across humanity, then I have no confidence that government, as a tool toward that end, will be any more effective. Similarly, I believe that a dangerous precedent is set by giving government the power to dictate morality, and bestowing that power creates a situation, in which I am confident that government will inevitably abuse the immense powers being acquiesced to it.

Since I do not believe that institutions can be inherently "moral," I do not believe in a consistently benevolent government. On the contrary, I fear that an all-powerful sovereign government will inevitably mirror the natural inclinations and flaws of the men, who ultimately wield its formidable powers. I will hold to my preferences for limited government and amoral institutions. Nothing in the arguments of others has ever convinced me that those concepts are out of place.

The Moral Being -

Morality is an individual trait. Governments (and institutions in general) should be amoral. That is not to say that institutions should be "immoral" (*i.e.* "without morals" or "evil"), but they should not strive to implement any particular moral code or religious beliefs.

Of course, there are some universally accepted (or nearly so) concepts of "right" and "wrong." However, where there is a marked divergence of opinions regarding the "rightness" of a specific act, government should resist the urge to intervene and choose sides. It is only when one person's exercise of a right materially interferes with the rights of another that government should intervene in order to keep the peace. As Zechariah Chafee said, "Your right to swing your arms ends just where the other man's nose begins."[125]

When one erects political philosophies upon supposedly "moral" foundations, the results are polarization and discord. The argument takes on the tenor of "right" versus "wrong." But, **whose** right and **who's** wrong?

Laws, policies, and government regulations should be based upon reason and rationality not social mores and personal whims. Government and politics should be based upon give-and-take among competing interests, a marketplace of ideas and policies. In such an environment, the pendulum inevitably swings to and fro.

At various times, the same individual may be a "winner" or "loser" in response to government actions, and one's relationship with government or the benefit received may change over time (or even be eliminated). Nevertheless, government policy should not be dictated by the identity of the beneficiary of government's largesse. The government should not pick winners and losers.

---

[125] The quote is often misattributed to the Justice Oliver Wendell Holmes – "Freedom of Speech in Wartime", 32 *Harvard Law Review* 932, 957 (1919).

There is no single constant path. Even if there were a certain path for any particular person, government is incapable of divining that singular path for the simultaneous benefit of more than 300 million citizens. When laws and policies evolve into birthrights and entitlements, governments become bloated, inefficient, ineffective, and corrupt.

The High Cost of "Morality" -

Anyone, who resists the compulsory and coercive taxing powers of government and opposes the growth of the Nanny State, is likely branded, "Greedy," by those, who favor active redistribution of wealth through government intervention. Producers, who are openly reluctant to shouldering the tax burden, are considered selfish, uncaring, or even immoral. However, to discredit the objections of those subjected to increased taxation is to infer that there are no individual property rights. Only nominal merit is given to the waning concepts of self-determination and personal responsibility. Such concepts are often seen as trite and outdated.

Instead, property is treated as though it belongs to the collective. Some members of the collective believe themselves entitled to a share of the cumulative wealth without due consideration of their contributions to their own well being or to the general welfare of the collective. Everyone wants the benefits, but few are ready, willing, and able to pay the associated costs. Everything, including freedom, has a "price," and we, as individuals and collectively as a society, must be willing to pay the incumbent price for the freedoms, liberties, protections, and entitlements that we receive through government or which are guaranteed by its protections.

The "Social Contract" breaks down when citizens attempt to remove the cost element from the equation and to eliminate the *quid-pro-quo* transaction. Citizens cannot and should not expect to have something for nothing. One should not expect a prescribed standard of living just for breathing. If one does not contribute to his own well being and that of others, then he should not expect the "village" to provide him support and comforts.

Similarly, persons should not expect the cumulative burdens and costs of a life poorly lived to fall upon the collective of society. There are costs and consequences associated with repetitive bad life choices, and those costs should be borne by the individuals making those choices not society in general.

Common Ground -

Few people would advocate against advancement of the species. Nearly no one would refuse to offer a helping hand to an individual, who is clearly in need. I do not think that the "ideals" of the politically polarized groups are widely divergent, and I do believe in a duty to aid one's fellow man. However, I think that political philosophies can and do differ significantly on the extent to which those ideals can be achieved realistically, and persons disagree as to the mechanisms and tools that should be used in pursuit of those ideals.

I accept imperfection and unfairness as inevitable facts of life, and I do not feel it incumbent upon me to personally fix all of the ills of mankind. Furthermore, I am not arrogant so as to think that such powers are mine to exert over humanity. Government is similarly incapable of imposing a standard of living free from want for all citizens and to insulate those same citizens from all forms of disappointment and loss.

If one believes in the omnipotent God of the Judeo-Christian faiths, an extension of the "you are your brother's keeper" argument would be to question, "Why does God himself choose not to completely alleviate all need, loss and suffering among mankind?"

Upon witnessing first-hand the trials and hardships of mankind, Jesus, as the incarnate Son of God, with a single act could have cured all illness, sheltered all of the homeless, clothed all of the naked, and fed all of the starving. Nevertheless, He chose not to do so. In an exercise of omniscience, God and his Son, Jesus Christ, choose neither to remedy the suffering nor to cure the ills of mankind.

I can hardly see why one should be called "evil" for not sacrificing that which he has for the supposed betterment of persons far removed. The sufficiency of one's charity should be a matter between a man, his conscience, and his God. It should not be a matter over which government and fellow citizens hold sway.

Misplaced Faith -

Liberals and Progressives seem to harbor a much higher level of idealism and faith in the immediate potential of humanity than I am able to muster. Similarly, they hold much greater confidence in the capabilities and benevolence of government than I believe to be safe. Ultimately, an arrogant and unrestrained government will prove true the adage, "Power corrupts, and absolute power corrupts absolutely."

If I am wrong, then the burden remains upon humanity to diverge from the paths of strife and suffering, which mankind has traveled for millennia. If those who favor a more powerful and intrusive government are wrong, then God help us all, since no lesser being could possibly intervene to reverse the course.

Any arguments to the contrary generally hinge upon the belief that government (institutions) or the collective will of the people can "fix" humanity. I believe that individual human beings, living their own lives to the best of their personal abilities, represent the only hope for humanity. Ayn Rand believed that productive work was the highest goal of humanity:

> *Productive work is the central purpose of a rational man's life, the central value that integrates and determines the hierarchy of all his other values.*[126]

In living lives well, persons will have less need for and dependence upon government. It is only at the individual level that human beings can truly evolve and develop.

Liberals and progressives believe that government is a dependable, pliable, and benevolent tool to be used in furtherance of some Utopian ideal. I believe that such faith in the institution of government is without an adequate foundation and that the presumed successes are without any sustained historical precedent. I believe that efforts by government in

---

[126] Rand, Ayn, "The Objectivist Ethics," *The Virtue of Selfishness*, p. 25 (1961).

furtherance of moral ideals are at best vain and misguided, and at worst, they are dangerous and counterproductive.

Conclusion -

I would like to believe that humanity is collectively evolving in a manner contrary to millennia of human history and experience, but nearly all evidence points to the fact that the course and eventual fate of humanity remains unchanged. Putting "faith" in mankind to fundamentally change his bestial nature is at least as disconcerting as succumbing to the supposed vice of religion. I am much more confident in the established nature of mankind to be selfish, corrupt, and devious. Those are the traits, which I believe government is most likely to adopt, rather than the much more rarefied traits of charity, compassion, grace, and humility.

Human beings are slow to grow beyond their base instincts, and persons are reluctant to embrace the reason, intellect, and free will, which differentiate our species from lower order animals. With knowledge, comes responsibility for choosing between good and evil, as well as the potential for blame and fault. Many persons would prefer to remain blissful in their collective ignorance rather than to show initiative and to risk failure.

Reason, intellect, and free will are the greatest gifts given by our Creator to the human species (and conversely among the greatest curses). With information and knowledge, comes responsibility, and we cannot shirk personal responsibility for our own well being by choosing to live our lives in ignorance and dependent upon the charity of others. For these reasons, I look to my God every day for the wisdom and guidance to live my life to the best of my abilities.

The gifts bestowed upon us should not be squandered by blindly following a rutted path. Instead, we should follow our own reason and rational thinking toward enlightenment; however, we should not become arrogant and overconfident in our abilities so as to succumb to hubris.

It is always good to remember that the best planned course nearly always requires corrections. To that end, it is much easier for an individual to veer onto the "Road Less Traveled"[127] than it is to expect the whole of humanity to follow a poorly charted and often solitary path. Rather than placing my faith in any institution or government, I prefer to place my hopes for the future in the collective power of those, who seek out truth, enlightenment, and reason. Only such persons are likely to positively affect the course of human development.

Two roads diverged
    in a wood and I—
I took the one
    less travelled by.
And that has made
    all the difference.
        ~ Robert Frost.

---

[127] I recommend to the reader not only the classic poem, "The Road not Taken," by the renowned author, Robert Frost, but also *The Road Less Traveled* series of books by the psychiatrist and author, Dr. M. Scott Peck.

APPENDIX

[W]e have almost succeeded in leveling all human activities to the common denominator of securing the necessities of life and providing for their abundance.

Whatever we do, we are supposed to do for the sake of "making a living;" such is the verdict of society, and the number of people, especially in the professions who might challenge it, has decreased rapidly.

The only exception society is willing to grant is to the artist, who, strictly speaking, is the only "worker" left in a laboring society.

Hannah Arendt (1906–1975), U.S. philosopher.
The Human Condition, Ch. 17 (1958).

WASHINGTON'S "FAREWELL ADDRESS"

I have already intimated to you the danger of parties in the State, with particular reference to the founding of them on geographical discriminations. Let me now take a more comprehensive view, and warn you in the most solemn manner against the baneful effects of the spirit of party generally.

This spirit, unfortunately, is inseparable from our nature, having its root in the strongest passions of the human mind. It exists under different shapes in all governments, more or less stifled, controlled, or repressed; but, in those of the popular form, it is seen in its greatest rankness, and is truly their worst enemy.

The alternate domination of one faction over another, sharpened by the spirit of revenge, natural to party dissension, which in different ages and countries has perpetrated the most horrid enormities, is itself a frightful despotism. But this leads at length to a more formal and permanent despotism. The disorders and miseries which result gradually incline the minds of men to seek security and repose in the absolute power of an individual; and sooner or later the chief of some prevailing faction, more able or more fortunate than his competitors, turns this disposition to the purposes of his own elevation, on the ruins of public liberty.

Without looking forward to an extremity of this kind (which nevertheless ought not to be entirely out of sight), the common and continual mischiefs of the spirit of party are sufficient to make it the interest and duty of a wise people to discourage and restrain it.

It serves always to distract the public councils and enfeeble the public administration. It agitates the community with ill-founded jealousies and false alarms, kindles the animosity of one part against another, foments occasionally riot and insurrection. It opens the door to foreign influence and corruption, which finds a facilitated access to the government itself through the channels of party passions. Thus the policy and the will of one country are subjected to the policy and will of another.

There is an opinion that parties in free countries are useful checks upon the administration of the government and serve to keep alive the spirit of liberty. This within certain limits is probably true; and in governments of a monarchical cast, patriotism may look with indulgence, if not with favor, upon the spirit of party. But in those of the popular character, in governments purely elective, it is a spirit not to be encouraged. From their natural tendency, it is certain there will always be enough of that spirit for every salutary purpose. And there being constant danger of excess, the effort ought to be by force of public opinion, to mitigate and assuage it. A fire not to be quenched, it demands a uniform vigilance to prevent its bursting into a flame, lest, instead of warming, it should consume.

***

It is important, likewise, that the habits of thinking in a free country should inspire caution in those entrusted with its administration, to confine themselves within their respective constitutional spheres, avoiding in the exercise of the powers of one department to encroach upon another. The spirit of encroachment tends to consolidate the powers of all the departments in one, and thus to create, whatever the form of government, a real despotism. A just estimate of that love of power, and proneness to abuse it, which predominates in the human heart, is sufficient to satisfy us of the truth of this position. The necessity of reciprocal checks in the exercise of political power, by dividing and distributing it into different depositaries, and constituting each the guardian of the public weal against invasions by the others, has been evinced by experiments ancient and modern; some of them in our country and under our own eyes. To preserve them must be as necessary as to institute them. If, in the opinion of the people, the distribution or modification of the constitutional powers be in any particular wrong, let it be corrected by an amendment in the way which the Constitution designates. But let there be no change by usurpation; for though this, in one instance, may be the instrument of good, it is the customary weapon by which free governments are destroyed. The precedent must always greatly overbalance in permanent evil any partial or transient benefit, which the use can at any time yield.

***

As a very important source of strength and security, cherish public credit. One method of preserving it is to use it as sparingly as possible, avoiding occasions of expense by cultivating peace, but remembering also that timely disbursements to prepare for danger frequently prevent much greater disbursements to repel it, avoiding likewise the accumulation of debt, not only by shunning occasions of expense, but by vigorous exertion in time of peace to discharge the debts which unavoidable wars may have occasioned, not ungenerously throwing upon posterity the burden which we ourselves ought to bear.

- GEORGE WASHINGTON (1796)

J. Wesley Casteen was born in Fort Riley, Kansas just prior to his father and namesake mustering out of the United States Army. He moved with his parents back to their hometown in eastern North Carolina where he was reared along with a younger brother.

Wesley graduated from James Kenan High School in Warsaw, North Carolina and attended college at Wake Forest University, where he received his undergraduate degree (B.S.) in Accounting. He passed the Certified Public Accountant (CPA) examination and worked in public accounting before returning to Law School.

He graduated *cum laude* with a *Juris Doctor* (J.D.) degree from the Norman A. Wiggins School of Law at Campbell University, and he has practiced law throughout the state of North Carolina. In 2010, Wesley received an advanced academic law degree (LL.M.) with a concentration in Taxation from the University of Alabama, where he graduated *cum laude*.

Wesley speaks regularly at continuing education seminars for both attorneys and CPA's, and he has served as an adjunct Professor at the UNCW-Cameron School of Business, where he teaches Taxation.

His writings have been published in various professional publications and newspapers. He received specialty designations from the American Institute of Certified Public Accountants (AICPA), including being Accredited in Business Valuations (ABV) and Certified in Financial Forensics (CFF).

Wesley presently lives and practices law in Wilmington, North Carolina, and his practice is concentrated in the areas of: Business Law, Commercial Transactions, Estate Planning, Taxation, and Civil Litigation.

Wesley has been active in numerous civic and professional organizations. He served on committees of the N.C. State Bar, including leadership positions with the Tenth (10th) District Bar, where he was President in 2009. He has served on committees and in leadership positions with the North Carolina Association of CPA's (NCACPA), including service on the Board of Directors. He presently serves on the NC CPA Foundation's Board of Directors.

Wake Forest University
PRO HUMANITATE
1834

Campbell University
AD ASTRA PER ASPERA

Alabama Crimson Tide

527

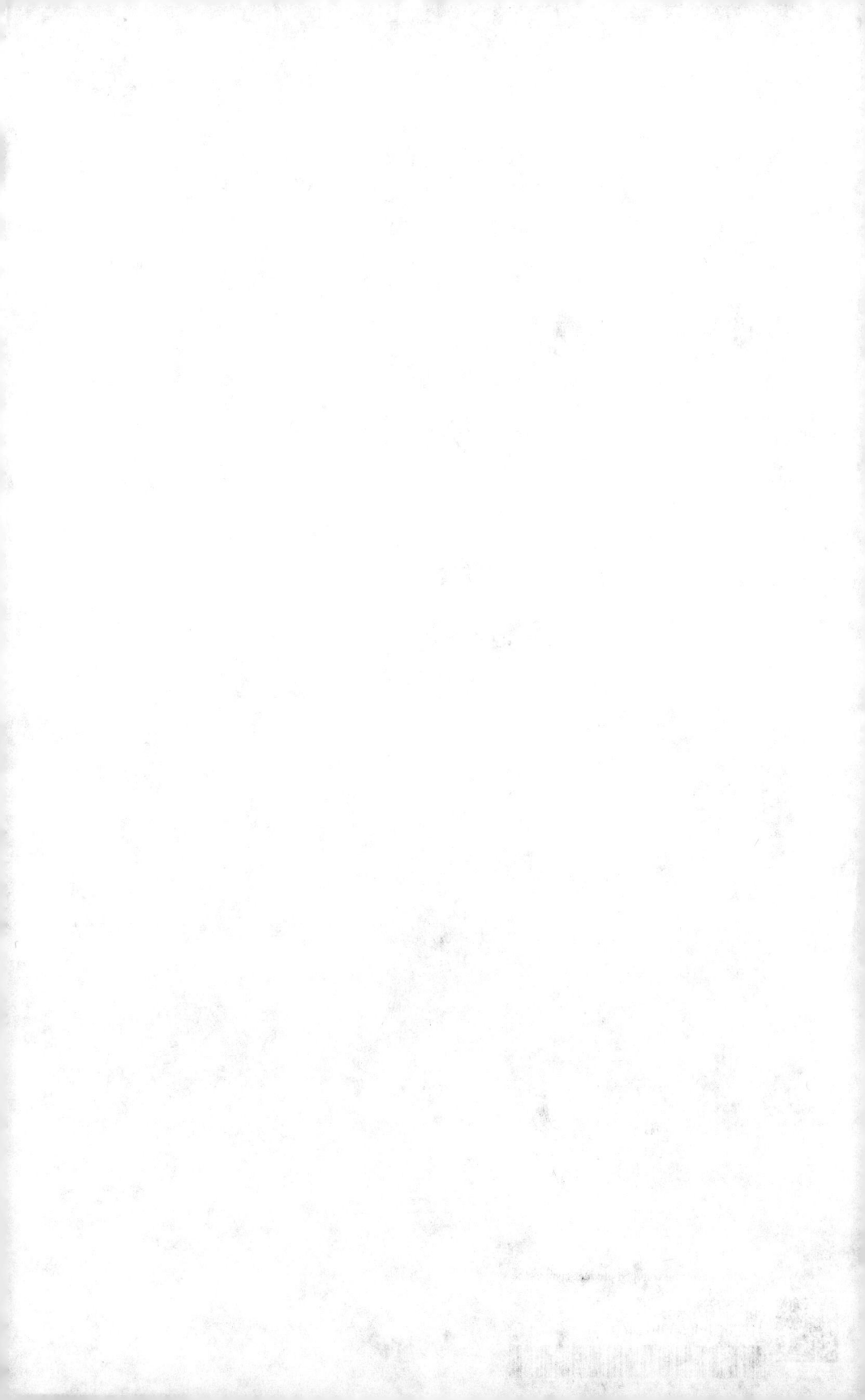

www.ingramcontent.com/pod-product-compliance
Lightning Source LLC
Chambersburg PA
CBHW062147270326
41930CB00009B/1469